The Growth of Latin American Cities

BY

WALTER D. HARRIS, Jr.

IN COLLABORATION WITH *Humberto L. Rodriguez-Camilloni*

ATHENS

OHIO UNIVERSITY PRESS

1971

Dedicated to the People of Latin America

Contents

Illustrations

FIGURES

GRAPHS

MAPS

PLATES

TABLES

APPENDIX
(TABLES)

Preface

THERE is no doubt that the urban place must be considered as a major element in the social and economic development of the Latin American region. In writing this book the concern has been less with a country-by-country description of the growth of specific cities than with the patterns of urban growth in the various regions of the Latin American continent. Because these patterns have in many cases been influenced by the preexisting urban systems dating back to pre-Columbian and Colonial times, the book begins with a survey of the geographic setting and historical development of Latin American cities from pre-Columbian days to the present.

The single most significant factor in the expansion of urban and metropolitan areas in Latin America in recent decades has been the phenomenal increase in the rate of population growth through most of the southern hemisphere, and the projections of the continuation of this trend in the future. A profile of population distribution and its relation to urban growth is presented next, followed by an evaluation of the role that rural-urban migration and industrialization have played in this development in Brazil, Costa Rica, Ecuador, Honduras, and México.

The rate of urbanization and some of the socio-economic problems associated with it are discussed with reference to Chile and Perú, and this is followed by a description of urban systems within a regional context as manifested in the cluster of countries which constitute the region of Central America—the regional setting here being more significant than national boundaries.

Associated with the growth of cities has been a startling expansion of metropolitan areas. This is illustrated by a discussion of seven metropolitan areas that have been selected both because they share certain similarities and at the same time demonstrate some unique characteristics.

The focus in Chapter 7 is narrowed to an evaluation of the effect of population growth and the proliferation of peripheral settlements on urban structure in Latin America, with a detailed description of the evolution and character of the barriadas in Lima, Perú.

The book concludes with some generalized observations on the physical structure of cities in Latin America, including a discussion of trends in residential patterns by income groups; of the location of industry and commerce; and of the nature and form of city centers.

Those who have worked in this area will be familiar with the problem of obtaining comparable statistics for the various Latin American countries. Nor is this surprising, since more than a score of countries comprise this region of the world, and many of them are at different stages of development, a situation that is reflected in the nature and immediacy of the statistical material available. However, the chief focus of this book has been on general trends and patterns rather than on minute data for individual cities.

It is the author's hope that his efforts in this volume will bring wider recognition of the importance of the urban place as the crucible in which the social and economic future of modern Latin America will be forged.

As anyone who has undertaken a venture of this kind will appreciate, this work could never have been completed without generous help and thoughtful criticism from my colleagues and students.

Grateful acknowledgment is made to the many former students from Latin America who, during a period spanning a decade, carried on research both a Yale University and at the Inter-American Housing and Planning Center (CINVA) in Bogotá. Without their contributions, enthusiasm, and unique insights, this book would not have been possible.

Specific acknowledgment goes to my former staff colleagues at the Pan American Union during 1960–1965, German Framinan, Philip Huber, Blanca L. Garin, Jose Alberto Rivas, and Alan Smith, for their research on Latin American cities, on which many of the historical sections of this book are based; to my former student, Mario E. Martin, whose 1966 MCP research paper is largely the basis for Chapter 5; and to Alfredo Rodriguez Arranz, Sofia Giles, and Julio Rojas Munoz, whose student research papers while at Yale contributed greatly to the sections on Chilean urban ranking, Peruvian urban ranking, and urban form.

Special mention must be made of Humberto L. Rodriguez-Camilloni, student, friend, and now colleague, for his patience, tenacity of purpose, and contributions to this work during the more than five years that went into its preparation; of Jaime Valenzuala Galvez, former student, later research assistant, for his contributions to the early stages of statistical calculation and organization; and of Alfred Stark, Yale College 1971, bursary research assistant, for his recent assistance in graphic presentations, proofreading, statistical checking, and loyalty to the undertaking.

Finally, the author's thanks go to Mrs. Sophie Powell for her patience and accurate typing and to Mrs. Fannia Weingartner whose editorial judgments and labor have contributed substantially to the realization of this work.

W. D. H., Jr.

The Growth of Latin American Cities

1

Geographical Setting and Historical Development of Latin American Cities

Geography and Climate

THE study of the growth and change of urban places in Latin America requires reference to both the physical geography and the urban history of this large and important world region. The land area occupied by the twenty republics of Latin America extends from the Rio Grande in northern México to the Tierra del Fuego in Chile, covering a total area of approximately 20,540,000 square kilometers. The longest distances measured from the extremes north-south and east-west are approximately 11,200 and 4,200 kilometers, respectively. More than 200,000,000 people live in this area in almost every kind of topographic and climatic zone.

Given their many differences, the one characteristic shared by all of the twenty republics of Latin America is the fact that they were all colonized by a Latin European country: Argentina, Bolivia, Chile, Colombia, Ecuador, Paraguay, Perú, Uruguay, Venezuela, México, Costa Rica, Guatemala, Honduras, Nicaragua, El Salvador, Panamá, Dominican Republic and Cuba by Spain; Brazil by Portugal; and Haití by France. Although this book deals with Latin America at large, regional distinctions are often made among the following: México, Central America, the Caribbean islands and South America. References to the continent of South America embrace the ten mainland countries below Panamá[1] (see map 1.1).

The Andes extend longitudinally through the South American continent forming the mountain chain which gives rise to the

[1] The Guianas are not included. The British Guiana became free under the name of Guyana in 1966; the French and Dutch Guiana (Surinam) are still linked to their mother countries.

Bolivian plateau (*Altiplano* or High Plains) and to the high Colombian and Venezuelan valleys. Separating South America from the Central American isthmus and the rest of meso-America are the jungles of Darién and Chocó. Another mountain range, volcanic in character, rises in Central America and in México branches off to form the Mexican plateau, averaging 2,000 meters above sea level in altitude. The Brazilian and Guiana Highlands, which form the other two major mountain regions of Latin America, are geologically older than the Andes but lower in altitude.

The Pacific coast of Central and South America is low, with the exception of the south of Chile. Its altitude generally does not exceed 300 meters above sea level. On the eastern Atlantic coast of South America this coastal border is broken at three major points by a large system of rivers: the Orinoco plains in Venezuela, the Amazon jungle in Brazil, and the Pampas of the La Plata River in Argentina.

More than two-thirds of the total area of Latin America lies in the tropical and subtropical zones. Yet the climate is largely influenced by the geographical systems. Temperate climates and satisfactory conditions for life are found on the plateaus. High temperatures and heavy rains make some portions of the coasts and plains of Central America and the northern part of South America uninhabitable. However, the lowlands below the Tropic of Capricorn on the South American continent are extremely fertile. In several places on the Pampa in Argentina, the humus reaches a depth of 100 meters. The only major desert zone is found in the middle region of the South American Pacific coast. It extends from the north of Chile (*Punta de Atacama*) to the border between Perú and Ecuador. Other semi-desert regions with little precipitation during certain times of the year are found in the south of Argentina and parts of México and Brazil. The insular part of Latin America on the Caribbean Sea is another geographically distinct region. It is formed by the emerging part of a mountain chain which unites the extreme northern Andes with the coast of Florida in North America. This region is characterized by a tropical climate with seasonal periods of hurricanes and rain.[2]

Within this extremely diversified geographical setting the three major pre-Columbian civilizations, Aztec, Mayan and Incan, de-

[2] Gilbert J. Butland, *Latin America* (New York: John Wiley & Sons, Inc., 1966), pp. 8–15.

MAP 1.1

PHYSIOGRAPHY OF LATIN AMERICA

LEGEND

	Cool Humid Forested Lands
	Selvas (Hot Humid Forested Lands)
	Tropical Humid & Dry Parklands
	Scrub Bush & Dry Forest Lands
	Llanos (Tropical Grasslands)
	Pampa (Temperate Grasslands)
	Hot Desert Lands
	Cold Grasslands
	Semi-Desert Lands
	Mediterranean Lands
	Plateau Lands With Principal Ranges
	Andean Mountain System
	Intermontane Basins

* Not Included (See Guianas)

MEXICO
GULF OF MEXICO
La Habana
Port-au-Prince
DOMINICAN REPUBLIC
Mexico City
CUBA
Santo Domingo
HONDURAS
HAITI
GUATEMALA
Tegucigalpa
CARIBBEAN SEA
Guatemala City
NICARAGUA
EL SALVADOR
COSTA RICA
Caracas
VENEZUELA
San Salvador
Managua
San Jose
PANAMA
Panama City
Bogota
ECUADOR
Quito
COLOMBIA
Amazon Rivers
Guayaquil
PERU
Lima
BRAZIL
La Paz
Brasilia
BOLIVIA
PACIFIC OCEAN
PARAGUAY
Rio de Janeiro
Asuncion
Sao Paulo
ARGENTINA
CHILE
ATLANTIC OCEAN
Santiago
URUGUAY
Buenos Aires
Montivideo
ANDES MOUNTAINS

veloped and flourished in physical isolation from one another. Geographically these cultures were confined mainly to the highlands of the Mexican plateau and the Peruvian Andes.[3] The Europeans who started colonization in the Caribbean areas, México, and Perú (1496–1550), faced the problem of protecting and populating a physically varied environment. Mountain chains, almost impenetrable jungles, and very few navigable rivers made it impossible to establish an efficient system of communication. Later, many of these same physical barriers restricted the consolidation of colonial urban centers which often enjoyed better communications with their mother countries than with each other. This was true, for example, of those early urban centers which developed around the ports of Buenos Aires in Argentina, Montevideo in Uruguay, Rio de Janeiro in Brazil, and Lima-Callao in Perú.

Pre-Columbian Period (to 1500)

Of the pre-Columbian cultures that flourished in America, only the Aztecs in the Valley of México and the Incas in the Peruvian Andes had reached a high peak of development at the time of the arrival of the Spanish conquerors. In the case of the Mayan culture only a handful of ruins remain, barely enabling us to realize the greatness of such ancient First Empire centers as Copán, Palenque, Tikal, Chichén-Itzá, Uxmal and Mayapán.[4] The few Second Empire Mayan centers in use at the time of the conquest, such as Tayalsal, were only small religious settlements of little administrative or commercial importance.

Most archaeologists maintain that the Mayan center (city) was a ceremonial rather than a true urban center (fig. 1.1). Indeed, there is little archaeological evidence to suggest that the Mayan centers were cities in the contemporary sense of the word as were the Incan and Aztec centers. Most of the buildings found in Mayan centers were temples, pyramids and ceremonial structures. Apparently the location of the Mayan centers was primarily dictated by the considerations of religious strategy rather than by any other factor.

[3] Preston E. James, *Latin America* (New York: The Odyssey Press, 1959), p. 15.
[4] Donald Robertson, *Pre-Columbian Architecture* (New York: George Braziller, 1963), pp. 39–41.

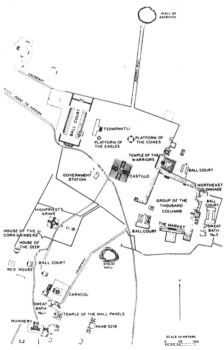

FIG. 1.1 *Chichén Itzá, drawing of site. Site plan of central section. Reprinted from Tatian Proskouriakoff,* An Album of Major Architecture *(Washington, D.C.: Carnegie Institution, 1946). Reprinted courtesy of the Carnegie Institution.*

This may explain the inaccessibility of the places chosen for settlement during the two Mayan periods: first in the virgin jungles in the southern part of the peninsula and in Guatemala and Honduras; and later in the semidesert zone in the north of Yucatán. None of these Mayan centers seems to have been visited by the first European expeditions, nor to have had any influence on the routes that these expeditions took to penetrate and explore the Central American isthmus. On the other hand, the Aztec and Incan cities definitely influenced the directions taken by the Spanish explorations.

Religion, the idea of God, was the inspiring element and dominant factor in Aztec life.[5] Everything was religious in its essence and so everything important was, in one form or another, dedicated to religion. In this sense, the Aztec approach to town planning and building resembled that of the Mayas. But because they lacked the political means to absorb the populations they had conquered into their empire, the Aztecs never did succeed in imposing either political or architectural unity throughout their domain. Instead they borrowed and adapted many forms and methods from the peoples they had conquered, so that Aztec town planning came to be a composite of elements drawn from the Olmec, the Mayas, the Zapotec, the Mixtec, and, above all, the Toltec.

At the time of Cortés' arrival in Veracruz in 1519, the Aztec Empire extended from the Valley of Anahuac to Oaxaca, and from the Gulf of México to Michoacán (see map 1.2). The total population may have been over 10 million. The city of Tenochtitlán (fig. 1.2) the capital of the Empire, has been considered as one of the better designed pre-Columbian cities. The architectural magnificence of the Temple and the Palace of Montezuma, described by the Spanish Conquistadors, remains legendary, though nothing is left of them today.[6] Tenochtitlán was the first administrative center, but the Aztec territory comprised other important cities which had themselves previously been centers of other cultures such as Atzcapozalco, Tlacopán, Tula and Cholula. The Spaniards totally destroyed the Aztec capital, but chose the same site for the foundation of México City in 1521 (fig. 1.3).

[5] Ibid., p. 11.

[6] See the great Temple of Tenochtitlán as reconstructed by Ignacio Marquina from descriptions by Spanish conquerors and existing Aztec monuments in Paul F. Damaz, *Art in Latin American Architecture* (New York: Reinhold Publishing Corporation, 1963), p. 23.

MAP 1.2

Pre-Columbian Mayan and Aztec Urban Centers. Maps 1.2, 1.3 from Victor Von Hagen, The Ancient Sun Kingdom of the Americas (Cleveland: The World Publishing Co., 1961).

FIG. 1.2 *Drawing of the reconstruction of Tenochtitlán. Reprinted from Ignacio Marquina,* El Templo Mayor de México *(México: Instituto de Antropología, 1960). Reprinted by permission.*

In South America, the Conquistadors found the most organized pre-Columbian civilization of the continent. Centralized in the city of Cuzco, the Incan Empire extended from the southern part of Colombia (Pasto) to the northern provinces of Argentina, and from the Pacific coast to the border of the Andes with the Amazon jungle (map 1.3). A highly developed road system connected Cuzco with a series of towns such as Tambomachay, Pisac, Calca and Ollantaytambo, which served as administrative and commercial subcenters. Machu Picchu, the most interesting of these centers, is located at the summit of an almost inaccessible mountain and overlooks the majestic Urubamba Canyon (see fig. 1.4). This stone city, undiscovered by the Spanish Conquistadors and unknown to the rest of the world for more than 400 years, was found in 1911 by the American archaeologist, Hiram A. Bingham.[7] This "Lost City of the Incas" is situated 2,090 meters above sea level, its ruins covering more than

[7] See George Kubler, "Machu Picchu" in *Perspecta 6, The Yale Architectural Journal* (1960): 49–55.

FIG. 1.3 *Plan of México City, 1556. From Gian Battista Ramusio,* Delle Navigationi et Uiaggi, *vol. 3 (Venice, 1606).*

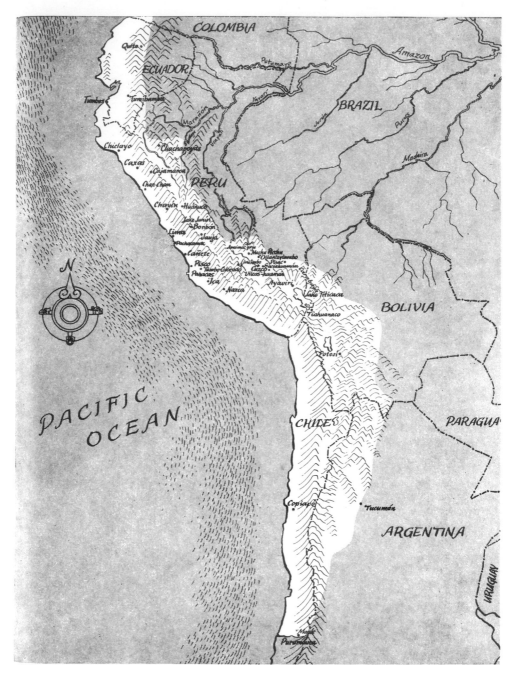

MAP 1.3
The Principal Pre-Columbian Incan Centers

Machu Picchu, Perú. Photo by author.

MACHU PICCHU

1. The gateway to the city. This is the only formal entrance.
2. Terraces, agricultural *andenes*. These "hanging gardens" were banked with soil; crops were grown here and watered by aqueducts.
3. Stairway of the fountains; these supplied the city with water from an aqueduct brought a mile from the city. It is composed of sixteen descending fountains (although often referred to as "baths").
4. One of the residential sections of the clans.
5. The sacred plaza and the Temple of the Three Windows.
6. The Intihuatana, "hitching-post-of-the-sun".
7. Northern terraces and road to Huayna Picchu.
8. The semi-circular Temple, the "Palace" of the Nustas, the Chosen Women.
9. Houses of the clans.
10. A clan section of the "Three Doors".
11. The royal Mausoleum, where gold-decked mummies were placed.
12. The place of the stairways and the cemeteries.

five square kilometers. The city was reached during Incan times by a wide stone road winding through the heights with large hanging bridges over deep abysses. Thus, inaccessible from the lower parts of the Urubamba Canyon and hidden among the thick vegetation of the Andes, Machu Picchu probably became the refuge of the last Incas, following the conquest of Cuzco by Pizarro. Two urban systems were thus described running longitudinally north-south and parallel to each other: one road linked the urban centers on the coast, and the other, the urban centers between the Andes. These two systems facilitated the efficient political and administrative organization of the empire and later served to define the almost identical urban colonial system.

Practically no major pre-Columbian center—with the possible exception of Cuzco in Perú—survived the impact of the conquest. Nevertheless the pre-Columbian center exerted a considerable influence on the colonial cities that were superimposed on them by the European colonizers. Moreover, this influence has extended down to the present century, for the tendency toward the centralization of political and economic life that characterized the pre-Columbian and colonial urban centers has persisted in the principal Latin American cities of today.

Colonial Period (1500–1800)

The builders of the colonial cities in Latin America paid more attention than had their pre-Columbian predecessors to the relationship of the various urban centers to the main capital city. This relationship concerned them more than the relationship of a potential urban center to the immediate region around it. As a result, the colonial urban centers were often peripheral to the actual physical area that they dominated. The fact that they functioned as gateways to the colonization fronts made their rank or degree of importance dependent upon their facilities for communication with foreign ports. The urban centers existing at the time of the arrival of the Conquistadors lost their original economic basis and for the

---

(LEFT)

FIG. 1.4 *Site plan of Machu Picchu ruins. Reprinted from "A Guide to Machu Picchu" by Victor von Hagen, 1949. Reprinted by permission of the author and Frederick Farnam Associates, Inc.*

most part disappeared or dropped to a lower rank, as was the case with Cuzco. When the location of the old centers coincided with the needs and interests of the colonizers, the new centers were re-founded on the ruins of the old, as in the case of México City (see map 1.4).

In 1573, Philip II, King of Spain, proclaimed the Ordenanzas sobre Descubrimiento Nuevo y Población, embodying the legal and working basis for urban planning in the American colony and establishing the principle that the colony's urban problems were to be subject to the attention of the Spanish Crown.[8] He dictated in detail the conditions that should determine the sites of new cities, specifying that they should have "good ports of entry and exit by land and sea, and be easily accessible by road and ship, so that one can enter and leave easily, do commerce and govern, aid and defend." [9] This appropriately summed up the functions that the new settlements were to carry out during the first part of the Colonial Period. The colonial cities were thus established in preferential order along the coast: Veracruz (1519), Santa Marta (1529), Maracaibo (1529), Cartagena (1533), Guayaquil (1535) (see fig. 1.5), Callao (1537), Valparaiso (1544), Recife (1526), Puerto Seguro (1500), Olinda (1535), Bahia (1549) and Santos (1536). The cities not founded on the coast generally served as loading or storage centers for merchandise in transit: México City (1521), Bogotá (1538), La Paz (1548), Cochabamba (1536), Asunción (1537) and Santiago (1541) (see fig. 1.6).

The plan of the Spanish colonial city was based on the idea of a central plaza with regular blocks extending outward in the direction of each of the four sides. This plaza, referred to as plaza mayor or plaza de armas, was the site of the main political and religious buildings, namely, the government palace, the cathedral and the town hall.[10] This pattern was followed again and again throughout Spanish Latin America. Santo Domingo (see fig. 1.7), founded in 1496 overlooking the Ozama River, was the first colonial city where the gridiron pattern was used. Lima and México City were two later examples.

---

[8] Altamira y Crevea, *Ensayo sobre Felipe II* (México City, 1950).
[9] *Laws of the Indies*, Book IV, title VII, "Provisions which declare the order to be kept in the Indies in new discoveries and settlements," 1573.
[10] Robert C. Smith, "Colonial Towns of Spanish and Portuguese America," in *Journal of the Society of Architectural Historians* 14(1955):4.

MAP 1.4

Cities Founded in America, 1496–1776

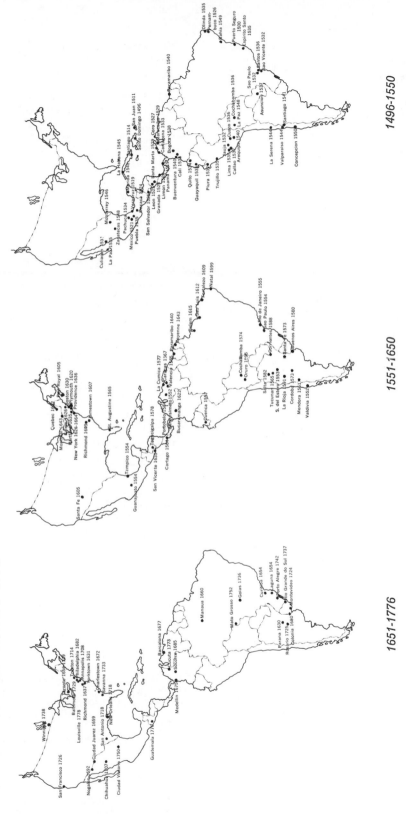

1496–1550

1551–1650

1651–1776

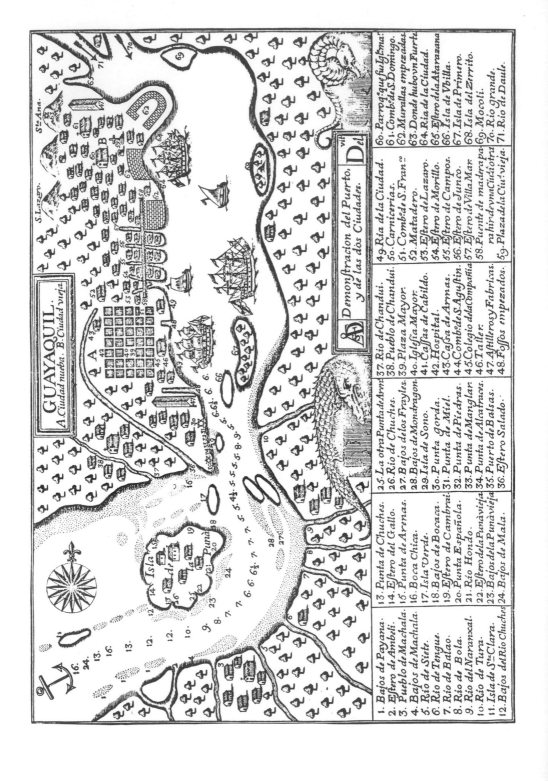

FIG. 1.5 *Plan of Guayaquil, 1937. Reprinted from Pedro Hidalgo Gonzalez,* Monografía Sintetica de Guayaquil *(City Council of Guayaquil, 1937). Reprinted by permission of the author.*

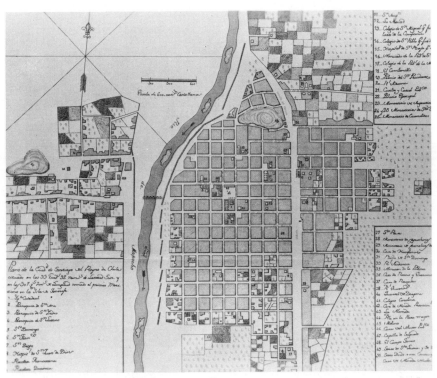

FIG. 1.6 *Plan of Santiago de Chile, 1793. Reprinted from Carlos Pena Oteagui,* Santiago de Siglo en Siglo *(Santiago: Empresa Editora Zig-Zag, 1944).*

In contrast to the city of Tenochtitlán—which had been totally destroyed by Cortés in 1521 and later became the site of México City—Cuzco, situated in a high valley surrounded by austere mountains proved impervious to the efforts of the Conquistadors to raze it to the ground: the Incan walls were so solid that they could not be destroyed (fig. 1.8). As a result, the new colonial city arose on the foundations and walls of the ancient center, the Incan masonry being incorporated into the new construction.[11]

[11] Wolf Schneider, *Babylon is Everywhere* (New York: McGraw-Hill Book Company, Inc., 1963), pp. 272–73.

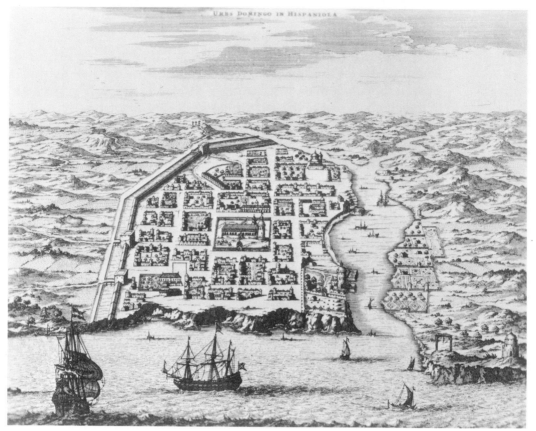

FIG. 1.7 *Plan of Santo Domingo, 1671. Reprinted from Montanus Arnoldus*, De Nieuwe en Onbekende Weerld *(Amsterdam, 1671).*

Valparaiso, Chile, followed the siting requirements laid down by the Spanish Crown. It did not, however, follow the ordinances for the internal layout as is evident from fig 1.9. There were times when the location and form of a town were largely dictated by strategic demands. The fortified cities of Cartagena (fig. 1.10) and Buenos Aires (fig. 1.11)—a city built anew—are two examples. Still another type of colonial city was built in Paraguay by Jesuit missionaries, who developed small isolated towns—reduciones—to convert the Indians. These reduciones were constructed and maintained by communal labor, and included up to seven thousand inhabitants. They represented a miniature version of the gridiron plan. Although

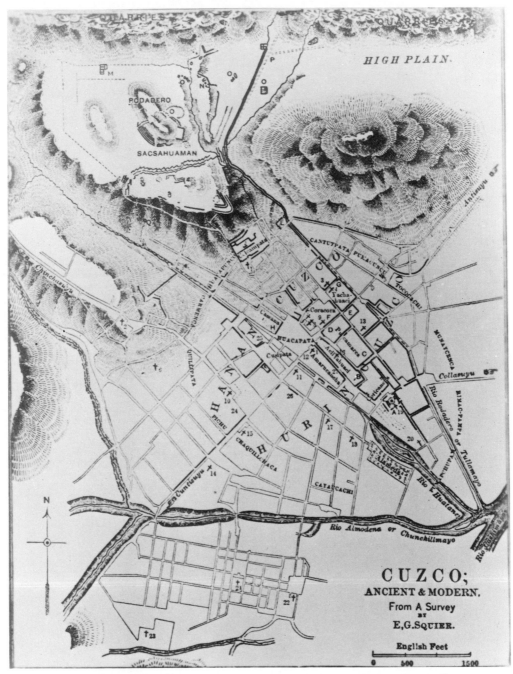

Fig. 1.8 *Plan of Cuzco, Perú, in the second half of the eighteenth century. Reprinted from* E. G. Squier, Peru, Incidents of Travel and Exploration in the Land of the Incas *(New York: Harper and Brothers, 1900). Reprinted by permission of the publisher.*

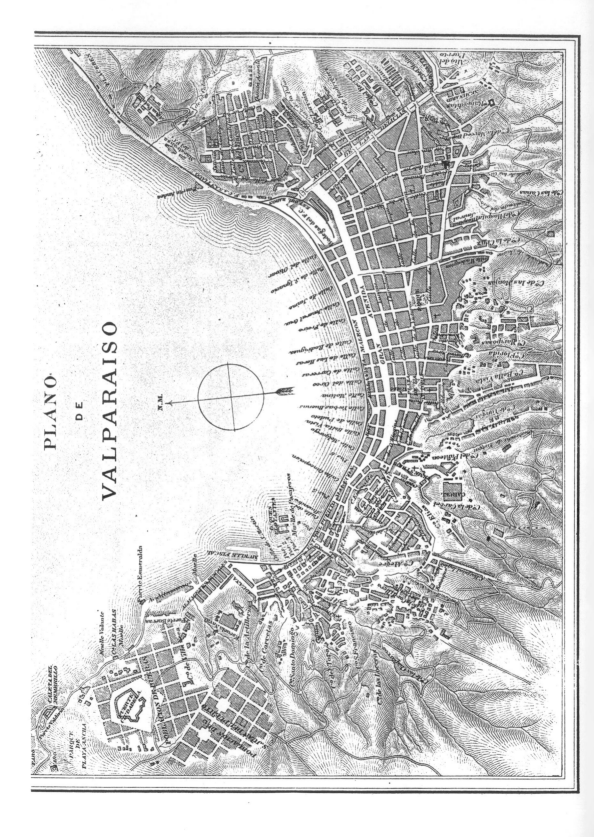

PLANO

DE

VALPARAISO

(LEFT)

FIG. 1.9 *Map of Valparaíso, 1903. Reprinted from Enrique Espinoza,* Geografía Descriptiva de la Republica de Chile *(Barcelona: Imprenta, Litografía Encuadernación, 1903), pp. 208–09.*

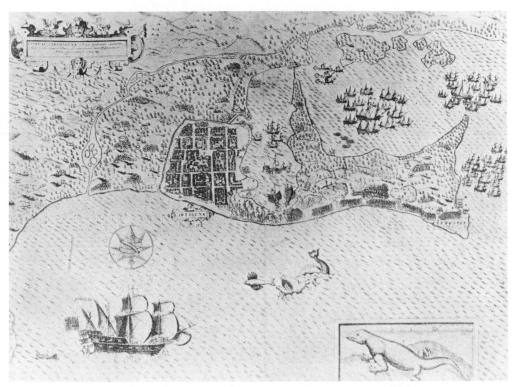

FIG. 1.10 *Plan of Cartagena, 1586. Reprinted from Enrique Marco Dorta,* Cartagena de Indias la Ciudad y Sus Monumentos *(Seville: Escuela de Estudios Hispano–Americanos de Seville, 1951).*

the Jesuit missions of Paraguay have almost entirely disappeared, it is possible to reconstruct their general layout from a 1793 engraving portraying the plan of Candelaria (fig. 1.12), which was considered a model for other towns of its type.[12]

In Brazil, the pattern of city planning was somewhat different, the idea of the central plaza being absent. In Bahia, for example, the whole skyline of the city is rendered extremely picturesque by the

[12] R. C. Smith, "Colonial Towns."

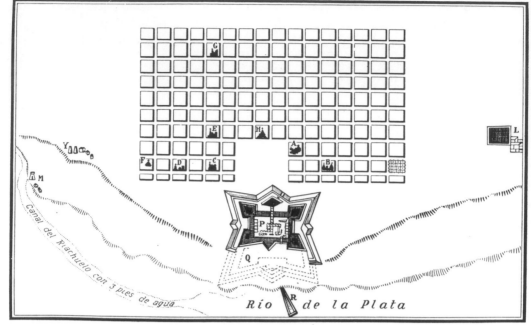

FIG. 1.11 *Plan of Buenos Aires, 1708. Reprinted from* Documentos y Planos Relativos al Periodo Edilicio Colonial de la Ciudad de Buenos Aires, *vol. 1 (Buenos Aires: Municipalidad de la Capital, 1910).*

variety of levels and the irregularity of the plan. The architecture was adapted to the irregularity of the topography and streets of different widths intersect at several irregular angles.[13]

The Spanish urban tradition transplanted its principal political institution to America, the *ayuntamiento*.[14] Through this institution the Spanish Crown consolidated its power over the subject people and succeeded in exercising absolute control over the large parti-

[13] The horizontal movement of the *bandeirantes* was a decisive factor in the development of Brazilian towns. The Paulistas or inhabitants of the captaincy of São Paulo comprised the most enterprising element in colonial Brazil. With the object of securing Indian slaves and discovering mines and precious metals they organized great expeditions into the interior, known as *bandeiras*. At times these expeditions were veritable treks or migrations in which entire families took part and which lasted for a period of years.

[14] The Spanish name for municipal government. In Spain and in her American colonies the *ayuntamiento* consisted of the official members, and of *regidores* or regulators, chosen in varying proportions from the *hidalgos* or nobles and the *pecheros* or commoners.

tions of land. This administrative centralization increased the importance of the capitals of the colonies and provinces as centers of power—an effect which persisted into the Republican period.

Portuguese colonization differed from the Spanish in some respects. A system of large land ownership was introduced in Brazil from the start, without the centralized administrative control typical of the Spanish system. The plantations were the centers of the principal economic activities, while the cities remained almost exclusively the places of residence for Portuguese who had recently arrived from the mother country. Bahia, which became the capital of Brazil in 1549, and Recife were both surrounded by large agri-

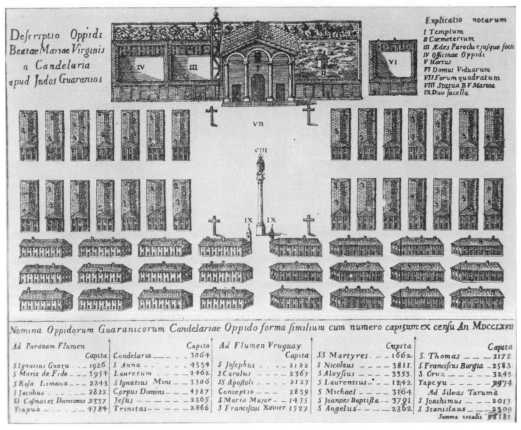

FIG. 1.12 *Plan of the Jesuit mission of Candelaria, Paraguay, 1767. Reprinted from P. Josephus Emmanuel Peramas,* De Vita et Moribus Tredecim-Virorum Paraguaycorum *(Faventiae, 1793).*

cultural plantations. It may be argued that the Portuguese colony was more rural than the Spanish colony and that the Brazilian cities did not have the prestige and power of their Spanish-American counterparts before the seventeenth century. But in Brazil as in Spanish America, the capital cities became the organization centers for all the colonization fronts. The expansion of bandeirantes from such centers as São Paulo, Bahia, and Pernambuco, for example, had a definite municipal and urban character (map 1.4).

The basic economic role of the colonial cities founded in America was the concentration and shipment of native products to the mother countries. Applying the principles of strict mercantilism, Spain and Portugal monopolized this commerce, making every effort to exclude other foreign countries. Until the end of the sixteenth century all commercial trade in South America was concentrated in the city of Lima, the capital of the Viceroyalty of Perú. However, at the beginning of the seventeenth century the city of Buenos Aires began to introduce other European products to the Spanish colony as a result of clandestine commerce initiated between Rio de La Plata and Brazilian ports in 1602. Eventually, Buenos Aires succeeded in gaining commercial hegemony over the southern part of the continent and this hegemony was recognized in 1776 when Buenos Aires became the capital of the Viceroyalty of Rio de La Plata. Only during the eighteenth century, after the rise of the Bourbon dynasty, did Spain revise its ideas about the government and economy of its colonies. This change in policy brought about economic expansion in Spanish America by encouraging the exploitation of native products other than minerals and by opening more ports to foreign commerce.

The estimated population in Spanish America around 1570 comprised about 160,000 persons of European origin, 7,500,000 Indians and 40,000 Negroes. At the end of the Colonial period (1825) the population of Latin America was estimated at 3,419,000 Europeans and Creoles, 7,830,000 Indians, 5,532,000 Mestizos and Mulattoes and about 2,000,000 Negroes.[15] A comparison of both estimates indicates a relatively greater increase in the groups of the population that supplied hard labor—the Mestizos, Negroes, Mulattoes, and Indians. The presence of Indian labor inspired, even in the Spaniards

[15] "Tendencias de Localización y Crecimiento de la Población Urbana Latinoamericana," Unpublished mimeograph (Washington, D.C.: Pan American Union, 1964), p. 7.

of working-class origin, the desire to settle down in the cities and live off the rent from land worked by semiforced labor. At the same time the commercial boom in urban centers, especially in the capitals, attracted a greater immigration from the mother country, and by the end of the eighteenth century, the Spanish-American cities had more power, wealth, and rank than the Anglo-Saxon and French cities in the north. For example, México City, which had 30,000 inhabitants at its founding in 1524 and occupied an area of 270 km.², had increased to an area of 771 km.² at the end of the eighteenth century and its population of 120,000 exceeded that of Port Royal, Philadelphia, Charleston, Boston and Quebec combined. Table 1.1 shows the population estimate of various cities on the

TABLE 1.1

POPULATION OF SELECTED LATIN AMERICAN
AND OTHER WORLD CITIES

CITIES	POPULATION, c. 1800	POPULATION, c. 1960
Paris	547,000	7,369,000
Lisbon	180,000	817,000
Madrid	160,000	2,259,000
Rome	153,000	2,188,000
Milan	135,000	1,582,000
México City	120,000	4,816,000
Barcelona	115,000	1,557,000
New York [a]	79,000	14,114,000
Lima	53,000	1,845,000
Rio de Janeiro	43,000	4,691,000
Buenos Aires	40,000	6,751,000
Caracas	40,000	1,492,000
Montevideo	6,000	1,202,000
Washington, D.C. [a]	3,000	1,808,000

SOURCE: 1800, José V. Montesino Samperio, *La Población del Area Metropolitana de Caracas* (Caracas: Demografía Venezuela, 1956); 1960, *Demographic Yearbook 1963* (New York: United Nations, 1964), Table V–3.
NOTE:
  a. Urbanized area.

continent around 1800 as well as the population of the most important European capitals at the same time. The growth of the principal centers in the middle of the eighteenth century became evident in urban expansion and improvement projects such as those undertaken in Rio de Janeiro (fig. 1.13) by de Andrade, in México City by the Count of Revillagigedo, in Lima by Ambrosio de O'Higgins (fig. 1.14) and in Buenos Aires by the Viceroy Vertiz.

RIO DE JANEIRO
ET ENVIRONS.
Echelle 1: 100.000

kilomètres

0 ————————————— 3

——— Chemin de Fer

---- Limite de l'impôt prédial urbain

Dessiné d'après les indications du Baron de Rio-Branco, par A. Lévy, 21 rue Vandamme

Rougeron, Vignerot, Sc.

N.B. Les rues principales sont seules indiquées.

OCÉAN ATLANTIQUE

BAIE DE RIO DE JANEIRO

NICTHEROY

RIO DE JANEIRO

Pão de Assucar

(LEFT)

FIG. 1.13 *Plan of Rio de Janeiro and its surroundings, 1889. Reprinted from E. Levasseur,* Le Brésil *(Paris; H. Lamirault et Cie, Editeurs, 1889).*

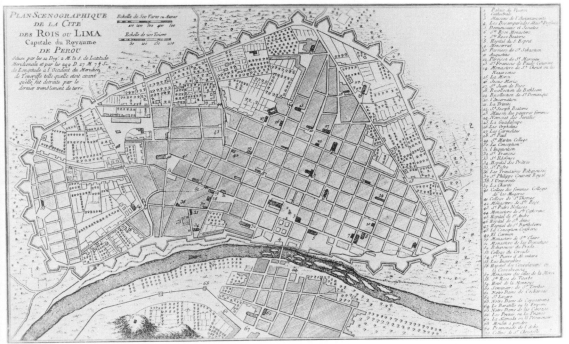

FIG. 1.14 *Plan of Lima, Perú, 1756. Reprinted from Juan Bromley and Jose Barbagelata,* Evolución Urbana de Lima *(Lima: Concejo Provincial de Lima, 1945), by permission of the publisher.*

Republican Period (1825–1900)

Following the successful Wars of Independence (1816–1825) most of the Latin American colonies became independent republics ceasing to be a colonial dependency of European powers—hence the term the Republican period.

Urban development during the Republican period was marked by the growth of almost all the cities and the establishment of a few small settlements near the various national borders for tactical or military reasons. Most of these cities had been founded during the

Colonial period and now continued their natural growth, though generally in a disorganized and haphazard way. Urban growth took place in all directions, whenever the topography and the physical characteristics of the terrain permitted it. Among the principal growth factors were the immigration influx from Europe to some of the large cities (especially on the Atlantic coast), and later, the growing attraction of the cities for the indigenous rural population.[16] Urbanization and the beginnings of industrialization became co-factors in the development of Republican cities. It is important to bear in mind that although Latin American industrial development started at the end of the eighteenth century it did not proceed with any impetus until after World War II.

The Independence movement of the nineteenth century, the subsequent civil wars, and the final consolidation of the new Latin American republics influenced the development of the Latin American cities in two important ways. In the first place, the large colonial cities, especially the capitals of the newborn nations became centers of national politics and foreign commerce free from mercantilistic restrictions. Secondly, demographic urban growth increased as a result of internal rural migrations to the cities coupled with immigration from Europe. The Latin American cities which in colonial times had functioned as centers from which population moved into the interior to expand colonization efforts now became places of refuge for those fleeing from the interior to escape the disorders of the postcolonial civil wars. At the same time the large ports of entry on the South American continent, which experienced a boom following the removal of the Spanish trading restrictions, attracted foreign immigrants in search of new opportunities.

Around 1826 about one-third of the population in America lived in the United States and Canada; one-third in México, Central America and the Antilles; and one-third in South America. After the middle of the century (1870), the population of the United States tripled from 10 million to 35 million inhabitants. The population of the United States was then approximately equal to that of Latin America, but twice as much as that of South America. The South American country that showed the highest index of growth was Brazil, where the estimated population during the struggle for independence had doubled to 10 million in 1872. Although the demo-

---

[16] P. E. James, *Latin America*, pp. 22–23.

graphic data for the nineteenth century in Latin America is scarce and often unreliable, it may be stated that the population in the rest of the American countries generally did not double between 1826 and 1870. However, after 1870 demographic growth was intensified in the countries that received European immigrations, such as Argentina, Uruguay and Brazil. These Latin American countries, as well as the United States, show higher indexes of growth than the rest of the American nations. Yet when the absolute population figures are compared by country with those of the principal cities, it can be observed that in Argentina, Uruguay and Brazil, the concentration is in the urban centers, whereas in the United States the population is more uniformly distributed throughout the country. The total population of the United States grew from 35 million in 1870 to 100 million in 1918; in Argentina from 1.7 million in 1869 to 7.8 million in 1914; in Brazil from 9.9 million in 1872 to 30.6 in 1920; in Colombia from 2.3 million in 1870 to 5.8 million in 1918; in Chile from 1.8 million in 1865 to 3.7 million in 1920; in México from 12.6 million in 1895 to 15.1 million in 1910; and in Venezuela, from 1.7 million in 1873 to 2.3 million in 1920.[17]

During the period between 1870 and 1918 African immigration to America diminished considerably, but European immigration increased. The United States received the largest portion of this immigration—some 20 million, out of which 50% migrated to the United States between 1904 and 1914. About four million immigrants entered Argentina and three million entered Brazil. This immigrating population was selective not only in regard to countries, but also in regard to places selected for settlement within those countries. Thus the majority of immigrants established themselves in the most important urban centers. The cities of Buenos Aires and its zone of immediate influence in Argentina, and São Paulo in Brazil were the centers of the greatest concentration of immigrants.[18] São Paulo increased its total population from 23,253 inhabitants in 1872 to 129,409 in 1914. It is significant that the proportion of foreigners with regard to the total population increased from 8% to 25% during the same period. Around 1897 the Italian immigrants were in a 2 to 1 ratio with regard to the Brazilian natives. Buenos Aires in turn, increased from 187, 126 inhabitants in 1869 to 1,575,814

[17] "Tendencias de Localización," p. 7.
[18] P. E. James, *Latin America*, pp. 297–99, 405–06.

in 1914, showing the most notable example of urban growth during that period.

The industrial development and professional opportunities offered by the urban centers of Brazil, Argentina and Uruguay made these Latin American countries the major targets of European immigration. However, the majority of the Latin American countries remained on the margin of this immigration movement. Population growth in countries like Perú, Ecuador, Bolivia and Guatemala stemmed primarily from an increase in the native Indian population; México, Honduras, Nicaragua, El Salvador, Colombia, Venezuela, Paraguay and Chile showed a significant growth in their mestizo populations; and the same could be said of the regional populations of Colombia and Venezuela.

The economic and political dominance of the Latin American capital cities during the nineteenth century contributed to the development of transportation systems centered around them. The economic base of these cities was characteristically agriculture, cattle raising, and mining, rather than manufacturing. These factors impeded the formation of new cities in the interior and encouraged the centralization of urban growth oriented to the capital.

The owners of large rural properties usually lived in the capital cities where they spent the profits they had earned through agriculture. Others left the country reinvesting little or nothing in the centers of production. Economic liberalism, transplanted without special regard for local conditions, helped to concentrate the money in urban centers in response to the city's demand for imported manufactured products. During the second half of the nineteenth century and during the twentieth, the coexistence of agrarian dominance and urban capitalism facilitated investment by overseas interests and at the same time encouraged the development of single-crop export products, such as coffee. The social and economic conditions in the rural areas of the Latin American countries, aggravated by the intensification of single-crop agricultural production which offered only seasonal employment, gave rise to periodic large interregional migrations of rural workers to the urban centers. The cities, for their part, held a double attraction for the rural population due to the increase in services which the demands and economic power of the upper classes made possible, more physical conveniences, and the possibility of economic security. The capital cities appeared more attractive because proximity to the centers of power offered the rural migrants a better opportunity to exert political pressure on their governments.

The Twentieth Century

The most distinctive characteristic of the Latin American population during the twentieth century has been its remarkable growth. Such population explosions are not new to the modern world. The industrial and agricultural revolutions in eighteenth- and nineteenth-century Europe had also produced a phenomenal growth in population. But in Latin America, the population explosion has not merely accompanied, but has in fact, often preceded industrialization and the effective modernization of agriculture. Moreover, while the growth occurring in other parts of the world, especially in Asia, is taking place in areas that are already saturated and have a relative scarcity of arable land, in Latin America land resources remain ample, even when considered in relation to the underdeveloped technology that characterizes most of its agriculture.

Between 1850 and 1900 the population of Latin America practically doubled, and between 1900 and 1940 it increased from 33 to 63 million. In the past 20 years it has exceeded 200 million, and it is quite possible that it has now reached 300 million. This would represent an increase of 100% in 30 years, as compared to the 40 years necessary to register a similar increase in the first part of this century and to 50 years in the latter half of the previous century. The rate of population growth in the American countries, with the exception of the United States and Canada, has been steadily increasing. During the decade 1920–30 there was a 20% population increase, rising to 24% in 1940–50 and 29% during 1950–60. As a result of this rate difference, the population of Latin America went from 4% of the world population in 1900 to the 7% which it constitutes today. It is probable that this figure will reach 8% in this decade.

The second distinctive characteristic of the Latin America population is the remarkable growth, both absolute and relative, of the urban center. In most of the hemisphere the urbanization process is occurring under conditions of slow industrialization and agricultural backwardness. The result is a serious lack of harmony between changes in the economic structure and changes in the urban-rural population composition. Above all, the growth of the cities is sustained by large migrations from the rural areas. The volume of the population shifts, in most cases, does not appear justified either by the relative surpluses created as a result of progress in agricultural technology or by the magnitude of the real demand for urban labor. Of greater importance than these factors are those created by the social and economic conditions of the rural areas and the general attraction that the cities hold for the inhabitants of these areas.

The third distinctive characteristic of the Latin America population is its remarkable geographic and sociocultural mobility. The magnitude of this phenomenon is indicated by the urban growth attributable to migration, the shift from certain rural areas to others, and by spontaneous settlement. Geographic and sociocultural mobility are frequently related. Particularly in the less developed and less dynamic areas, geographic displacement is usually the primary condition for obtaining sociocultural mobility. Thus internal migrations and the phenomenon of urbanization have been highly dynamic factors in the development of Latin America.

Few cities have been founded in Latin America during the last fifty years. The building of new cities like Brasilia in Brazil (see fig. 1.15), Ciudad Guayana in Venezuela (see fig. 1.16) and Chimbote in Perú was undertaken by the national governments primarily in the interests of overall economic policy. As a result, the location of these cities was in every case dictated by the natural resources of the region. The prime purpose was the establishment of industrial complexes that could process these natural resources, as in the case of Chimbote, fish processing and, in the case of Cuidad Guayana, iron. This concept is quite different from the founding concept of the colonial period and even of the pre-Columbian civilizations where the main purpose was either the creation of strategically located military outposts or the establishment of spearheads from which religion and political power could be carried beyond the frontiers.

In the case of Brasilia, one should remember that Brazil's urban and industrial growth had developed mainly along the southeastern coast, encompassing all the large cities of the country; the interior had remained almost desolate. The foundation of Brasilia near the geographical center of the country was originally planned as a means of opening up the interior to new forces of development and growth. It was hoped that the establishment of the political government in a new seat of power would attract the necessary population and,

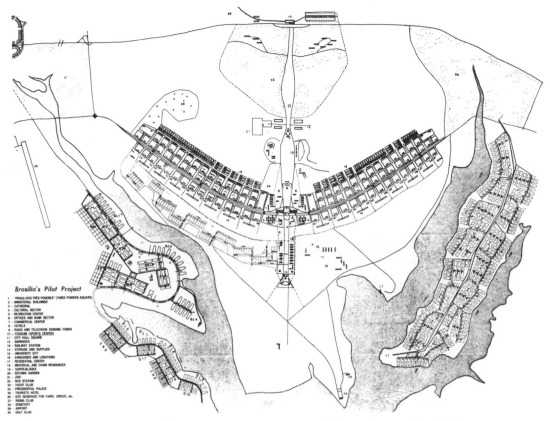

Brasilia's Pilot Project

1 - "PRAÇA DOS TRÊS PODERES" (THREE POWERS SQUARE)
2 - MINISTERIAL BUILDINGS
3 - CATHEDRAL
4 - CULTURAL SECTOR
5 - RECREATION CENTER
6 - OFFICES AND BANK SECTOR
7 - COMMERCIAL CENTER
8 - HOTELS
9 - RADIO AND TELEVISION SENDING TOWER
10 - STADIUM (SPORTS CENTER)
11 - CITY HALL SQUARE
12 - BARRACKS
13 - RAILWAY STATION
14 - STORAGE AND SUPPLIES
15 - UNIVERSITY CITY
16 - EMBASSIES AND LEGATIONS
17 - RESIDENTIAL CENTER
18 - INDIVIDUAL AND CHAIN RESIDENCES
19 - SUPER-BLOCKS
20 - BOTANIC GARDEN
21 - ZOO
22 - BUS STATION
23 - YACHT CLUB
24 - PRESIDENTIAL PALACE
25 - TOURISTS HOTEL
26 - SITE RESERVED FOR FAIRS, CIRCUS, etc.
27 - RIDING CLUB
28 - CEMETERY
29 - AIRPORT
30 - GOLF CLUB

FIG. 1.15 *Pilot plan for Brasilia. Reprinted from "Historia de Brasilia," published by the Banco de Lavorira de Minas Gerais, Belo Horizonte, Brazil. Published by permission.*

therefore, corresponding services and commerce, plus all sorts of industrial enterprises. Taking advantage of the surrounding natural resources and of the new transportation facilities provided, the aim was to connect this region with the most important cities of the country. The case of Ciudad Guayana was different in the sense that this time it was the discovery of rich iron ore deposits in the north central part of Venezuela that encouraged the foundation and development of a series of urban settlements around the rising industrial complex. Chimbote has grown and urbanized at an almost unbelievable rate in the last decade (1950–60). The development of the fishing industry in this port on the north Peruvian coast has attracted thousands of immigrants from all parts of the country. Its population grew from 10,000 in 1945 to more than 150,000 in 1965.

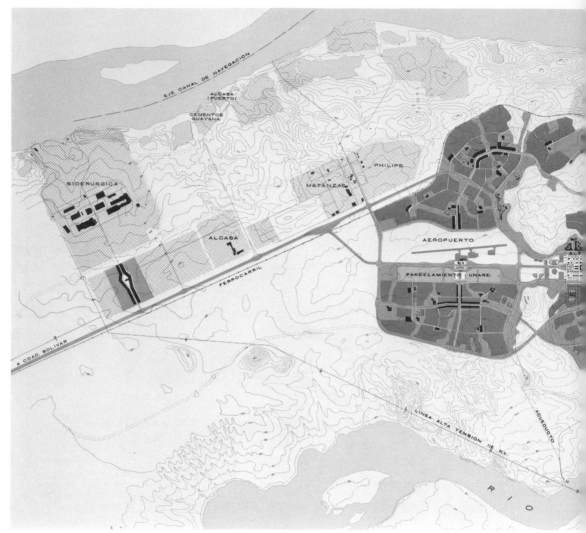

FIG. 1.16 *Map of modern Guayana, Venezuela. Published by permission of Corporación Venezolana de Guayana.*

The percentage of population residing in cities of 20,000 or more and 100,000 or more inhabitants is smaller for Latin America than for Europe, the United States, Canada or Oceania, but greater than for Asia or Africa. In making this comparison it is necessary to take into account the different ways according to which an area is classi-

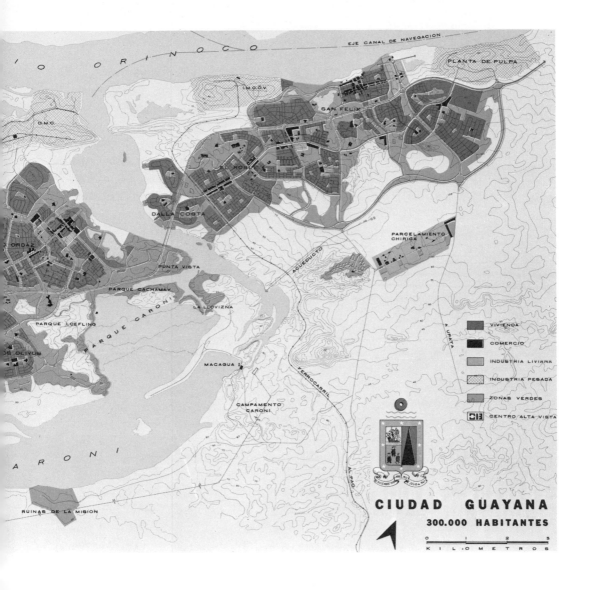

CIUDAD GUAYANA

300.000 HABITANTES

fied as urban in the censuses of the various countries. In this study, cities of fewer than 5,000 inhabitants are considered small; those with from 5,000 to fewer than 20,000 inhabitants are considered medium; from 20,000 to fewer than 100,000, large; and more than 100,000 capitals or metro-cities. As of 1950, in 12 Latin American countries the largest proportion of total urban population is found in the cities classified as capitals.[19] These include or coincide with

[19] *Economic and Social Survey of Latin America, 1961* (Washington, D.C.: Pan American Union, 1964), 2:276.

the political capitals of those countries. In four countries, El Salvador, Honduras, Nicaragua and Perú, the largest proportion of total urban population is found in the cities of 5,000 or less inhabitants.

The high percentages of population clustered in larger urban centers can be accounted for in various ways. In some cases a country is uniformly populated and the percentage of its urban population is distributed homogeneously, with a tendency to some concentration in the larger cities. In other cases, the percentages may indicate a polarization of the population, with one part concentrated in the large cities and the other part living in small towns, and an absence of intermediate medium cities. This situation frequently implies the coexistence of two sociocultural systems and two social structures, one with highly developed industrial and commercial characteristics and the other with agrarian and artisan characteristics. In many cases these two systems and structures are superimposed without being integrated.

In Latin America the small cities have thus far been district centers where primary economic activities predominate. The typical small city has a market place, a traditional industry, and a trade especially related to the surrounding area. The prevailing technical and economic level corresponds to that of the rural area served. In relation to the rest of the country, the volume of industrial activity in these small cities has increased rather slowly because many activities of a traditional nature are being displaced. The degree of displacement is directly related to the opening of communication routes. These localities have been continuously swelled by the inflow of surplus rural agricultural population, while the lack of opportunities encourages, to a greater or lesser extent, the outflow of the older inhabitants toward larger cities. If the rural immigrants do not find housing available, or if they have no means of obtaining it, they proceed to construct their own dwellings just as they did where they came from. The gradual growth of population and of more or less improvised housing increases the need for public services but the low income level of these communities makes it difficult to adequately finance such services.

The medium cities share many of the characteristics of the smaller ones, except that their rate of growth is much more varied, ranging from sharp increases to little or no increase, or at times even declines in population. The highest indices are generally found in the large cities, and, above all, in the capitals. However, in certain very densely populated metropolitan areas the surrounding suburban areas have shown a tendency to grow more rapidly than the centers. For example, there is evidence that population growth in México City itself has been less than that in the adjacent areas; this is typical of large cities in the more developed countries. However, in many large Latin American cities the population increased much more rapidly than within the urbanized areas. In general, the annual rate of growth has been higher in cities of 20,000 and more inhabitants than in the rest of the country. The growth rate in localities with more than 100,000 inhabitants has also been uniformly greater than the rate of growth in those with populations ranging from 20,000 to 100,000. In quite a few cities of more than 100,000 inhabitants the average annual rate of growth has been over 4%. This means, in effect, that if the rate remains constant the population will have doubled within 20 years.

Most observations in this book, therefore, are made with reference to the large cities, and, in the majority of the cases, to the capitals of the Latin American countries, largely because most of the available reliable data is limited to these first-rank cities. In view of this limitation our observations do not pretend to be representative of the typical Latin American city. The population, economic, and social characteristics of the capital city are generally quite distinct from those of the lower-rank cities of the rest of a given country. The range of variation among the capitals of different countries, however, diminishes the significance of this distortion. Thus one can more readily compare Managua, the capital of Nicaragua, having 234,600 inhabitants with Buenos Aires, capital of Argentina, with a population twenty-five times greater, 6.7 million, and with equivalent differences of complexity, than with another city in Nicaragua.

The Latin American cities today are undergoing rapid growth and change. Some of this development is characteristically native, a dramatic example being the proliferation of squatter settlements. Some of it is induced and imitative, inspired by developments abroad. A great many of the changes can be considered as the natural response to technological improvements, the industrialization of cities, changing commercial patterns, improvements in highway construction, a higher standard of living, and the increasing popularity of private automobiles. Most of the factors that have conditioned the recent growth of Latin American cities differ from those that were important in previous periods. This is dramatically demonstrated by the expansion of the cities into peripheral areas that were long considered as unsuitable for urban development. Of particular interest is the fact that while in North American and European cities suburbanization has been associated with the movement of high-income groups from the central city districts to the outskirts in Latin American cities the suburbs also include large numbers of low-income residents who have settled on the periphery. Indeed, as will become evident in the course of this book, in Latin American cities the areas with the highest population densities are often found on the peripheries of the urban centers rather than in the traditional central core of the city.

The increase of population and its redistribution as the result of internal migrations have been among the prime factors responsible for the growth of Latin American cities in recent decades. We begin then, with an analysis of urban population distribution and of demographic growth in Latin America.

2

Distribution of Urban Population

Population Distribution

POPULATION distribution throughout Latin America, both among the various countries and within each country, is extremely uneven. While large areas have a population density of less than one person per square kilometer, some small Central American countries (for example, Haití and El Salvador) show a population density in excess of 100 persons per square kilometer. High densities are also found in regions surrounding large metropolises, especially along the Atlantic coast. One such large population center clusters around the mouth of the La Plata River including the region around Buenos Aires in Argentina along one bank and the region around Montevideo in Uruguay on the other. Yet another population center surrounds both Rio de Janeiro and São Paulo in Brazil. Each of these concentrations comprises about 10 million inhabitants—a number that exceeds the total population of most of the individual countries of Latin America (see table 2.1, p. 45). One major explanation for these concentrations along the Atlantic coast is that, like the northeastern United States, this coastal area attracted massive European immigration toward the end of the nineteenth and at the beginning of the twentieth century.

Map 2.1, Population Density in 1960 and 1966,[1] shows that with the exception of México and Colombia, the large Latin American

[1] SOURCES: 1960 figures from Department of Social Affairs, *Economic and Social Survey of Latin America, 1961* (Washington, D.C.: Pan American Union, 1964), table 16, 2:224. Figures for 1966 from Economic Commission for Latin America, *Statistical Bulletin for Latin America*, vol. 2, no. 2 (New York: United Nations, Sept. 1966). (Commission henceforth referred to as ECLA.)

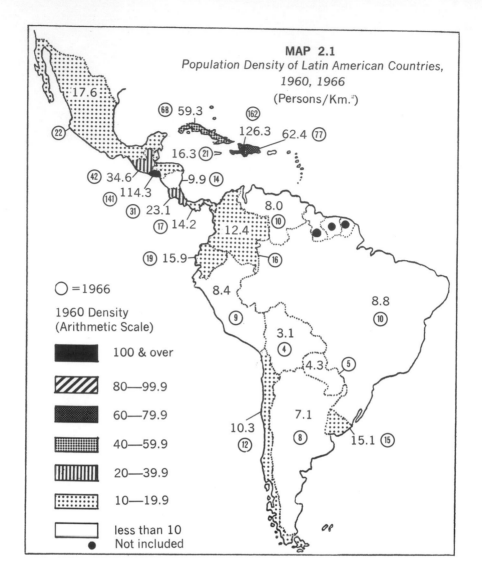

MAP 2.1

Population Density of Latin American Countries,
1960, 1966

(Persons/Km.²)

○ = 1966

1960 Density
(Arithmetic Scale)

■	100 & over
▧	80—99.9
▨	60—79.9
▦	40—59.9
▥	20—39.9
⫶	10—19.9
□	less than 10
●	Not included

countries such as Argentina, Brazil, Perú and Venezuela had a population density considerably below 11.0 in 1960 and 13.0 in 1966, which were the average densities for Latin America as a whole, indicating that settlement within the various countries is very much scattered over wide areas, only small portions being thickly populated. Ranked according to population density in 1966, the countries of Latin America fall roughly into the following order (see map 2.1): Group 1: Haití (162 persons per square kilometer), and El Salvador (141 persons per square kilometer)—both in the Caribbean; Group 2: the Dominican Republic (77), Cuba (68), and Guatemala (42). Group 3, comprising the largest number of countries, includes: Costa Rica, México, Honduras, Ecuador, Panama, Colombia, Uruguay, and Chile—in which the density falls between 12 and 31 persons per square kilometer. Nicaragua, with a density of 14 also comes within this group but is remarkable in having such low density compared to the neighboring Caribbean countries which head this list. Group 4 includes Brazil, Venezuela, Perú and Argentina, all with densities of approximately 9 persons per square kilometer. Group 5, countries with the lowest densities, consists of Paraguay (5) and Bolivia (4), both of which are in the interior of South America.

If one compares the 1960 density figures with those for 1950 (see map 2.2) one sees that, in absolute figures, El Salvador, the

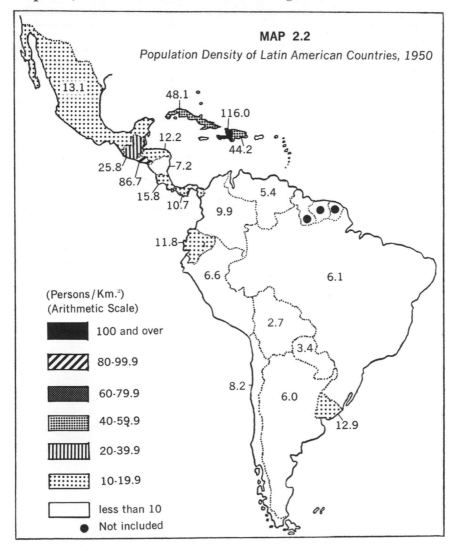

MAP 2.2

Population Density of Latin American Countries, 1950

13.1

48.1

116.0

12.2

44.2

25.8

7.2

86.7

15.8

10.7

9.9

5.4

11.8

6.6

6.1

(Persons / Km.²)
(Arithmetic Scale)

██	100 and over
▨	80-99.9
▦	60-79.9
▤	40-59.9
▥	20-39.9
⠿	10-19.9
☐	less than 10
●	Not included

2.7

3.4

8.2

6.0

12.9

Dominican Republic, Cuba and Haití experienced the highest increase of persons per square kilometer during this ten-year period.[2] The differences in density for these countries within the ten-year span were 27.6, 18.2, 11.2, and 10.3, respectively. Bolivia, Paraguay, Argentina and Perú, on the other hand, showed the lowest increase of population density with differences of 0.4, 0.9, 1.1 and 1.8, respectively, for the 1950–1960 period. Changes in density distribution between 1960 and 1966 continued the same trend. Haití, El Salvador, the Dominican Republic and Cuba again showed the highest increase of persons per square kilometer, with density differences of 36, 27, 15 and 9, respectively, within the six-year period. Perú, Argentina, Paraguay and Bolivia also showed the lowest increase of population density, all with differences of 1 person per square kilometer for this period.

What accounts for these variations in population density, and what problems do they pose? In many cases the answer to the first of these questions is to be found in the prevailing natural physical and climatic conditions. The scattered population in Brazil, for example, is partially accounted for by the presence of the Amazon jungle in the interior of that country. Only recently has the development of this region been consciously sponsored by the government in its plan for decentralization.[3] Indeed, this was one of the fundamental aims of the creation of the new capital of Brasilia, almost at the geographical center of the country. Natural conditions similarly account for the scattering of population in the highlands of Perú, Bolivia, and Ecuador, on the coastal deserts of Perú, in the cold rainy regions of southern Chile, and in the Patagonian region of Argentina.

The uneven distribution of population throughout a country presents two major problems, that of scattered settlement, and that of

---

[2] SOURCE: *Economic and Social Survey, 1961*, table 16, 2:224.

[3] In 1953, President Juscelino Kubitschek included among the aims of his administration the transfer of Brazil's capital (then Rio de Janeiro) to the Central Plateau, in obedience to a constitutional provision of 1946. Perhaps the single most convincing argument for the construction of Brasilia was that it could open up the vast and empty interior lands of the nation. As an instrument for regional development, Brasilia would serve this purpose in several ways because the opening of the Amazon region would provide job opportunities as well as an expansion of the national income and production. The construction of Brasilia has yet to achieve these goals, but the long-term benefits are expected to crystallize in the future. For the time being, most of the construction has been internal. Efforts to stimulate regional growth have not yet been extended beyond the provision of highway links from the coast to Brasilia.

densely populated areas with a high rate of population increase. Scattering population over large areas makes the provision of various services such as roads, educational networks and associated regional community services physically difficult and financially costly. The lack of existing services in turn discourages private development, because in the absence of roads, trained personnel, and closely linked populous communities, the potential of profit for private investors is slim. Thus only government can summon the political and economic resources to undertake the development of such areas, and to some degree, this has been done in the Carretera Marginal de la Selva in Perú.[4]

Urban Population Growth

The obverse of underpopulation—the high concentration and rapid rate of increase of population within a limited space (found at its extreme in Haití)—creates yet another problem. In these

[4] The Carretera Marginal de la Selva, Marginal Forest Highway, was first proposed in 1957 by Perú's President Fernando Belaunde Terry. The Highway, now under construction, will be a 3500-mile road to benefit the four Andean countries along its route—Colombia, Ecuador, Perú and Bolivia. It will run along the forested eastern foothills of the Andes, from Colombia's border with Venezuela to Santa Cruz, Bolivia. The total cost has been estimated at $494 million. A summary of the direct benefits and costs are given in the following table:

The Carretera Marginal de la Selva: Summary of Direct Benefits & Costs					
	Colombia	*Ecuador*	*Perú*	*Bolivia*	*Total*
Annual value of farm production in full development (Millions)	$35,118	13,960	36,409	13,084	98,571
Regional product at full development (Mil.)	$58,530	23,267	60,682	21,807	164,286
Per capita product, zone of influence	$ 194	56	114	63	(avg.) 103
Total population in area at full development (Thousands)	302	412	530	348	1,593
Hectares made available (Mil.)	2,430	1,640	1,718	1,605	7,392
Cost of highway and other works (Mil.)	$ 113,1	81,3	227,8	71,8	494

SOURCE: *Traffic Quarterly*, April, 1966.

cases the rapidity of population increase outstrips the planning and provision of housing and related social services, so that once again, though for different reasons, these services are inadequate to the needs of the population. The degree to which a large proportion of the population is concentrated within a relatively small proportion of the total area of many Latin American countries is demonstrated by the fact that 50% of the total population occupies ⅛ of the land area of Colombia, 1/11 of the area of Brazil, 1/20 of the area of Chile, and only 1/40 of the areas of Argentina and Paraguay.[5] Moreover, the urban population of Latin America is growing at a much faster rate than the total population. While in the last decade of 1950–1960 the total population increased about 30%, the growth of urban population was in the magnitude of 56%.[6] In general, the percentage of urban population increased at a faster rate in countries with intermediate levels of urbanization in 1950, and at a slower rate in countries such as Chile, Argentina and Uruguay that already had more than 50% of their population in urban areas. Table 2.1 shows the general distribution of urban and rural population in Latin America from 1950 to 1980. Urban population as a percentage of the total population of each individual country is also indicated.

Thus the most urbanized countries in 1950 were those falling within the triangle of the southern part of Latin America: Uruguay with 79% of its population urban, Argentina with 64%, and Chile with 54%. Immediately following were: Cuba (50%), Venezuela (48%) and México (46%). At the intermediate level were: Colombia (36%), Panamá (35%), and Perú (31%), followed by Brazil (30%), Costa Rica (29%), Nicaragua and Paraguay (28%) and Ecuador and El Salvador (27%). Showing the lowest levels of urbanization were Bolivia (25%), Guatemala (24%), Dominican Republic (21%), Honduras (17%), and Haití (10%).

The average of urban population for Latin America in 1950 was 39% so that the continent was still predominantly rural. These percentages are represented geographically on map 2.3.[7] By 1960, however, the average percent of urban population for Latin America as a whole had risen to 46%, though the pattern of urbanization

[5] ECLA, *Preliminary Study of the Demographic Situation in Latin America*, E/CN 12/604 (New York: United Nations, April 1961), p. 9.

[6] Unless otherwise indicated, urban population is defined as 2,000 or more inhabitants per locality, the remainder being considered as rural (see table 2.1).

[7] Based on table 2.1.

TABLE 2.1

URBAN AND RURAL POPULATION OF LATIN AMERICAN COUNTRIES,
1950 TO 1980
(Thousands)

COUNTRY AND AREA	1950	1955	1960	1965	1970	1975	1980
Argentina	17,189	19,122	20,956	22,909	24,937	27,068	29,334
Urban	11,038	12,657	14,161	15,767	17,431	19,179	21,043
Rural	6,151	6,465	6,795	7,142	7,506	7,889	8,291
% urban	64.2	66.2	67.6	68.8	69.9	70.9	71.7
Bolivia	3,013	3,322	3,696	4,136	4,658	5,277	6,000
Urban	778	915	1,104	1,345	1,652	2,040	2,514
Rural	2,235	2,407	2,592	2,791	3,006	3,237	3,486
% urban	25.8	27.5	29.9	32.5	35.5	38.7	41.9
Brazil	52,178	60,453	70,309	81,300	93,752	107,863	123,566
Urban	16,083	21,526	28,329	36,026	44,926	55,207	66,779
Rural	36,095	38,927	41,980	45,274	48,826	52,656	56,787
% urban	30.8	35.6	40.3	44.3	47.9	51.2	54.0
Chile	6,073	6,761	7,627	8,567	9,636	10,872	12,300
Urban	3,327	4,005	4,861	5,791	6,850	8,024	9,274
Rural	2,746	2,756	2,766	2,776	2,786	2,848	3,026
% urban	54.8	59.2	63.7	67.6	71.1	73.8	75.4
Colombia	11,679	13,441	15,468	17,787	20,514	23,774	27,691
Urban	4,253	5,574	7,134	8,958	11,161	13,865	17,193
Rural	7,426	7,867	8,334	8,829	9,353	9,909	10,498
% urban	36.4	41.5	46.1	50.4	54.4	58.3	62.1
Ecuador	3,197	3,691	4,317	5,036	5,909	6,933	8,080
Urban	878	1,100	1,423	1,803	2,297	2,898	3,573
Rural	2,319	2,591	2,894	3,233	3,612	4,035	4,507
% urban	27.5	29.8	33.0	35.8	38.9	41.8	44.2
Paraguay	1,397	1,565	1,768	2,007	2,296	2,645	3,065
Urban	392	444	508	583	674	785	920
Rural	1,005	1,121	1,260	1,424	1,622	1,860	2,145
% urban	28.1	28.4	28.7	29.0	29.4	29.7	30.0
Perú	7,969	8,790	10,025	11,650	13,586	15,869	18,527
Urban	2,498	3,003	3,904	5,021	6,345	7,935	9,782
Rural	5,471	5,787	6,121	6,629	7,241	7,934	8,745
% urban	31.3	34.2	38.9	43.1	46.7	50.0	52.8
Uruguay	2,195	2,348	2,491	2,647	2,802	2,960	3,126
Urban	1,734	1,887	2,030	2,186	2,341	2,499	2,665
Rural	461	461	461	461	461	461	461
% urban	79.0	80.4	81.5	82.6	83.5	84.2	85.3

COUNTRY AND AREA	1950	1955	1960	1965	1970	1975	1980
Venezuela	4,974	6,049	7,331	8,722	10,399	12,434	14,827
Urban	2,422	3,414	4,611	5,844	7,300	9,052	11,031
Rural	2,552	2,635	2,720	2,878	3,099	3,382	3,796
% urban	48.7	56.4	62.9	67.0	70.2	72.8	74.4
Total South America	109,864	125,542	143,988	164,761	188,489	215,695	246,516
Urban	43,403	54,525	68,065	83,324	100,977	121,484	144,774
Rural	66,461	71,017	75,923	81,437	87,512	94,211	101,742
% urban	39.5	43.4	47.3	50.6	53.6	56.3	58.7
Costa Rica	801	984	1,206	1,467	1,769	2,110	2,491
Urban	232	297	377	494	647	836	1,071
Rural	569	687	829	973	1,122	1,274	1,420
% urban	29.9	30.1	31.3	33.7	36.6	39.6	43.0
El Salvador	1,868	2,142	2,490	2,914	3,417	4,022	4,730
Urban	515	595	721	892	1,105	1,378	1,708
Rural	1,353	1,547	1,769	2,022	2,312	2,644	3,022
% urban	27.6	27.8	29.0	30.6	32.3	34.3	36.1
Guatemala	2,805	3,258	3,765	4,343	5,053	5,906	6,942
Urban	674	886	1,124	1,403	1,780	2,262	2,885
Rural	2,131	2,372	2,641	2,940	3,273	3,644	4,057
% urban	24.0	27.2	29.9	32.3	35.2	38.3	41.6
Honduras	1,428	1,660	1,950	2,315	2,750	3,266	3,879
Urban	249	321	432	593	797	1,051	1,367
Rural	1,181	1,339	1,518	1,722	1,953	2,215	2,512
% urban	17.3	19.3	22.2	25.6	29.0	32.2	35.2
Nicaragua	1,060	1,245	1,477	1,754	2,083	2,474	2,938
Urban	297	383	502	638	819	1,047	1,343
Rural	763	862	975	1,116	1,264	1,427	1,595
% urban	28.0	30.8	34.0	36.4	39.3	42.3	45.7
Panamá	797	923	1,055	1,209	1,387	1,591	1,823
Urban	282	363	447	548	669	811	975
Rural	515	560	608	661	718	780	848
% urban	35.4	39.3	42.4	45.3	48.2	51.0	53.5
Total Central America	8,759	10,212	11,943	14,002	16,459	19,369	22,803
Urban	2,247	2,845	3,603	4,568	5,817	7,385	9,349
Rural	6,512	7,367	8,340	9,434	10,642	11,984	13,454
% urban	25.7	27.9	30.2	32.6	35.3	38.1	41.0

COUNTRY AND AREA	1950	1955	1960	1965	1970	1975	1980
Cuba	5,508	6,127	6,797	7,523	8,307	9,146	10,034
Urban	2,753	3,261	3,816	4,423	5,083	5,792	6,546
Rural	2,755	2,866	2,981	3,100	3,224	3,354	3,488
% urban	50.0	53.2	56.1	58.8	61.2	63.3	65.2
Haití	3,380	3,722	4,140	4,645	5,255	6,001	6,912
Urban	340	401	513	683	927	1,274	1,749
Rural	3,040	3,321	3,627	3,962	4,328	4,727	5,163
% urban	10.1	10.8	12.4	14.7	17.6	21.2	25.3
México	26,366	30,612	36,018	42,681	50,733	60,554	72,659
Urban	12,144	15,397	19,741	25,268	32,105	40,626	51,340
Rural	14,222	15,215	16,277	17,413	18,628	19,928	21,319
% urban	46.1	50.3	54.8	59.2	63.3	67.1	70.7
Dominican Republic	2,243	2,587	3,030	3,588	4,277	5,124	6,174
Urban	482	634	834	1,096	1,435	1,874	2,444
Rural	1,761	1,953	2,196	2,492	2,842	3,250	3,730
% urban	21.5	24.5	27.5	30.5	33.6	36.6	39.6
Total Latin America	156,120	178,802	205,916	237,200	273,520	315,889	365,098
Urban	61,369	77,063	96,572	119,362	146,344	178,435	216,202
Rural	94,751	101,739	109,344	117,838	127,176	137,454	148,896
% urban	39.3	43.1	46.9	50.3	53.5	56.5	59.2

SOURCE: ECLA, *Statistical Bulletin for Latin America*, vol. 2, no. 2 (New York: United Nations, August 1965), p. 10.

according to country remained very similar to that of 1950. The most urbanized countries were still Uruguay, Argentina and Chile, with 81%, 67% and 63% urban population, respectively (see map 2.4[8]). Venezuela, however, had moved very close to this group with 62% of its population urban. A second group was formed by Cuba (56%), México (54%), Colombia (46%), Panamá (42%), Brazil (40%), Perú (38%), and Nicaragua (34%), followed closely by Ecuador (33%), Costa Rica (31%), El Salvador (29%) and Paraguay (28%). The countries with the lowest levels of urbanization remained in the same decreasing order as in 1950, namely: the Dominican Republic (27%), Honduras (22%) and Haití (12%).

It is estimated that by 1965, the population living in localities of 2,000 inhabitants or more had already surpassed the population in

[8] Based on table 2.1.

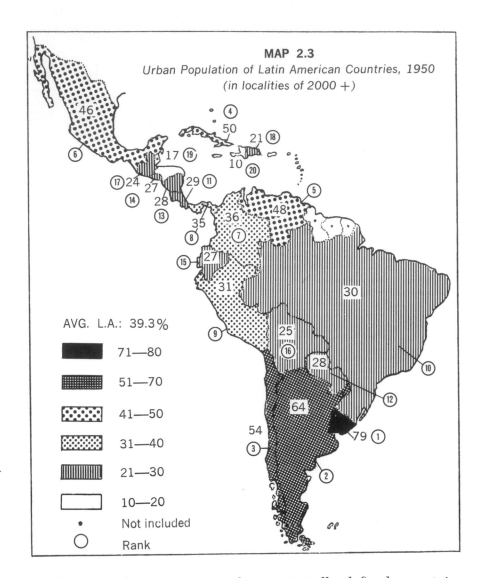

MAP 2.3

Urban Population of Latin American Countries, 1950
(in localities of 2000 +)

AVG. L.A.: 39.3 %

- ■ 71—80
- ▦ 51—70
- ▨ 41—50
- ▧ 31—40
- ▥ 21—30
- □ 10—20
- • Not included
- ○ Rank

rural areas.[9] This, in a region characteristically defined as not industrialized, is a strange phenomenon. The explanation is, that in
Latin America, as opposed to most European countries or the United
States, the industrialization of cities is only one reason for urbanization, and, often, not the most important one: "It is at least doubtful
that the marked trend towards concentration in Latin America's
large cities can be attributed to economic factors alone. An 'urban
bias' may be inherent in Latin civilization, or illusions may be widely
held about the social and cultural advantages of the metropolis.

[9] ECLA, *Statistical Bulletin for Latin America*, vol. 2, no. 2, table 4, p. 10.

Small-town residents may be more attracted to some of the leading cities than economic grounds would warrant. Entrepreneurs may often neglect, and even disdain, existing development opportunities in some of the smaller towns." [10]

The period 1950–1960 indicated that the countries urbanizing most rapidly were Venezuela, with a 90% increase of urban population followed by Brazil with 76%, and Honduras with 74%. Still at a higher level of urbanization than Latin America as a whole were

[10] ECLA, *Demographic Situation in Latin America*, p. 49.

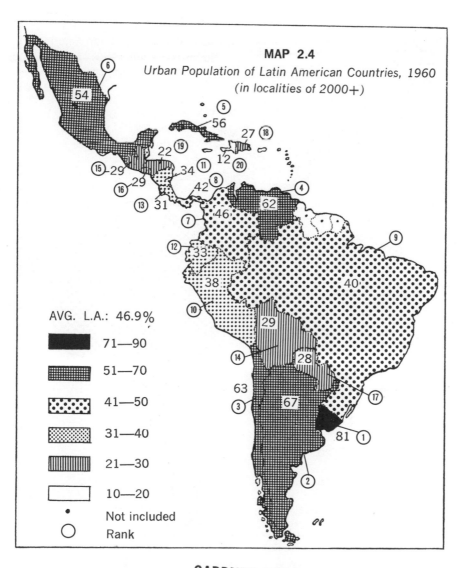

MAP 2.4

Urban Population of Latin American Countries, 1960
(in localities of 2000+)

AVG. L.A.: 46.9%

- 71—90
- 51—70
- 41—50
- 31—40
- 21—30
- 10—20
- • Not included
- ◯ Rank

the Dominican Republic (73%), Nicaragua (69%), Colombia (67%), and Guatemala (66%); and Costa Rica, México and Ecuador, with 62% each. Urbanizing at a similar level to the Latin American region as a whole were Panamá and Perú, with 58% and 56%, respectively. Haití, Chile, Bolivia and El Salvador increased their urban population more slowly, at 50%, 46%, 41% and 40%, respectively. Argentina and Uruguay were the countries urbanizing at the lowest levels, with only a 28% and 17% increase, respectively, for the given decade.

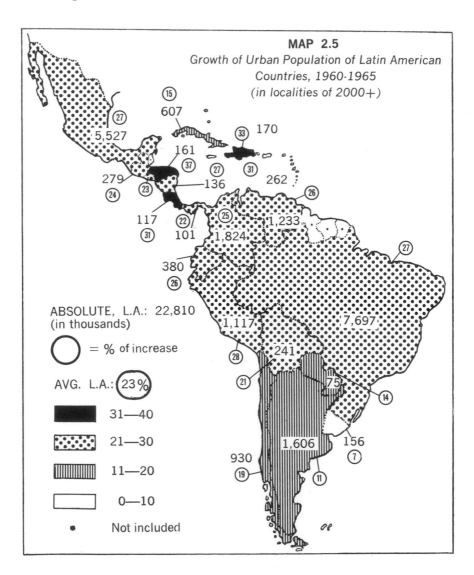

MAP 2.5

Growth of Urban Population of Latin American Countries, 1960-1965

(in localities of 2000+)

ABSOLUTE, L.A.: 22,810
(in thousands)

◯ = % of increase

AVG. L.A.: ⟨23%⟩

■ 31—40

▦ 21—30

▥ 11—20

▢ 0—10

• Not included

During the period 1960–1965 Latin America increased its urban population by 23%. The highest percentage increases of urban population were those of Honduras (37%), Haití (33%), the Dominican Republic (31%) and Costa Rica (31%). Still at a higher level of urbanization than Latin America as a whole were Perú (28%), México (27%), Brazil (27%), Nicaragua (27%), Venezuela (26%) and Ecuador (26%). Argentina and Uruguay continued to show the lowest percentage increases in urban population with only 11% and 7% increases, respectively, during the five-year period (see map 2.5).[11]

As the data of growth of urban population demonstrates, the total increase of population in Latin America as a whole, as well as in most of the individual countries, has been due largely to increases in population living in cities. Indeed, 70.6% of the total population growth in Latin America between 1950 and 1960 can be attributed to the growth of the population of cities of 2,000 inhabitants or more. The extreme case is Uruguay, where there is practically no increase of rural population, or in other words, where urban growth is 100% of the total national population growth. Countries like Argentina, Chile, Venezuela, Colombia, Cuba and México present a very similar picture with over 75% of their total growth attributable to urban growth. Revealing a situation most characteristic of Latin America as a whole are Brazil, Perú and Panamá, with about 63% to 68% of their growth due to growth in urban population. Lower than this average are the remaining countries, with the lowest figure for Haití, in which only 22% of the total growth was due to growth in the cities.

The increase of population in Latin America between 1960 and 1965 generally continued the trend of the previous decade, with 72.9% of the total growth attributed to the growth of urban population (see map 2.6).[12] Uruguay again showed an urban growth representing 100% of the total national population growth. Chile, Venezuela, Cuba, México and Argentina had over 80% of their total growth attributable to urban growth. Still much below the average for Latin America as a whole were El Salvador, Haití and Paraguay, with only 40%, 33% and 31% of their respective total population growth due to growth in urban places of 2,000 inhabitants or more.

[11] Based on table 2.1.
[12] Based on table 2.1.

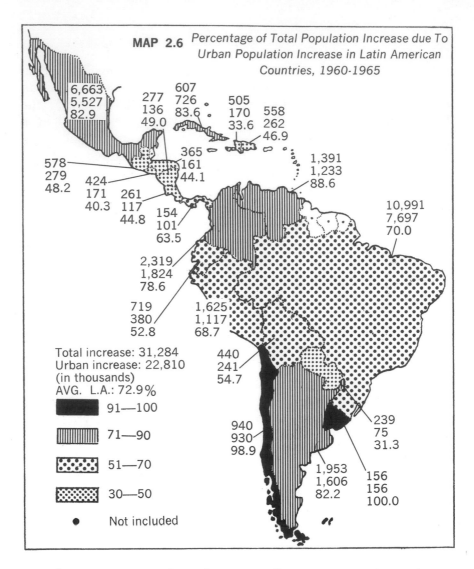

MAP 2.6 *Percentage of Total Population Increase due To Urban Population Increase in Latin American Countries, 1960-1965*

6,663
5,527
82.9

277
136
49.0

607
726
83.6

505
170
33.6

558
262
46.9

578
279
48.2

424
171
40.3

261
117
44.8

365
161
44.1

154
101
63.5

1,391
1,233
88.6

10,991
7,697
70.0

2,319
1,824
78.6

719
380
52.8

1,625
1,117
68.7

Total increase: 31,284
Urban increase: 22,810
(in thousands)
AVG. L.A.: 72.9%

440
241
54.7

940
930
98.9

239
75
31.3

1,953
1,606
82.2

156
156
100.0

91—100

71—90

51—70

30—50

●   Not included

Urbanization is a relatively recent phenomenon in Latin American countries, dating in general from the second quarter of the present century. The only exceptions are Argentina and Uruguay, which experienced early urbanization as a result of large migrations from Europe.

The censuses (1950, 1960) and estimates for 1965 (the most recent statistics allowing for comparisons of the various countries) suggest that the most urbanized countries in Latin America are generally those with the highest degree of economic development. But at the same time it is significant that the fastest rates of urbanization during 1950–1960 occurred in the countries that had been

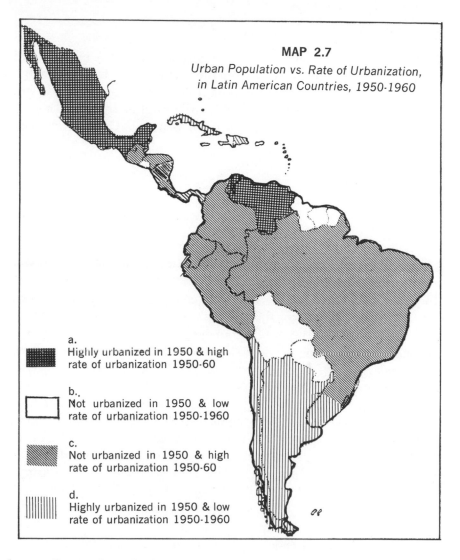

MAP 2.7

*Urban Population vs. Rate of Urbanization,
in Latin American Countries, 1950-1960*

a.
Highly urbanized in 1950 & high
rate of urbanization 1950-60

b.
Not urbanized in 1950 & low
rate of urbanization 1950-1960

c.
Not urbanized in 1950 & high
rate of urbanization 1950-60

d.
Highly urbanized in 1950 & low
rate of urbanization 1950-1960

least urbanized at the beginning of that period. Thus there is, as a
rule, a reverse correlation between the percentage of urban population within a country in 1950 and the growth of urban population
in that country during 1950–1960. Closer study, however, reveals
several exceptions to this rule. At the one extreme are (a) the
countries that were already highly urbanized in 1950 and continued
to show a high rate of urbanization during 1950–1960, namely,
México and Venezuela. At the other extreme are (b) the countries
which were predominantly rural in 1950 and continued to show a
low rate of urbanization in 1950–1960. Much more numerous, however, were the countries that followed the rule, namely, (c) those

that were predominantly rural in 1950 and showed a high rate of urbanization in 1950–1960—Costa Rica, Honduras, Dominican Republic, Guatemala, Brazil, Colombia, Ecuador, Nicaragua and Perú —and (d) countries that were highly urbanized in 1950 and showed a low rate of urbanization in 1950–1960: Uruguay, Cuba, Chile, and Argentina (see map 2.7).[13]

Demographic Growth

The population of Latin America is growing at a faster rate than that of any other region of the world. The Annual Rate of Growth (ARG) for Latin America as a whole is about 2.7% but, for some of the Caribbean and South American countries, the ARG is about 3.5%. During the 1950–1960 period, Latin America experienced a total population growth of about 30.6%. Countries whose populations were growing at a faster than average rate were, first, Venezuela, with a total increase of 46.6% at an ARG of 3.9%, followed by Costa Rica with 46.2% (3.9% ARG) and the Dominican Republic with 41.1% (3.5% ARG). At levels still higher than the average were Brazil, Nicaragua and Ecuador growing at about 36% each; and México, Guatemala, Honduras, Panamá and El Salvador, at 32 to 34%. Lower than the average were: Perú, Chile, Colombia, Cuba and Paraguay, with a 20 to 30% increase and Argentina and Uruguay with around 18% growth. Bolivia and Haití were the countries growing at the slowest ARG of about 1.4% or a total growth of about 14% (map 2.8).[14]

In the previous decade of 1940–1950, the total population of Latin America grew only 24.6%, at an average rate of 2.2% per year (see map 2.9).[15] The fastest growing country was Venezuela with a total 34% total increase and an ARG of 3%, followed by México with a 30.1% total increase and an ARG of 2.7%. A second group of countries whose population during 1940–1950 grew at a faster rate than obtained for Latin America as a whole comprised

[13] SOURCES: ECLA, *Demographic Situation in Latin America,* p. 49 and ECLA, *Geographic Distribution of the Population of Latin America and Regional Development Priorities,* E/CN, 12/643 (New York: United Nations, February 1963). See also table 2.1.
[14] SOURCE: Dept. of Social Affairs, *Economic and Social Survey,* 2:216, table 2.1.
[15] SOURCE: Dept. of Social Affairs, *Economic and Social Survey,* 2:216.

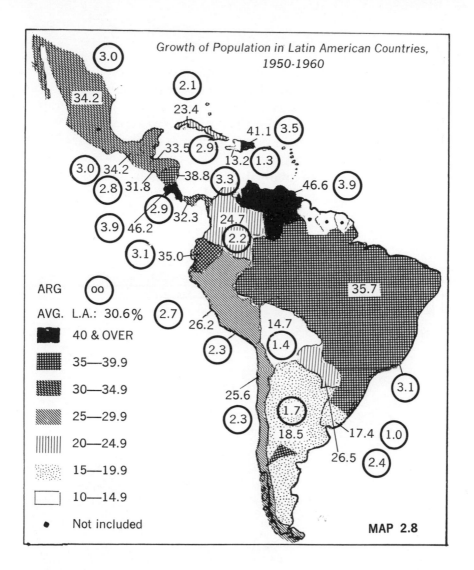

Growth of Population in Latin American Countries, 1950-1960

ARG

AVG. L.A.: 30.6%

- ⬛ 40 & OVER
- 35—39.9
- 30—34.9
- 25—29.9
- |||||| 20—24.9
- 15—19.9
- 10—14.9
- ● Not included

MAP 2.8

the Caribbean countries of Guatemala, Nicaragua, Costa Rica, Panamá, the Dominican Republic, and the South American countries of Ecuador, Brazil and Paraguay—all showing a total increase of about 25% and an ARG of around 2.5%. An intermediate group was formed by Honduras, Cuba, Colombia and Perú, with about a 20 to 25% increase at an ARG of 2.0%. Even lesser increases were observed in the southern countries of Argentina and Chile, and two Caribbean countries, El Salvador and Haití—all showing no more than a 10% to 20% increase. The country with the least population growth was Uruguay, with a total increase of only 11.7%, and an ARG of 1.1%.

The problems caused by rates of population growth as high as those of the 1950–1960 period are numerous. If a country is to maintain the existing living standard for its population, its high rate of population growth must be matched by a high proportion of its current income going into investments that will generate rapid economic growth. This is all the more necessary because not only will there be a high ratio of totally dependent children to working adults in a country with rapid population growth, but also the education of the high proportion of youngsters in the population will require

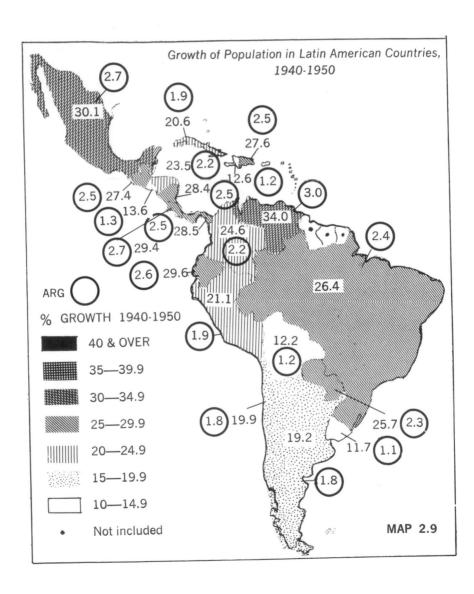

Growth of Population in Latin American Countries, 1940-1950

MAP 2.9

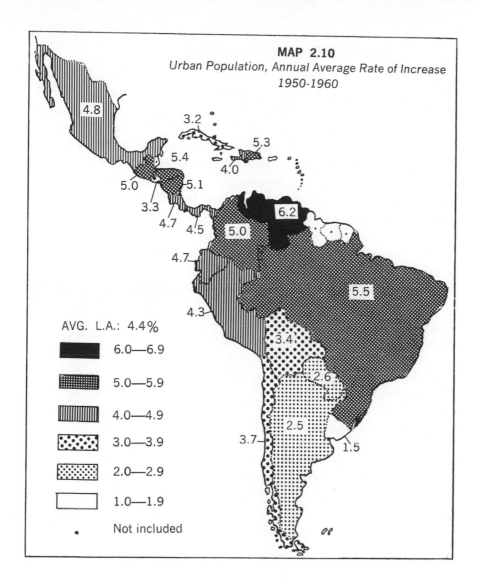

MAP 2.10

Urban Population, Annual Average Rate of Increase
1950-1960

AVG. L.A.: 4.4%

■	6.0—6.9
▦	5.0—5.9
▥	4.0—4.9
⦂	3.0—3.9
⦂	2.0—2.9
☐	1.0—1.9
•	Not included

heavy government expenditures as well. The Economic Commission
for Latin America estimates that if a high rate of economic growth
is to be retained while population growth continues at a rate even
higher than the present, Latin America must by 1975 expand its
industrial production by 400% and its agricultural production by
120%. It will have to find jobs for a labor force that will by then
have increased by 35 million, and, only 5 million of these new jobs
can be anticipated from the agricultural sector.[16] The implications

[16] Department of Economic and Social Affairs, *1963 Report on the World Social
Situation* (New York: United Nations, 1963), p. 123.

of all of this for the urban areas are considerable. Thus there will be a need for heavy investment in urban areas not only to create jobs but also to provide adequate housing and services for ever-increasing urban populations. As it is, most Latin American countries have been unable to keep up with the constantly growing demand for proper housing in urban areas. As we shall see (Chapters 7 and 8) it is this gap between supply and demand that has led to the creation of the squatter settlements that flourish around many of the large urban areas such as in Lima, Perú, Rio de Janeiro, and Caracas, Venezuela.

Urban population in Latin America seen in terms of the Annual Average Rate of Increase (AARI) for each individual country is shown geographically on map 2.10.[17] Close to the AARI for Latin America as a whole (4.4%), are the AARI for Perú (4.3%), for Panamá (4.5%), for Ecuador (4.7%), and for Costa Rica (4.7%). The highest AARI in urban population is found in Venezuela (6.2%) and Brazil (5.5%) followed by Honduras (5.4%) and the Dominican Republic (5.3%).

The contrast with the annual average rate of increase of rural population in Latin America for the same period is sharp (see map 2.11).[18] In every case, the AARI is considerably lower; the highest being that of Costa Rica, 3.7%. The AARI of rural population for Latin America as a whole is 1.4%. Close to this average are those of México (1.3%), Brazil (1.5%), Bolivia (1.5%) and Panamá (1.7%). The lowest rural annual average rate increases are those of Cuba (0.8%), Chile (0.7%) and Venezuela (0.6%). Uruguay presents an extreme case with an AARI of 0.0% for the decade of 1950–1960.

It is important to observe that whereas the urban population in Latin America as a whole is growing at an annual average rate of

[17] Based on table 2.1. The annual average rate of increase is computed by dividing the increase of the intercensal period by the mean population (defined as the mean average of the first and last census population figures for each period) and by the intercensal period expressed in years: $\mathrm{AARI} = \dfrac{(\text{Pop. 1960} - \text{Pop. 1950})}{\dfrac{(\text{Pop. 1960} + \text{Pop. 1950})}{2} \, 10} \times 100$

[18] Based on table 2.1.

4.4%, the populations of the larger cities are increasing at even higher rates:

	Population (In Thousands)[19]		Annual Average Rate of Increase
	1950	*1960*	
São Paulo	2,449	4,369	5.6%
Caracas	790	1,492	6.2%
Guayaquil	267	568	7.2%

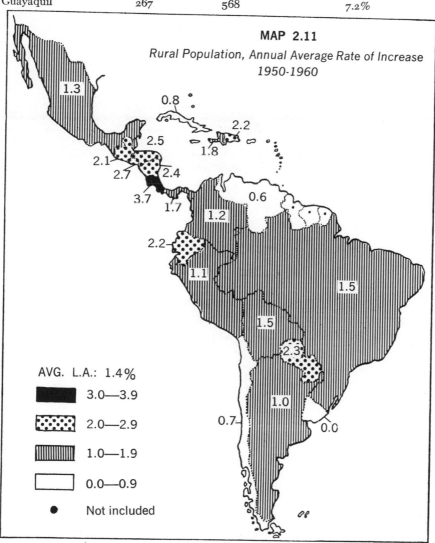

MAP 2.11

Rural Population, Annual Average Rate of Increase
1950-1960

AVG. L.A.: 1.4%

████ 3.0—3.9

▒▒▒ 2.0—2.9

‖‖‖ 1.0—1.9

☐ 0.0—0.9

● Not included

[19] Metropolitan areas.

Brasilia, a planned city. © *Manchete.*

The metropolitan areas of some of the national capitals have doubled their populations during the past decade and the already existing gap between the resources available to these areas and the expenditures required to provide an adequate physical setting for their inhabitants has widened even further.

While the population explosion and increased urbanization which have become typical of Latin America in recent years have finally attracted attention, what is not always noted is that much of the increase in urbanization is spontaneous, occurring in a completely unplanned way. Much of the increasing population in urban areas can be traced to migrants from rural areas who have simply "squatted" in the peripheral areas of various cities.

The squatter phenomenon, a striking characteristic of Latin American urbanization, is discussed in more detail in Chapters 7 and 8. Here it is sufficient to mention that the enormous population growth of Latin America is dramatically reflected in the proliferation of squatter houses on the outskirts of cities as well as in previously occupied spaces of the existing urban texture. The presence of such unused areas within the confines of cities can be explained in several ways. These lots may have remained idle because of natural site disadvantages—hilly slopes, swampy land, floods, proximity to railroad lines or noxious industrial areas. In other cases such land was simply retained by owners in the expectation that it would eventually become more valuable (without any extra investment for development) because as urban growth progressed there would be a greater demand for it. In varying degrees this type of land speculation—merely holding on to land and waiting for its value to increase over time—while not unknown in other countries is fairly common in countries with less advanced economies. Often lacking an organized channel for investment in commerce and industry such as is provided by the stock exchanges of developed economies, men of means put their savings into large land holdings which by their concrete nature appear to offer security. Such land, standing idle and unoccupied, attracts settlement by squatters coming from rural areas who cannot afford to pay for housing at all, arriving, as they do, with absolutely no resources.

Comparison with Other World Regions

The phenomenon of urbanization in Latin America can be better understood if considered within the context of the same process in other regions of the world. As shown by map 2.12, Latin America's population grew at the rate of 2.9% average per year in 1963–1967, or 1.0% faster than the average rate of 1.9% for the world as a whole during the same period.[20] Within Latin America, population

[20] Based on table 2.3.

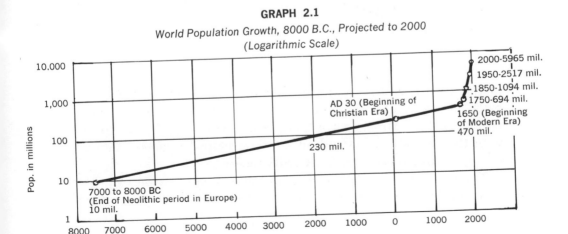

GRAPH 2.1

World Population Growth, 8000 B.C., Projected to 2000
(Logarithmic Scale)

GRAPH 2.2

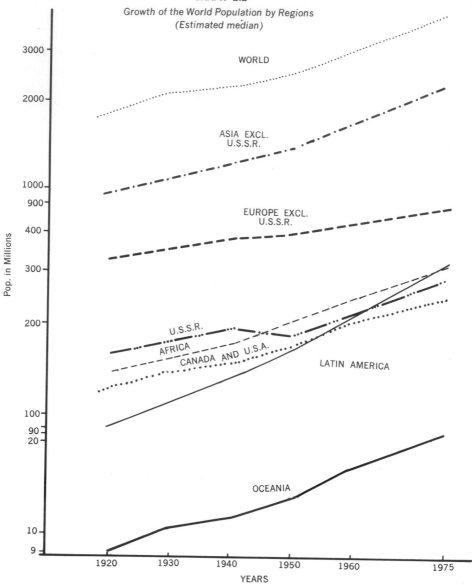

Growth of the World Population by Regions
(Estimated median)

of the areas near the tropics is growing at even faster rates, 3 to 3.2% per year. This is a common pattern for all underdeveloped regions such as Africa (2.5%), and South Asia, (2.4%), compared with the low rates of growth of more developed regions—Europe, 0.8%, North America, 1.3%, USSR, 1.2%.

The rapid growth of population in Latin America is, in fact, part of a world-wide phenomenon. World population figures for most of man's history cannot be considered as very reliable, since no censuses were taken until very recently; but it has been estimated that at the end of the Neolithic period in Europe (8000 to 7000 B.C.), the population of the earth was about 10 million people (see graph 2.1). By the beginning of the Christian era (A.D. 30) it is reasonable to assume that it had increased to 210 or 250 million, about half of this located in the Far East outside the Roman Empire, which included about a quarter of the total. The rest was dispersed through the northern countries of Europe, America and Oceania. By 1650, usually considered as the beginning of the modern era, the total population was about 470 million. One century later, in 1750, the population had increased to about 694 million, with average decennial increases of 2.7 to 3.2%. These figures indicate the speeding up of the population increase since the beginning of the modern era— an increase which continues to the present. In 1850 world population was 1,094 million, with average decennial increases of 4.5 to 5.3%; by 1950, it had reached 2,517 million, with average decennial increases of 6.5 to 8.3%. The validity of these averages is questionable, but it cannot be denied that the growth of world population during the last four centuries is something unusual in history, especially the rate of increase during the last decades. In the decade of 1940–1950, world population grew by a total of 9.7%; in the decade of 1950–1960, this figure rose to 19.0%.

At present, world population is growing at a faster rate than at any other time in history. It took all of recorded history for the world population to amount to about 1,500 million by the turn of the twentieth century; but it took only the past sixty years to double that figure, and according to U.N. projections, by the year 2000 (only thirty more years) the present population will have doubled again. In Latin America, this speeding up has been still more acute. By the turn of the century, Latin America had reached a population of about 63 million people; in less than forty years, this doubled (130 million in 1940); and by 1967 (or about 25 years later), the 1940 population had doubled, the U.N. estimating it to be 259 million in 1967 (see graph 2.2).[21] According to U.N. estimates, in another twenty-five years Latin America will again double its present population. Population estimates and projections for the world and major regions between 1650 and the year 2000 are given in table 2.2.

[21] SOURCE: *Economic and Social Survey of Latin America, 1961* (Washington, D.C.: Pan American Union, 1964), 2:369.

TABLE 2.2

POPULATION ESTIMATES AND PROJECTIONS FOR
THE WORLD AND MAJOR REGIONS, 1650–2000
Total Pop. (millions)

YEAR	WORLD	AFRICA	NORTH AMERICA	LATIN AMERICA	ASIA	EUROPE	OCEANIA	USSR
1650	470	100	1	7	257	103 [a]	2	1 [b]
1750	694	100	1	10	437	144 [a]	2	1 [b]
1850	1,094	100	26	33	656	274 [a]	2	1 [b]
1900	1,550	120	81	63	857	308	6	115
1920	1,830	139	117	90	990 [a]	486 [a]	8.8 [a]	—
1930	2,070	164	134	108	1,120	355	10	179
1940	2,295	191	144	130	1,244	380	11.1	195
1950	2,517	222	166	163	1,381	392	12.7	180
1960	2,990	273	199	212	1,651	425	15.7	214
1963	3,160	294	208	231	1,748	437	16.8	225
1967	3,420	328	220	259	1,907	452	18.1	236
1970	3,574	346	227	282	2,000	454	18.7	246
1980	4,269	449	262	374	2,404	479	22.6	278
1990	5,068	587	306	488	2,840	504	27.0	316
2000	5,965	768	354	624	3,307	527	31.9	353

SOURCES: Data for 1650–1900 and 1920 (except data for 1900 of Europe and USSR):
U.N. Population Division, "The Past and Future Population of the World and its
Continents," paper presented at the World Population Conference, Rome, 1964.
Other data for 1650–1900: ECLA, *Preliminary Study of the Demographic Situation*
(April 1961). Data for 1930–1963: *Demographic Yearbook, 1964*, 16th issue (New
York: United Nations, 1965). Data for 1970–2000: Economic and Social Council,
World Population Prospects for the Year 2000 (New York: United Nations, 1965);
data for 1967: *U.N. Demographic Yearbook, 1967* (New York: United Nations, 1968).
NOTES:
    a. Including USSR
    b. Included in Europe

In absolute figures, this growth is also significant. While in 1900
the population of Latin America represented about 4% of the world
population, by 1967 this percentage had almost doubled to 7.6%.
By the year 2000, it is estimated that this proportion will increase
to 10.5% (see table 2.3). What is true of Latin America is also true,
to a lesser degree, of the underdeveloped regions of the world.
Population pressures are increasing precisely in those countries that
have the least resources to cope with them. Africa's population is
growing at an annual average rate of 2.5%, having doubled the
population attained by 1900 in little more than fifty years. The
prospect is for a doubling again in the 1990s or in about twenty
years. The population of Asia as a whole is growing at 2.0% a year,

TABLE 2.3

THE GROWTH OF WORLD POPULATION BY REGION

		WORLD	AFRICA	ASIA	EUROPE	LATIN AMERICA	NORTH AMERICA	OCEANIA	USSR
1650	Share of world population (%)	100.0	21.3	54.7	21.9	1.5	0.2	0.43	—[a]
1900		100.0	7.7	55.3	19.9	4.1	5.2	0.39	7.4
1963		100.0	9.3	55.3	13.8	7.3	6.6	0.53	7.1
1967		100.0	9.6	55.8	13.2	7.6	6.4	0.53	6.9
2000		100.0	12.9	55.4	8.8	10.5	5.9	0.53	5.9
1958–63	Rate of pop. growth (%)	1.8	2.3	1.8	0.9	2.7	1.6	2.1	1.6
1960–63		1.9	2.5	1.9	0.9	2.8	1.6	2.2	1.6
1963–67		1.9	2.5	2.0	0.8	2.9	1.3	1.9	1.2
1958–63	Birth rate o/oo	34	46	38	19	40	24	27	24
1960–67		34	46	38	19	40	21	26	21
1958–63	Death rate o/oo	16	23	20	10	14	9	11	7
1960–67		15	22	18	10	12	9	11	7
1958–63	Natural increase o/oo	18	23	18	9	26	15	16	17
1960–67		19	24	20	9	28	12	15	14
1958–63	Real inc. o/oo	18	23	18	9	27	16	21	16
1958–63	Nat. inc. real inc. o/oo	0	0	0	0	+1	+1	+5	−1
		0	0	0	0	3.9	6.7	31.0	5.9
Area (oooKm²)		135.761[b]	30.227[b]	27.621[b]	4.929	20.535[b]	21.515	8.532[b]	22.402
Density (Inhab/Km²)		23	10	63	89	11	10	2	10
Density 1967[b]		25	11	69	92	13	10	2	11

SOURCES: *Demographic Yearbook, 1964*, no. 16 (1965); and *Demographic Yearbook, 1967*, no. 19 (1968).
NOTES:
  a. Included in Europe.
  b. Area (Km²) figures are slightly different.

but within it, that of South Asia is growing at 2.4%. Mainland China (growing at 1.4%) and Japan, at 1.0%, are responsible for the lowering of the average. Asia as a whole doubled its population attained by 1900 in about sixty years, about the same time that it took the world as a whole to do this. It will double again by the year 2000, as will the world figure.

These rates of growth are very high indeed when compared to the rates of more developed world regions. North America's population is growing at a present rate of 1.3% a year, Europe's at 0.8%, and the USSR's at 1.2%. The United States had a very fast growth during the last two centuries, in part due to heavy immigration from overseas. By 1750 the population of North America (including Canada) was about 1 million. For comparison, Latin America's population was then about 10 million. A century later, in 1850, however, while the population of Latin America had increased little more than three times, the population of North America had increased twenty-six times; and by 1900, it had surpassed the population of Latin America, with 81 million as against Latin America's 63 million. The growth of North America continued during the first decades of the present century, but at a less accelerated rate than in Latin America. By 1960, the growth rate had slowed down in North America while Latin America already had a larger population, 212, as opposed to 199 million. In the future, it is expected that North America will slow down even more, since by the year 2000 it will not yet have doubled its present population suggesting that the population of North America will be growing at a slower rate than that of the world as a whole.

Europe shows an even more acute slowdown. Its total population in 1900 was estimated to be 308 million (see table 2.2). By 1967 it had doubled only 46% of that figure, with a total population of 452 million. Projections for the year 2000 indicate a total population of 527 million. This is a minimal growth when compared with Latin America, which by then would not only have doubled its population of 1900, but increased it about ten times. Population growth in the USSR has been rather slow too, with a present rate of 1.2%, only slightly lower than North America. If we consider the population of the USSR in 1900 as being about 115 million, then it only doubled that figure by 1963, according to unofficial U.N. estimates (table 2.2). In other words, the USSR doubled its population at a rate six years slower than the world as a whole, and about twenty-six years slower than Latin America. By the year 2000 it will not have doubled again; and the projections of the U.N. indicate a future slower growth than any other region in the world, with the exception, perhaps, of Europe.

Oceania is a special case. Having the gross of its population in developed regions, it presents a relatively high rate of growth— 2.2% average for 1960–1963 and 1.9% for 1963–1967 (map 2.12). Australia and New Zealand alone accounted for 13.5 of the total population of 16.8 million of this region in 1963, at an average rate of growth of 2% a year. Though less in volume, the flow of immigration to Australia and New Zealand can be likened to that into the United States during the last century. In 1850 Oceania had about 2 million inhabitants; and by 1900 this had increased to about 6 million, primarily due to heavy immigration (see table 2.2). During the next 50 years Oceania doubled its total population to 12.7 million. It is estimated that a second doubling will occur by 1990 (within 40 years). In comparison, it is estimated that Latin America will have trebled its population during the same forty-year period.

Since growth rates are independent of the size of the population to which they refer, they may give a distorted impression if not qualified by the absolute figures. It may therefore be best to review the proportion of population living in different regions of the world in the past, and then to view projections for the future. This comparison yields a less dramatic picture than the previous one, but one that also reveals a diminishing share of the total population in the already developed regions, and an increasing share of that population in the developing ones. In 1650, the 7 million people that are estimated to have lived in Latin America represented about 1.5% of the total of 470 million estimated to have lived in the world at that time. During the next two and one-half centuries, that is, by 1900, the population of Latin America increased to represent a little more than 4% of the world population, or 63 million of 1,550 million for the world as a whole. In 1967, only six decades later, the population of Latin America was 259 million, or 7.6% of the 3,420 million living in the world. By the year 2000, its 624 million will represent 10.5% of the 5,965 million expected total world population. This figure is very significant, since by then Latin America would represent the third most populated region in the world, second only to

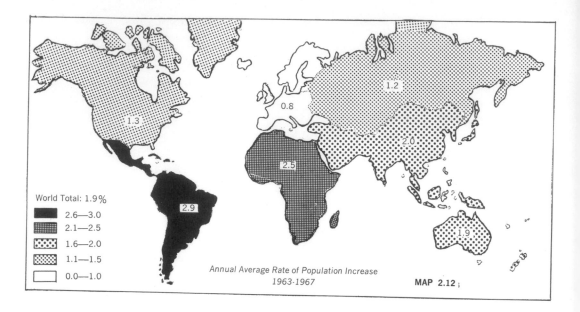

World Total: 1.9%

- ■ 2.6—3.0
- ▨ 2.1—2.5
- ▨ 1.6—2.0
- ▨ 1.1—1.5
- □ 0.0—1.0

Annual Average Rate of Population Increase
1963-1967

MAP 2.12

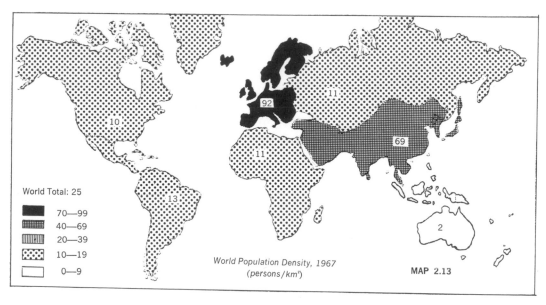

World Total: 25

- ■ 70—99
- ▨ 40—69
- ▥ 20—39
- ▨ 10—19
- □ 0—9

World Population Density, 1967
(persons/km²)

MAP 2.13

Asia and Africa. In 1960 it was only the fifth most populated region (or fourth, if another slightly lower estimate for the Soviet Union is used).

The proportion of people living in Africa is also increasing rapidly. In 1650, it accounted for 21.3% of the total world population. By 1900 there was a sharp drop to 7.7%, but from then on it has kept increasing constantly. Thus, in 1967, it was 9.6%, which made it the third most populated region, after Asia and Europe. By the year 2000, according to projections, it will surpass Europe, with a percentage as high as 12.9%. Asia has always been by far the most populated region of the world, and will continue to be so in the future. World population densities are shown on map 2.13:[22] Asia's share of the world population has changed slightly but the future pattern is not likely to suffer any radical change. In 1650 Asia represented 54.7% of world population; this percentage dropped slightly to 55.3% in 1900, but by 1967, the figure increased to 55.8%. By the year 2000 it is expected to drop again to 55.4%. This fluctuation represents a variation within the range of less than 2% over three and one-half centuries.

The demographic share of regions in a more advanced stage of economic development will decrease in the future, or will remain stationary, as in Oceania. Europe's share will then be more sharply reduced than in 1650, when its population represented 21.9% of the world population (see table 2.3). In 1900, Europe's population (not including the USSR) represented a share of 19.9%, and therefore it can be assumed that between 1650–1900, it either slightly increased, or remained constant. By 1967, however, its share had dropped to 13.2% and it is expected to further decrease in the year 2000, to 8.8%. The share of North America and the USSR will decrease somewhat less sharply. In North America it has been increasing up to the present, but will decrease in the future. In 1650, North America was responsible for 0.2% of the world population, in 1900, 5.2%, and in 1967, 6.4%. By the year 2000 it is expected to decrease to 5.9%. The USSR, in 1900 contained 7.4% of the world population, by 1967, this had decreased to 6.9%. It is expected to fall even more by the year 2000, to 5.9%.

Three of the chief factors to which the tremendous growth of world population can be attributed are: (1) improvements in health and wealth resulting in the reduction of mortality rates; (2) transportation improvements that have made it possible for masses of people to relocate and multiply in previously underdeveloped areas in a way that would not have been possible in the previous location, with its relatively fixed territory; and (3) technological progress that has been able to provide a means of livelihood for greater numbers of people. Above all, it must be noted that the reduction of mortality

[22] Based on table 2.3.

rates has not been accompanied by a reduction in birth rates. This fact alone is responsible for the main part of the growth of population in the various regions of the world.

The rates of population growth in the different regions of the world in the last decades are also primarily a reflection of this natural increase. In recent times, intercontinental migrations have had only a minimal effect, with the exception of Oceania, where immigration from Europe accounted for about 30% of its population increase. As can be seen in table 2.3, the figures for natural increase and real increase during the years 1958–1963 are practically the same for the different regions of the world—with the exception, again, of Oceania. In Latin America, only 3.9% of the population increase was due to migrations from other regions during this period. For Asia, Africa and Europe, there was no noticeable difference. For North America, only 6.7% of the growth was due to immigration. In the USSR there is a negative difference, indicating outward migration. The figures for natural increase during the years 1960–1967 show that Latin America has the highest natural increase, with an annual average of 28 per thousand. Second is Africa, with 24 per thousand; and next on the list are: Asia, with 20 per thousand; Oceania, with 15 per thousand; North America, with 12 per thousand; and finally Europe, with only 9 per thousand. The average for the world as a whole was 19 per thousand.

3

Urbanization in Latin America

THE term urbanization as used in different context by historians, sociologists, city planners, and the public has acquired a whole cluster of associations.[1] It is used here in a strictly limited sense to designate an increase in the proportion of a population living in relatively permanent places with high density concentrations of inhabitants. Thus, an apparently simple way to measure the degree of urbanization of a region or country would be to compare the proportion of its population living in urban places with that living in rural areas.

What makes this method somewhat less simple is the fact that despite the urgings of the International Statistical Institute there has been no international agreement as to the minimum number of inhabitants required to designate an area as eligible for classification as urban. Not only does the numerical requirement vary from country to country, but there are, as well, differing notions as to what other characteristics must be possessed by an area for it to qualify as urban rather than rural.[2] In its technical and demographic

---

[1] H. L. Browning, "The Demography of the City," *The Urban Explosion in Latin America*, ed. G. H. Beyer (Ithaca: Cornell University Press, 1967), p. 72, discusses Louis Wirth's classic essay on "Urbanism as a Way of Life" and suggests that the concept of urbanism is expansive and elusive because it attempts to identify the consequences, both personal and social, of life in urban environments, especially when viewed cross-culturally.

[2] In Latin America, for example, Perú, Chile, Ecuador and Colombia all define an urban area according to their own system. Perú: Capitals of departments, provinces, districts and other populated centers the number of whose inhabitants exceeds the average for the capital (2,500 inhabitants), provided such centers do not have typical rural characteristics. Chile: Municipalities and towns (places of 5,000 inhabitants or more) possessing definite urban characteristics. Places with larger population numbers but which do not possess urban characteristics are therefore not considered. Ecuador: Administrative centers of provinces and cantons. Colombia: Centers of more than 1,500 inhabitants which are seats of municipalities or districts.

publications, the United Nations has chosen to classify any built-up area with a population of over 2,000 as urban.[3] But it is important to realize that these characteristics may not reflect the urban-rural pattern of a particular country as well as does its own system of classification, which corresponds more immediately to actual conditions in that country. But given these limitations of available statistics for the different Latin American countries, we can nevertheless establish the proportion of people living in a predominantly rural environment as opposed to the proportion living in an environment that is predominantly urban, for each country. And this can in turn be used to measure a more complex phenomenon of social change.

The urbanization process in Latin America is, of course, part of a world phenomenon not confined to recent decades. The trend toward centralization and the phenomenon of urbanization in general have traditionally been associated with a parallel process of economic and industrial development. In Europe, for instance, the massive migration of population from the country to the city was a direct response to the great demand for labor generated by the factory system which grew out of the Industrial Revolution. While rural-urban migration as an accompaniment of industrial development has also played an important role in Latin American urbanization in recent decades it has not done so to anywhere near the same degree as in Europe. Countries which have in no way reached a stage of industrial development comparable to that enjoyed by many European countries in the nineteenth century have nevertheless experienced an even greater rate of urbanization. Clearly other factors have played an equal or even larger role in the transformation of Latin America in recent years. One of the most important of these is simply the worldwide biological phenomenon of an excess of births over deaths.[4] Given this natural cause for total population increase within a country we can expect that some of that increase will be revealed in an increase of urban population. The proportion of total population increase reflected in the population growth of

[3] See ECLA, *Statistical Bulletin for Latin America*, vol. 2, no. 2.

[4] In Costa Rica and México, for instance, Kingsley Davis found that about 50% of the urban population growth is due to mere natural birth, about 20% to rural-urban migrations, and the rest to the combined effect of both. See his "The Urbanization of the Human Population," special issue *Scientific American* vol. 213, no. 3 (September 1965): 50.

specific urban areas will vary from country to country according to the role played by other factors such as rural-urban migration and general economic as well as industrial expansion. We turn first to the relationship between urbanization and rural-urban migration.

Urbanization and Rural-Urban Migration

The present urban growth in Latin America is unprecedented in the history of the twenty republics. Moreover, its consequences go beyond creating political and economic instability and embrace every facet of Latin American life. A significant element in this transformation of most Latin American countries is the rural-urban migration. Since Latin America is by no means a monolith, some countries are more affected by this demographic movement than others. Nevertheless, certain general conclusions can be drawn.

Probably the prime impetus for rural-urban migration is economic —the desire for a higher standard of living, for the opportunity to earn more money. The average rural migrant sees the urban place as offering a panacea for all his problems; he sees it as offering unlimited opportunities, especially for unskilled labor which is, so he is told, in great demand. Moreover, when he does get to an urban place he is not as much at a disadvantage as one might suppose. H. L. Browning, for example, has questioned the validity of the general belief that migrants are usually unable to compete effectively with the native born in urban centers because of their lack of training. The following conclusions drawn from a study based on the 1960 Mexican census of the Distrito Federal suggest that: "Contrary to expectation, migrants, those born outside the Distrito Federal, do *not* differ greatly in most respects from the native population in some socioeconomic characteristics. The major exception is education, in which migrants, especially workers, are much inferior to the natives. This does not seem to have much effect, surprisingly, when it comes to occupational and income differences in which natives are superior, but the difference is not large. And when standard of living indicators are taken from the census data (availability of running water in households, sewage facilities, separate

bathrooms, ownership of radio and TV), there is virtually no difference between the two groups." [5]

The pull of economic opportunities, of industrial jobs, exerted by
urban places is all the stronger given the low agricultural productivity of much of Latin America. The traditional agricultural areas
have not increased their productivity sufficiently to match the increase in population. Even when the governments have attempted
to direct indigenous rural populations into unsettled fertile regions
by sponsoring colonization programs, their success has proved
limited.[6] Table 3.1 shows the very close statistical relationship between the rise in per capita income and the decline in the proportion of the labor force engaged in agriculture.

TABLE 3.1

POPULATION ENGAGED IN AGRICULTURAL OCCUPATIONS
IN SPECIFIED LATIN AMERICAN COUNTRIES

CONTINENT AND COUNTRIES	PERCENTAGE 1930–44	1945–62 (AVERAGE)	PER CAPITA GNP 1961 (US $)
North America			
United States	19	7	2,790
Latin America			
Venezuela	50	32	644
Argentina	—	20	533
Uruguay	—	14	449
Chile	35	28	348
México	65	54	297
Colombia	72	54	287
Costa Rica	63	55	278
Brazil	67	58	268
El Salvador	75	60	191
Guatemala	71	68	184
Paraguay	—	54	129

SOURCE: Rosenstein-Rodan, "Review of Economics and Statistics," *FAO Statistical
Yearbook* 43 (1961): 107–38.

[5] Browning, "Demography of the City," p. 91.
[6] The Pacific Coast resettlement program of Guatemala and the various colonization
programs in Perú, including San Lorenzo i Piura, are notable examples. See also G.
Prendle, *Paraguay* (London: Oxford University Press, 1967), regarding Japanese
and German settlers in Paraguay.

Given the present population densities in Latin America, the gap between actual and potential agricultural productivity is needlessly large, for the high percentage of migration from rural to urban areas creates an increased demand for agricultural raw materials to support the growing urban population and to meet the increasing needs of expanding industry. If agricultural productivity does not keep pace with industrial expansion it becomes necessary to import raw materials from abroad—a burden that falls most heavily on the industrial sector. Clearly industrialization and improvement in agricultural productivity must go hand in hand to insure a balanced economic development.[7]

Although possibly less important than the economic factor, social reasons also play a considerable role in the present migratory patterns. With the breakup of the *latifundia*—land holdings—in the rural sector, the peasant loses his patron and protector. In the city he often finds a surrogate in the church or government. Moreover, the urban centers provide a freer political atmosphere and greater opportunities for education—if not for oneself, at least for one's children. Obviously, there is no single motive for migration to urban centers, and in each country there will be a combination of different economic and social motives inducing large portions of the population to take this step.[8]

The various patterns of internal migration and the multiplicity of motivations responsible for them are revealed in the following sta-

[7] B. Higgins, "The City and Economic Development," *The Urban Explosion in Latin America*, p. 122.

[8] Most of the migration patterns in Latin America can be correlated with the four categories postulated by E. G. Ravenstein in the nineteenth century: a) the local migrant; b) the short-journey migrant; c) the long-journey migrant; d) the migrant by stages. To summarize his conclusions: 1) The great body of migrants only proceed a short distance, and there takes place shifting or displacement of the population in the direction of the great centers of commerce and industry. 2) The process of absorption [goes] on in the following manner: The inhabitants immediately surrounding a town of rapid growth flock into it; the attractive force makes its influence felt, step by step, to the most remote corner of the [country]. Migrants enumerated in a certain center of absorption will consequently grow less with the distance [from, and proportionately to,] the native population which furnishes them. 3) The process of dispersion is the inverse of that absorption. 4) Each main current of migration provides a compensating countercurrent. 5) Migrants proceeding long distances generally go . . . to one of the great centers of commerce or industry. 6) The natives of towns are less migratory than those of the rural part of the country. 7) Females are more migratory than males. See Walter Isard, *Methods of Regional Analysis: An Introduction to Regional Science* (New York: John Wiley & Sons, 1960), pp. 67–8.

tistical presentation of population movement in five Latin American countries.

Internal Migrations: Brazil, Costa Rica, Ecuador, Honduras, and México

Data from the censuses of 1950 and 1960 allow for a comparison of statistics for internal migrations within departments, states, or provinces according to the specific name assigned by each country to its major administrative unit (see Bibliography, entries for census publications). In the case of a particular administrative unit, the difference between the figures for the in-migratory population and the out-migratory population (net migratory remainder) does not include the number of deaths of migrants which occurred during the period of the censuses. Nor does it include the movement by stages or movement of a temporary nature which occurred during the same time. Nevertheless, the figures present a fairly accurate means for determining the general direction of the migratory movement of the population. In the maps that follow, the index of migration used is the percentage of net migration or 100 percent net migratory remainder divided by the population based on the latest census figures. The sign $(+)$ indicates in-migration; the sign $(-)$, out-migration. The methods used to estimate the internal migrations were chosen according to the best information available. In the case of México, for example, it was possible to use a direct method based on the census data according to place of residence as opposed to place of birth. For Honduras, on the other hand, it was necessary to calculate an average of sex and age figures.

BRAZIL

In Brazil, internal migrations have been directed both from rural to urban areas and between rural areas (see map 3.1). The general tendency of the migratory movement has been from the states along the Atlantic Coast to the interior states, the major exceptions being Fernando de Noronha, Paraná, Amapá and Maranhao which had positive percentages of net migration between 13% and 43%. It is significant that most of the large cities (100,000 and more inhabitants) in Brazil are located on the coast. However, these cities often

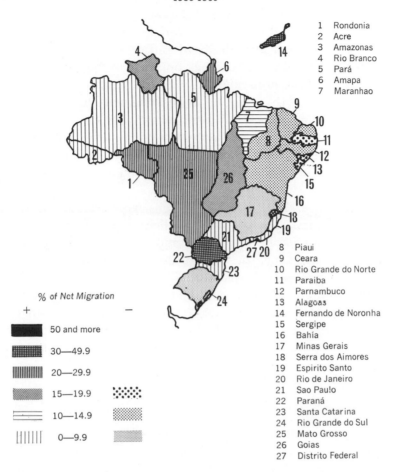

MAP 3.1

Brazil: Net Migratory Movement by State
1950-1960

1 Rondonia
2 Acre
3 Amazonas
4 Rio Branco
5 Pará
6 Amapa
7 Maranhao

8 Piaui
9 Ceara
10 Rio Grande do Norte
11 Paraiba
12 Parnambuco
13 Alagoas
14 Fernando de Noronha
15 Sergipe
16 Bahía
17 Minas Gerais
18 Serra dos Aimores
19 Espirito Santo
20 Rio de Janeiro
21 Sao Paulo
22 Paraná
23 Santa Catarina
24 Rio Grande do Sul
25 Mato Grosso
26 Goias
27 Distrito Federal

% of Net Migration

+   −

50 and more

30—49.9

20—29.9

15—19.9

10—14.9

0—9.9

do not account for a high percentage of the total urban population of their particular states. The southern region composed of the states of São Paulo, Paraná, Santa Catarina and Rio Grande do Sul attracted a large number of in-migrants. Between 1950 and 1960, the net migratory remainder accounted for a population increase of 1,656,300 inhabitants; 2,895,000 in-migrated to urban areas, 1,239,000 of these being migrants from rural areas of the same region. But only Paraná had a high percentage (32%) of net in-migration. The percentages of net in-migration in São Paulo and Santa Catarina were 4% and 1%, respectively. Rio Grande do Sul had a 4% increase of net out-migration. In Paraná, the proportion of migrants coming from other states was as high as ⅓ of the total.

The central-western region composed of the states of Mato Grosso, Goiás and the Federal District, also experienced a large migratory movement to both urban and rural areas. In-migrants to the urban areas added 474,000 as opposed to 159,300 to the rural areas. The net total of in-migrants, 633,800, represented 21% of the total population of the region for 1960. In relative figures, this region had the major proportion of in-migrants with respect to its total population. In the Federal District 100% of the population was composed of in-migrants. But this is explained by the fact that all of its population migrated from Rio de Janeiro to Brasilia in April of 1960.

The eastern and northeastern regions were characterized by an outward migratory movement. The first region had a population decrease of 979,300 between 1950 and 1960; the second region, a decrease of 1,392,100. In the northeastern region, the principal states of exodus were Pernambuco (501,700 migrants) and Ceara (344,700 migrants). Their respective capitals are the important ports of Recife (1,064,345 inhabitants) and Fortaleza (514,818 inhabitants). But the present migratory tendency suggests a predominant movement from the rural areas of these states to the urban areas of other, interior, states.

COSTA RICA

Costa Rica, like Brazil, has been characterized by a migratory movement from rural areas to urban areas and among rural areas. But migration is also occurring among urban areas (see map 3.2). The statistics reveal two main centers of attraction, the provinces of San José and Puntarenas, both located on the Pacific Coast. The positive net migratory remainders for the period 1950–1963 were 14,000 in San José and 13,100 in Puntarenas. The large migratory movement to the urban areas of the province of San José is mainly directed toward the capital of the country, with a total population of 320,478 inhabitants. The movement in Puntarenas, however, is exactly the reverse, since the rural areas of this province constitute the main focus of attraction. The explanation for the latter situation is primarily economic. The large banana plantations of this province are located in rural areas, and their increasing need for labor has attracted migration to these areas.

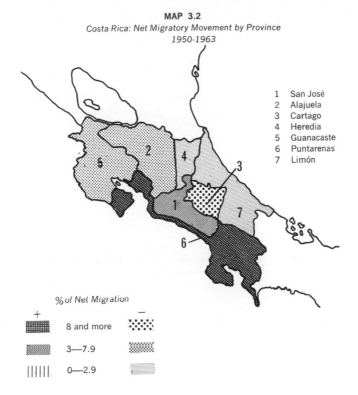

MAP 3.2
Costa Rica: Net Migratory Movement by Province
1950-1963

1   San José
2   Alajuela
3   Cartago
4   Heredia
5   Guanacaste
6   Puntarenas
7   Limón

% of Net Migration

+		−	
	8 and more		
	3—7.9		
	0—2.9		

All the other provinces of the country were characterized by an outward movement of population. Cartago and Alajuela, in the north central region, recorded a large exodus of population: Cartago lost 12,200 people and Alajuela; 8,700. The migratory movement was entirely directed to the urban and rural areas of San José and Puntarenas.

ECUADOR

Demographically, Ecuador may be divided into two vertical regions: a western region, including the coast and the sierra, which contains most of the population of the country (6,946,600 inhabitants), and an eastern or Amazonic region with fewer than 5 inhabitants per square kilometer (78,000 inhabitants). The concentration of urban and rural population in the west can be accounted for by geographical factors. The coast and the sierra are favored with a mild climate that stimulates urban settlement; in contrast, the Amazonic region is rainy and very humid. The two major transportation routes of the country, the Pan American Highway which runs north to south and the railroad which connects the sierra with the coast, also facilitate settlement in the western region.

The coastal region is the most important zone of in-migration to urban and rural areas (map 3.3). During the period 1950–1962, this area had a migratory movement of 280,000 people, the province of Guayas receiving the major increase. For the same period, this province increased its population by 153,400 in-migrants, representing 16% of its total population in 1962. The major reason for this is that this province contains Guayaquil, the most important port and largest city of the country (567,895 inhabitants). A large migratory

MAP 3.3

Ecuador: Net Migratory Movement by Province
1950-1962

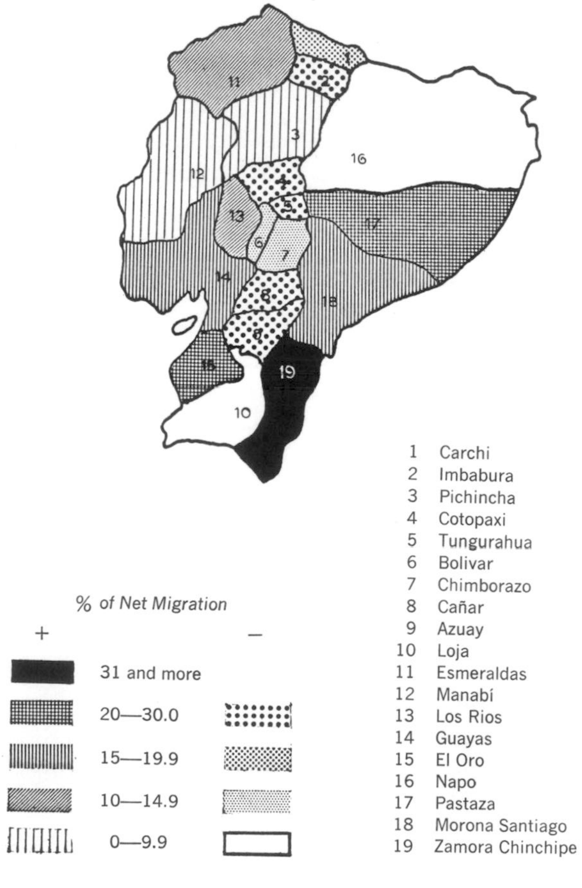

% of Net Migration

+   −

31 and more

20—30.0

15—19.9

10—14.9

0—9.9

1	Carchi
2	Imbabura
3	Pichincha
4	Cotopaxi
5	Tungurahua
6	Bolivar
7	Chimborazo
8	Cañar
9	Azuay
10	Loja
11	Esmeraldas
12	Manabí
13	Los Rios
14	Guayas
15	El Oro
16	Napo
17	Pastaza
18	Morona Santiago
19	Zamora Chinchipe

movement also took place in the coastal provinces of Manabí and Los Rios. In these two provinces, the migration was to both the urban and rural areas, each with a total movement of 40,600 and 34,800 migrants, respectively.

Outward migration from the sierra occurs every year on a larger scale. Between 1950 and 1962, 292,900 people abandoned the sierra. Only Pichincha, containing the capital, Quito, had a positive net migratory remainder of in-migrants from other provinces (34,700). The general migratory movement in this part of the country takes the form of people leaving the rural areas to settle in rural and urban areas on the coast.

HONDURAS

Honduras has two important departments of in-migration: Cortés and Francisco Morazán (map 3.4). In-migration to these departments is twice as high as it is to Santa Bárbara, next in order of importance. Santa Bárbara received 11,000 migrants, as opposed to Cortés and Francisco Morazán, which received 27,000 and 24,700 migrants, respectively. Cortés contains the principal port—also named Cortés—of the nation, and the second largest city of the republic, San Pedro Sula. The high level of industrial and commercial activity in both centers attracts migrants. The same holds for the department of Francisco Morazán, containing the capital of the country, Tegucigalpa.

Analyzing the figures according to sex, it can be seen that women tend to migrate in large numbers within the departments of Cortés and Francisco Morazán. The proportion was 134 and 178 women respectively, as opposed to 100 men. The department of Atlántida showed an equilibrium between the in-migrants of both sexes (111 women for each 100 men). Here migration probably occurred by couples or families. In Colón and Santa Bárbara, however, male in-migrants prevail. The proportion in each department was 227 and 233 men for every 100 women, respectively, or almost a 2:1 ratio. Youthful migrants largely account for in-migrant to the departments of Cortés and Francisco Morazán. In Cortés, young people of nine and between the ages of fifteen and twenty-four form the larger group. In Francisco Morazán, most in-migrants are in the twenty-year-old group.

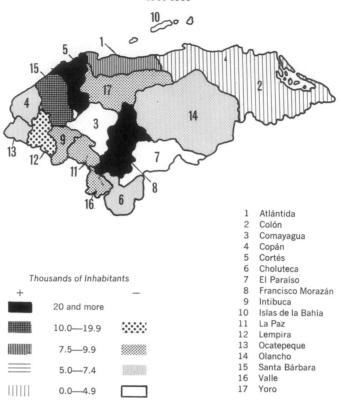

MAP 3.4
Honduras: Net Migratory Movement by Departments
1950-1960

Thousands of Inhabitants

+		−
◼	20 and more	
▦	10.0—19.9	⠿
▥	7.5—9.9	▨
▤	5.0—7.4	▦
‖‖‖	0.0—4.9	▭

1	Atlántida
2	Colón
3	Comayagua
4	Copán
5	Cortés
6	Choluteca
7	El Paraíso
8	Francisco Morazán
9	Intibuca
10	Islas de la Bahía
11	La Paz
12	Lempira
13	Ocatepeque
14	Olancho
15	Santa Bárbara
16	Valle
17	Yoro

MÉXICO

In México, figures indicate that the Federal District had the highest number of in-migrants during the period between 1950 and 1960 (528,691). Relatively large numbers of in-migrants were also recorded for the states of México (174,789), Baja California (153,084), Nuevo León (115,332) and Veracruz (102,826). On the other hand, an out-migration in Zacatecas should be noted, as it reveals a remigration of people who had arrived there before 1950 (map 3.5).

In most places of in-migration, there appears to be a male-female equilibrium. Only Durango and Tlaxcala show a large excess of female migrants, with 406 and 152 women for every 100 men, respectively. Male in-migrants prevail in Quintana Roo and Baja California Territorio Sur, but the excess of males over females is less marked than is the reverse situation noted above.

The states of Michoacán, Jalisco, Guanajuato and the Federal District registered the major exodus. During this period, 149,761 people born in Michoacán left the state. Exodus figures for Jalisco, Guanajuato and the Federal District were 111,569 110,180, and 110,159, respectively.

If migrants are classified by their place of destination, more than half of those leaving the Federal District went to the State of México, that is, the federal unit that contains the District. This seems to confirm the general tendency of people who reside in highly populated cities to move and establish themselves in places relatively close to these cities.

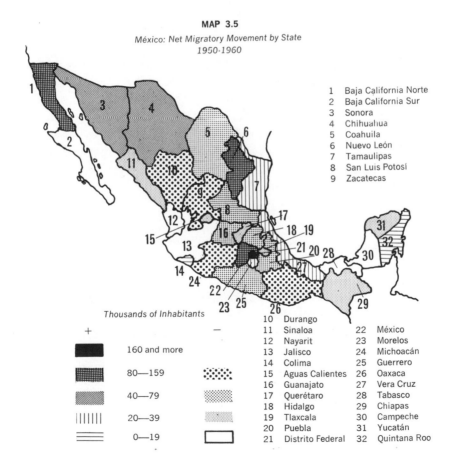

MAP 3.5

México: Net Migratory Movement by State
1950-1960

1 Baja California Norte
2 Baja California Sur
3 Sonora
4 Chihuahua
5 Coahuila
6 Nuevo León
7 Tamaulipas
8 San Luis Potosí
9 Zacatecas

Thousands of Inhabitants

+		—
■ 160 and more		
▨ 80—159	░░	
▨ 40—79	░	
‖‖‖ 20—39	░	
≡ 0—19	☐	

10 Durango
11 Sinaloa
12 Nayarit
13 Jalisco
14 Colima
15 Aguas Calientes
16 Guanajato
17 Querétaro
18 Hidalgo
19 Tlaxcala
20 Puebla
21 Distrito Federal

22 México
23 Morelos
24 Michoacán
25 Guerrero
26 Oaxaca
27 Vera Cruz
28 Tabasco
29 Chiapas
30 Campeche
31 Yucatán
32 Quintana Roo

SUMMARY

Internal migration in Latin America is occurring on at least three levels: (1) from rural areas to urban areas; (2) on a lesser scale, among urban areas and (3) among rural areas. The forces which could lead to migration from a rural setting to an urban one may very generally be thought of as a push-pull force. It seems clear that rural-urban migration results from some combination of the push and pull.[9] However, it is not hard to extend these concepts to interurban migration as well as to the less frequent inter-rural migration. The push factor represents the pressure of rural poverty and is generally reflected in low agricultural productivity, which, in turn, results from a lack of education and human energy. Land tenure arrangements that fail to provide incentive for capital improvements, or government price policies that discourage investment in agriculture are additional forces tending to direct rural people to the urban area.

The pull factors consist of a number of attractive urban opportunities. These opportunities include not only jobs and better salaries, but also opportunities for social interaction. It should be noted that the pull factor can also embrace migrating groups originating from comparatively rich rural regions. In any case, "the attractions of the city [urban place], in whatever form they may take for the migrant, are sufficient to pluck some people out of the rural population and deposit them in the city." [10]

Urbanization and Industrialization

It is generally assumed that industrialization can only take place in and around cities. This has largely been the case in Latin America, just as it was in Europe. Even when industrial plants are built in the countryside, they usually retain close ties to various essential facili-

[9] See Simon Kuznets, *Economic Growth and Structure* (New York: W. W. Norton & Co. Inc., 1965), and *Modern Economic Growth, Rate, Structure, and Spread* (New Haven: Yale University Press, 1966).

[10] Bruce H. Herrick, *Urban Migration and Economic Development in Chile*, (Cambridge, Mass.: The M.I.T. Press, 1965), p. 14.

ties in the cities.[11] Moreover, a form of urbanization, the building of housing adjacent to the plant, soon follows.[12]

Several studies by the ECLA have provided some data on urbanization and industrialization in Latin American countries. As stated before, the census definitions of urban areas do not permit an absolute comparative analysis of the degree of urbanization since definitions vary from country to country. It was therefore necessary to devise a measure of urbanization that would make it possible to compare levels in the different countries. For this purpose, urbanization is defined as a percentage of the total country population

TABLE 3.2

INDICES OF URBANIZATION AND INDUSTRIALIZATION FOR
SELECTED LATIN AMERICAN COUNTRIES

COUNTRY	CENSUS YEAR	URBANIZATION (%)	INDUSTRIALIZATION (%)
Argentina	1947	48.3	26.9
Chile	1952	42.8	24.2
Ecuador	1950	17.8	17.8
Venezuela	1950	31.0	15.6
Paraguay	1950	15.2	15.5
Bolivia	1950	19.7	15.4
Colombia	1951	22.3	14.6
Perú	1940	13.9	13.2
Brazil	1950	20.2	12.6

SOURCES: Pedro Teichert, *Revolución Económica e Industrial en America Latina, 1961,* ECLA, "Economic Bulletin of Latin America," no. 6, 1961.

living in places of 20,000 or more inhabitants. Industrialization is defined as a percentage of the economically active male population engaged in manufacturing, construction, gas and electricity production. Table 3.2 suggests (particularly in the cases of Ecuador, Paraguay, Bolivia and Perú) that the degree of urbanization is closely associated with the degree of industrialization, although the ratio of the two indices varies a good deal. But the number of cases is too small to provide a rank correlation of any high degree of re-

[11] See Chapter 4, pp. 119–22 on the correlation between urban location, natural resources and industrial activity.

[12] See Chapter 7, pp. 214–16 for an example of such urbanization.

liability. A stronger relationship would probably be evident if there were greater unanimity over the definition of industries in the censuses of the different countries.

This relationship would appear to confirm the traditional connection between industrialization and urbanization. However, B. Higgins has recently made a strong case against assuming that this connection is necessarily inevitable in the Latin American context. His reading of the ECLA studies led him to conclude that: "While it would appear that significant industrialization is not possible without some accompanying urbanization (although metropolitanization may not be absolutely necessary), it is less clear that urbanization is impossible without industrialization. There is substantial evidence that during recent decades the pace of urbanization has been faster than the corresponding rate of industrialization would require, especially in Latin America. This imbalance takes the form of urban unemployment, and urban low-productivity employment. Through the process of urbanization, in Latin America as in Asia and the Middle East, there has been a transfer of these . . . aspects of underdevelopment from the countryside to the city."[13]

Thus Higgins' interpretation of the ECLA figures suggests that the generally assumed connection between industrialization and urbanization—although valid to a degree—only tells part of the story of urbanization in Latin America. This becomes clear in the following case studies of urbanization in Perú and Chile.

[13] Higgins, "City and Economic Development," pp. 134–38.

4

Urbanization in Latin America: Perú and Chile

Rate of Urbanization

The following tabular data on Perú and Chile primarily take into account census data for 1950 and 1960. From table 4.1, which gives the total population and annual rate of increase (%) for each country, it can be seen that after the 1950s, the annual rate of increase for the two countries has been equally high: Perú (1960) 2.32%; Chile (1960) 2.30%.

TABLE 4.1

PERÚ AND CHILE: TOTAL POPULATION AND
ANNUAL RATES OF INCREASE, 1850–1961

	CENSUS DATE		TOTAL POPULATION	ANNUAL RATE OF INCREASE
Perú	1 VII	1850	2,001,203	—
		1862	2,487,916	1.83
	14 V	1876	2,699,106	0.58
	9 VI	1940	6,207,967	1.31
		1950	7,969,000	—
		1960	10,025,000	2.32
Chile	19 IV	1854	1,439,120	—
	19 IV	1865	1,819,223	2.15
	19 IV	1875	2,075,971	1.33
	26 XI	1885	2,491,886	—
	28 XI	1895	2,804,300	1.19
	28 XI	1907	3,228,558	1.18
	15 XIII	1920	3,823,510	1.30
	27 XI	1930	4,391,316	1.40
	28 IX	1940	5,094,353	1.50
		1950	6,073,000	1.77
		1960	7,627,000	2.30

SOURCE: *Demographic Yearbook*, 1955; 1963; figures 1950–1960, table 2.1.

Tables 4.2 and 4.3 show that urbanization in each country is, to a large extent, a function of the exceedingly rapid rate of total population growth. The growth of urban population in Perú and Chile, greater than the growth of total population, reached levels as high as 4.56% per year. For the period 1950–1960, however, Chile had an annual rate of increase of urban population that was less than twice the rate of growth of the total population.

TABLE 4.2

PERÚ AND CHILE: ARG OF URBAN POPULATION, 1876–1961
(percentage)

COUNTRY	INTERCENSAL PERIOD	AARI BY CITY SIZE		ARG URBAN POP.[b]	ARG TOTAL POP.[b]
		100,000+	20,000+		
Perú	1876–1940	2.1	1.9	—	1.31
	1950–60 [a]	—	—	4.56	2.32
	1955–61 [a]	8.0	—	—	—
Chile	1940–52	2.6	2.6	—	1.9
	1950–60	—	—	3.86	2.30
	1955–59 [a]	5.0	—	—	—

SOURCE: *Demographic Yearbook*, 1952; 1963.
NOTES: *a.* Estimated; *b.* table 2.1.

TABLE 4.3

PERÚ AND CHILE: POPULATION BY URBAN-RURAL CLASSIFICATION

CENSUS DATE		POPULATION				
		TOTAL	URBAN [a]	%	RURAL	%
Perú						
	1950	7,969,000	2,498,000	31.3	5,471,000	68.9
	1960	10,025,000	3,904,000	38.9	6,121,000	61.1
Chile						
	1950	6,073,000	3,327,000	54.8	2,746,000	45.2
	1960	7,627,000	4,861,000	63.7	2,766,000	36.3

SOURCE: Table 2.1.
NOTE: *a.* Urban population by definition. (See Chapter 2, fn. 6, p. 44)

In Perú the urban population at the observed rate of growth had doubled the rate of growth of the total population. The rate of urban growth has been higher in the larger metro-cities of 100,000 inhabitants or more, especially capital cities, than in the urban places of average size (20,000 or more). See Chapter 6 for an in-depth study of the growth of these metropolitan areas.

Urbanization in Perú

The country of Perú is located in the central part of the west coast of South America, occupying 1,249,049 square kilometers or some 6.5 per cent of the combined land area of the twenty Latin American republics. The national territory is divided longitudinally into three main geographic regions: 1) *the coast*, essentially a rainless desert strip crossed at irregular intervals by 52 rivers coursing down from the Andes, none of which is navigable. This region covers less than 12 percent of the country's area but contains nearly a third of the total population. Its export agriculture and industrial activity generates about 55 percent of the national income; 2) *the Sierra*, structured by the Andean spine consisting of three large chains of mountains running north to south, with inter-mountain valleys primarily dedicated to domestic farming. This region accounts for 27% of the national area and nearly 60% of the total population, but contributes only 40% of the national income, and; 3) *the Selva*, a sparsely populated region extending over the forested eastern slopes of the Andes and the flat lowlands of the Amazon basin, which covers 60% of the national territory but produces only 4% of the national income.

The 1960 estimated population of Perú was 10,025,000, which represented an annual growth rate of 2.32% since the previous estimate for 1950.[1] Projected at the same rate, Perú will by 1980 have some 18 million inhabitants. Most of the country's urban population is located on the coast, with 40% concentrated in Lima alone. The Sierra region's density is about 18 inhabitants per square kilometer, but its population is mainly rural. The Selva has a population density of only 1.5 per square kilometer. In 1960

---

[1] See also Chapter 2, map 2.9, tables 2.1, 4.1–4.3.

about 61% of Perú's total populaion was classified as rural (in 1940, 65% of the population had been rural).[2] However, the regional distribution of the rural population varies considerably. It is smaller, for example, on the coast, with only about one-third of the total population in the departments of Tumbes and Arequipa classified as rural. In the Sierra, on the other hand, in the departments of Cajamarca, Apurímac and Puno, the proportion of the rural population is considerably higher, ranging over 85.7, 80.7 and 81.6 percent, respectively.

The urban population in Perú is distributed among several cities and towns all of which are expanding rapidly. Lima, the national capital has a population of 1,845,910, representing an increase of 186 percent since 1940. Nine cities have more than 50,000 inhabitants: Arequipa (222,377), Trujillo (100,130), Chiclayo (95,667), Cuzco (79,857), Piura (72,096), Huancayo (64,153), Chimbote (59,990), Iquitos (57,777) and Sullana (50,171). Among these, the growth of Chimbote has been amazing, with an increase of over 1,314 percent in 20 years, due to fishing and mining activities which have developed in the region. Others, such as Chiclayo and Trujillo, also experienced a rapid expansion, of 203 and 171 percent, respectively.

A large proportion of the Peruvian population consists of descendants of the Incas who lived mostly in the Andean mountain range. One of the notable features in the complex social structure of Perú is the survival of pre-Columbian culture, production techniques, and consumer patterns among a large proportion of the population. The indigenous Indian population adheres to the collectivist and communal ties of the past and has found it difficult to adopt Western social and cultural patterns, particularly in respect to land tenure (see page 105). Illiterate for the most part, the major portion of this population has not felt the impact of the great changes that have taken place elsewhere in the country. In the contemporary social and economic development of Perú this division runs much deeper than the ordinary rural-urban dualism common to other low-income nations.

---

[2] It should be noted that the census definition of 1961 differs from that of 1940, since it classifies as urban some communities with predominantly rural characteristics.

HISTORICAL LOCATION OF URBAN PLACES

The Perú of today is still largely rooted in the past and its development continues to be influenced by historical circumstances. Many cities have been born, have had a period of development and greatness, and have died. Ruins scattered throughout the Republic of Perú testify to the past existence of great cities that have already moved through their life cycle. The urban pattern in Perú, consequently, has changed in the course of its long history. The severe earthquakes of 1970 without doubt will exert further influence.

The locations of cities during the Incan Empire had definite characteristics. Two principal systems of cities can be identified: one along the coast, and another along the Andes (see map 1.3). The system along the coast was formed by cities located in the river valleys and included Tumbes, Chicama, Chimú, Paramonga, Chancay, Pachacamac, Ica, Nazca, Tacna and other, smaller towns. Probably most of these cities were founded by other Indian cultures and annexed by the Incas in the course of their conquests. In the Andean system, the cities followed the natural formation of the Andes, paralleling the coast. These cities were also located mainly in the river valleys and included Cajamarca, Huamachuco, Chavín, Huánuco, Jauja, Ollantaytambo, Abancay, and finally, Cuzco, the capital city of the Incan Empire.

The economic orientation of Perú during the period of Inca rule was profoundly changed shortly after the conquest. The Spaniards were primarily interested in their overseas trade; and, as a result, the coast, which was remote from the center of economic activity under the Incas (the Sierra), now became the geographical focus and center for this activity. The Inca road systems connecting the Empire from north to south were abandoned in favor of short transverse roads which provided the shortest outlets to the sea and, therefore, foreign trade.[3] This led to the decline of many Inca cities, especially in the highlands, and the growth of new cities. The capital city of Lima was founded on the coast in 1535, and became the

[3] The Inca road system was divided into two longitudinal routes, one linking the Andean cities and the other linking the coastal cities. Some secondary or transverse roads connected both longitudinal routes which integrally structured the early pre-Columbian urban system.

center for political, social and commercial life that it remains today.

The Colonial period is often referred to as the urbanization period in Latin America. Francisco Pizarro alone founded 22 cities on the coast, the highlands and the eastern lowlands (ceja de selva). Their primary role, however, was defensive, part of the consolidation of the conquest. Under a decree issued by Viceroy Toledo in 1569, all Indians not previously assigned to some Spanish administrator were relocated in controlled villages (reduciones), many of which became the base for new cities. The imposition of the Spanish urban structure on the Incan towns gave rise to three basic types of cities: 1) Incan cities which later took on a Spanish appearance, such as Tumbes, Cajamarca, Huánuco; 2) juxtaposed cities or Spanish cities constructed on the foundations of a preexisting Inca city, as Cuzco, and; 3) newly created cities with specific political, commercial, and social functions, such as Lima, Trujillo, and Arequipa.

The wars of emancipation in Perú finally established the nation as an independent republic in 1821. During the first part of the Republican period the country areas were highly favored for the establishment of new settlements. On the coast and in the highlands, new cities were located in the valleys near farm lands, or near the newly developing mines. But the expansion of the coastal and Andean urban places basically took place within the two longitudinal systems established during the Colonial period.

Technological improvement since the second half of the nineteenth century brought new functions to the cities and produced new urban centers, especially those linked to transportation routes. Some important examples are La Oroya and Juliaca, railroad centers in the Sierra; Huancayo, intersection point of several routes, also in the Sierra; Mollendo, southern seaport and gateway to Bolivia through Arequipa, Cuzco and Puno; and Tingo María and Pucallpa, river ports in the Amazon basin. The Selva, which had never been dominated either by the Incas or the Spaniards became an important region for development during this period. Several attempts at colonization were made, especially in the central zone. New settlements appeared along the routes of penetration, and near the navigable rivers. This was the case for the colonies of Oxapampa and Pozuzo started by German immigrants during the last quarter of the nineteenth century. However, these colonies faced many difficulties and, mainly due to the lack of communication routes, they failed to fully accomplish their economic and social objectives. Other incentives for new settlements in this region were exploitation of the forests and, especially of rubber production in Iquitos.

Since the turn of the century, and especially since 1935, the development of transportation routes has encouraged the growth of new settlements. During the same period, most centers that were not on or near principal routes underwent little development. The Pan American Highway and other secondary roads benefited the coastal cities. The Andean railroads, Lima-La Oroya, La Oroya-Cerro de Pasco, La Oroya-Huancayo, contributed to the development of the inter-mountain valleys they connected, and the centers which they linked to the coast. In the Selva, cities were primarily benefited by the introduction of air transportation and the expansion of navigation on the larger rivers.

Since 1940, urbanization in Perú has been characterized by: (1) the concentration of population in three metropolitan areas located on the coast—Trujillo in the north, Lima in the center, and Arequipa in the south; (2) the fast growth of the towns in the Ceja de Selva, such as Pucallpa; (3) rapid urban growth as a result of economic push factors from the rural areas. (This pull to the cities tends to be divided between social and economic attractions.);[4] (4) the development of nodal centers along the transportation routes growing at the expense of smaller cities within their area of influence; (5) the primacy enjoyed by Lima over all other cities in the country. In the following analysis, urban places founded in Perú between 1940–1961 will be discussed according to the location, population size, rate of growth, economic base and relationship to major transportation links.

LOCATION OF URBAN PLACES IN RECENT DECADES

During recent decades, urbanization in Perú has been concentrated in only a few places. The identification of the resulting patterns of urban places can be made within the context of the country's three geographic regions (see map 4.1). The distribution of population ranges from scattered and isolated farms in the Sierra and Selva, to compact nuclei of urban places on the coast, climaxed by

[4] See Chapter 7, pp. 229–30 for questionnaire conclusions regarding migration to barriadas in Perú.

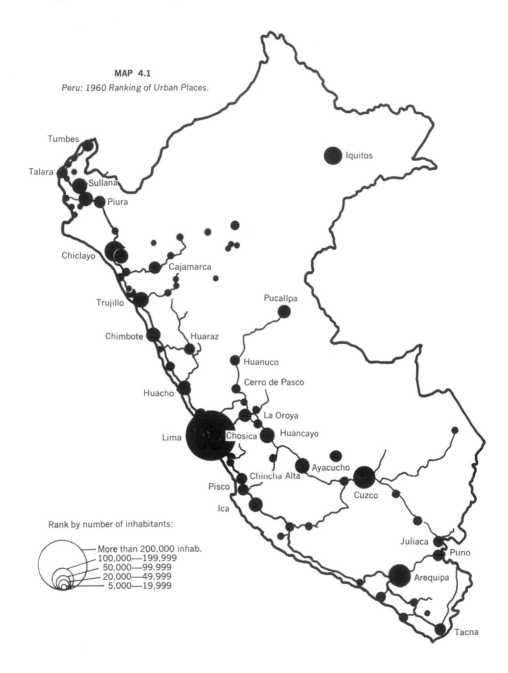

MAP 4.1

Peru: 1960 Ranking of Urban Places.

Tumbes

Iquitos

Talara

Sullana

Piura

Chiclayo

Cajamarca

Pucallpa

Trujillo

Chimbote

Huaraz

Huanuco

Cerro de Pasco

Huacho

La Oroya

Lima

Chosica

Huancayo

Ayacucho

Chincha Alta

Pisco

Cuzco

Ica

Juliaca

Puno

Arequipa

Tacna

Rank by number of inhabitants:

More than 200,000 inhab.
100,000—199,999
50,000—99,999
20,000—49,999
5,000—19,999

the larger metropolitan areas of Lima, Trujillo and Arequipa. Each region, to some extent, illustrates the following three-part urban settlement pattern. On the coast this pattern is clearly visible: (1) ports, located at irregular intervals along the coast (some of them like Chimbote and Talara enjoy natural protection); (2) agrarian-commercial cities, located in the irrigated valleys. Many of these valleys include more than one urban center; (3) mining cities, located near the working zone or within it such as the oil fields in the north, the iron mines in Marcona, and the copper mines in Toquepala. Coincidentally these mining cities are usually found in desert areas.

Similar types of urban settlements may be found in the Sierra, with the exception of ports, since there are no navigable rivers in this region. The largest centers of the region, Cuzco, Huancayo, Huaraz, are agrarian-commercial. Many centers in this region were founded by foreign companies. The most outstanding is Cerro de Pasco, which is connected by the railroad to La Oroya. La Oroya and Juliaca in Puno are the only important railroad centers in Perú. Arequipa, the second largest city in Perú, has the characteristics both of the coast and the Sierra. Like Lima,[5] Arequipa serves as a socio-economic center for the southern region.

In the Selva, most of the urban centers are agrarian-commercial and can also be typed according to their location along navigable rivers, land routes or airways. The more important of these centers, Pucallpa, Iquitos, Yurimaguas, are located on navigable rivers.

CLASSIFICATION OF URBAN PLACES ACCORDING TO POPULATION SIZE

In table 4.4, cities with a population above 20,000, are ranked according to the 1961 census (see Appendix, table 1 for ranking of cities over 5,000 inhabitants, 1961). For comparison, population figures for 1940 are also given. Growth indices are expressed as percentages of relative growth and annual rate of increase:

[5] Lima can be considered separately since it serves as a political, economic and social center for the entire nation.

TABLE 4.4

PERÚ: CITIES OF OVER 20,000 INHABITANTS, 1961

RANK	CITY	SIZE (HECTARES)	POPULATION 1940	POPULATION 1961	RELATIVE GROWTH %	ANNUAL RATE OF INCREASE %
1	Lima	15,000	645,172	1,845,910	186	5.1
2	Arequipa	1,031	76,871	222,377	189	5.2
3	Trujillo	300	36,958	100,130	177	4.9
4	Chiclayo	313	31,539	95,667	204	5.4
5	Cuzco	480	40,657	79,857	96	3.3
6	Piura	241	27,919	72,096	158	4.6
7	Huancayo	200	26,729	64,153	140	4.3
8	Chimbote	100	4,243	59,990	1314	13.6
9	Iquitos	300	31,828	57,777	82	2.9
10	Sullana	220	21,159	50,171	137	4.3
11	Ica	126	20,896	49,097	135	4.2
12	Talara		12,985	27,957	115	3.7
13	Tacna	160	11,025	27,499	149	4.5
14	Pucallpa	145	2,368	26,391	1014	12.1
15	Chosica		4,160	25,248	511	9.0
16	La Oroya		13,508	24,724	83	3.0
17	Huánuco		11,966	24,646	106	3.5
18	Puno	125	13,786	24,459	77	2.8
19	Ayacucho	160	16,642	23,768	43	1.7
20	Huacho	120	12,993	22,806	76	2.7
21	Cajamarca	127	14,290	22,705	59	2.2
22	Pisco	64	14,240	22,112	55	2.1
23	Cerro de Pasco	54	17,882	21,363	19	0.1
24	Tumbes	51	6,172	20,885	238	6.0
25	Chincha Alta	78	12,446	20,817	67	2.5
26	Juliaca	62	6,034	20,351	237	6.0
27	Huaraz	96	11,054	20,345	84	3.0

SOURCES: Dirección Nacional de Estadistica y Censos, Perú, *Censo Nacional de Población y Occupación, 1940* (Lima, 1944–1949); vol. 1, *Resúmenes General*; and *Demographic Yearbook* (New York, 1963).

This table indicates that there are few large and many small urban places in Perú. The largest are those considered as regional capitals, Lima, Arequipa and Trujillo, which are also communication centers. Their annual rate of increase (with the exception of Arequipa) is relatively high. A special case is presented by Pucallpa, on the Ucayali River, which shows an annual increase of 12.1%. In 1943 this city became a transportation link with access both to Lima and to the Amazon region. Chimbote, with an annual rate of increase of 13.6% is also a communication center and the point of origin of the railroad to Huallanca. However, its growth was stimulated as well by the development of new fishing and steel industries.

Other cities showing a high percentage of population growth fall into two groups: those located within the zone of influence of the metropolitan area of Lima, namely, Chosica and Huacho; and, those showing high annual rates of increase but comparatively small absolute growth, such as Pativilca, Ilo and Quillabamba.[6] There may be several causes responsible for their growth, but in most cases linkage to transportation systems seems the most likely reason. It may be observed from map 4.1 (which is based on table 4.4) that the fastest growing urban places parallel the coast and are located along the Pan American Highway.

Five ranks of cities are shown on map 4.1 according to population distribution. It is apparent that Lima influences the cities in the lower orders. In his "Law of the Primate City," concerning the relationship between the first two or three cities of a nation, Mark Jefferson observed that in 28 leading countries of the world, the largest city is more than twice as large as the next, whereas in eighteen more it is more than three times as large.[7] Urban primacy in Perú is reflected as follows:

	Largest City (Lima)	Second City (Arequipa)	Third City (Trujillo)
1940	100%	11.9%	5.7%
1961	100%	12.0%	5.4%

Lima claims 18.4% of the total population of the country and is close to four times the population of the four other largest cities added together. According to Jefferson, the primate city is not only disproportionately large, but also exceptionally expressive of the national political, social and economic character of the country as a whole. All these characteristics may indeed be appropriately applied to Lima.

URBAN PLACES CLASSIFIED ACCORDING TO BASIC ECONOMIC ACTIVITY

In Perú, as in most of the Latin American countries, it is somewhat difficult to precisely define each city according to its basic

[6] Between 1940 and 1961, Pativilca grew from a population of 1,142 to 15,325 at an annual rate of increase of 13.2%; Ilo grew from 1,043 to 9,986 at an annual rate of increase of 11.3%; and Quillabamba grew from 201 to 8,644, at an annual rate of increase of 19.6%.

[7] Mark Jefferson, "The Law of the Primate City," *The Geographical Review*, no. 2 (April 1939) 29:226–32.

economic activity. Each of the larger cities necessarily includes a variety of activities in its economic makeup. Iquitos, for example, has a very high percentage of its labor force engaged in agriculture, but due to its geographical location at the head of the Amazon River, is more important as a regional and transportation network center. Hence it is classified as a commercial city (see map 4.2). On the other hand, Puno is classified as an agricultural city, although it clearly lies on the transportation route to Bolivia and Argentina. Lima is the prime example of a city having a diversified economic base. It could be classified simultaneously as an agricultural, commercial and industrial city. For the sake of simplification, however, the cities are classified according to the following criteria: 1) *agricultural cities* which have at least 65% of their labor force engaged in agriculture and other primacy activities such as forestry, hunting, fishing, and mining; 2) *commercial cities* which have a high percentage of their labor force engaged in private or public services and utilities; and 3) *industrial cities* which have a large, active industrial labor force. Only four cities fall within this latter category. A study of map 4.2 suggests that a distinct spatial pattern exists for urban places. On the one hand, the traditional agricultural centers fall within the confines of the central Andean Cordillera. On the other, the commercial cities and regional centers complement the positions of the agricultural cities, surrounding them and forming an apex in the southernmost part of the country. The industrial cities follow the coastal line, with the exception of Arequipa which falls within the area of the agricultural cities. Its position can probably be best explained by its location along the major transportation artery which connects Perú with Bolivia and Argentina.

TRANSPORTATION LINKAGES: HIGHWAYS, RAILWAYS, AIR TRANSPORT

Transportation linkage is clearly one of the most important forces affecting the location and growth of the urban system. In one way or another transportation systems influence the origin, evolution, survival or death of urban places. This is particularly true in a country like Perú, where topography and physical geography also influence overall development and urban growth.

The present road system in Perú is formed by two major longitudinal highways, five transversal highways, and several other minor ones. The most important highway to the present is undoubtedly

MAP 4.2

Perú: Basic Economic Activity of Urban Places

Tumbes

Iquitos

Sullana
Piura

Chiclayo
Cajamarca

Trujillo

Chimbote
Huaraz

Huanuco

Cerro de Pasco

La Oroya

Lima-Callao
Huancayo

Ayacucho

Cuzco

Huancavelica

Pisco
Abancay

Ica

Puno

Arequipa

Moquegua

Tacna

Basic Economic Activity

◯ Agricultural Cities

⊕ Commercial Cities

⬤ Industrial Cities

Scale:
1:9,310,000

the Pan American Highway on the coast, which is 2,556 kilometers long. The other longitudinal road in the highlands is not yet complete, but will run to 3,290 kilometers. It is intended to be a modern version of the inter-Andean highway. Most of the penetration roads into the Selva and Sierra are now being constructed and improved.

The Ministry of Development and Public Works has established a National Plan of Roads, to be carried out between 1963 and 1970. This plan embraces penetration roads, roads to the capitals of the provinces, the completion of the longitudinal highland road and the Carretera Marginal de la Selva. This Marginal Highway in the Selva, presently under construction, is intended to create nuclei for colonization. This is to be achieved by incorporating 5 kilometers of land on each side of the road in preparation for settlement. The highway will connect populated centers in the Amazon region of Perú with Bolivia, Ecuador and Colombia. This highway will complement the network of navigable rivers since, with access to the important river ports, it will begin at points where the rivers become unnavigable. In Perú, the Marginal Highway will run a length of 2,603 kilometers, joining the valleys of Mayo, Huallaga, Pozuzo, Perené, Ene, Apurímac, Urubamba, Camisea and Madre de Dios, reaching the Ucayali River in Atalaya and Huallaga River in Yurimaguas.

During the present century, railroads in Perú have been deteriorating, their principal deficiency being that they are not integrated into a network, but remain as isolated systems. Even on the same line there are often changes in the gauge, as is the case on the Central Railroad that runs from Lima to Huancayo on a gauge of 1.435 meters and from there to Huancairlica on a gauge of 0.914 meters. The total railroad mileage in use has decreased rather than increased in recent years, from 4,425 kilometers in 1929 to only 3,263 kilometers at the present time. Of this total, 2,403 kilometers are operated by private enterprise and 860 kilometers by the government. In addition, 817 kilometers belong to private corporations but are used solely to transport their own products within their areas of operation. The principal lines are operated by the Peruvian Corporation. These are run from Callao to Huancayo (Central Railroad) and from Mollendo and Matarani to Puno and Cuzco (Southern Railroad). The Central Railroad is connected to another railroad from La Oroya to Cerro de Pasco operated by the mining corporation Cerro de Pasco. The lines connecting Lima and Lurín, and Ilo and Moquegua, for example, are in the process of being eliminated because they operate with large deficits. Their modernization is not justified because of the small number of passengers and the limited availability of freight.

Air transport in Perú is constantly expanding and increasing in importance. Four major commercial lines—SATCO, FAUCETT, APSA, LANSA—provide services along the coast and connect principal cities of this region with cities in the Sierra and the Selva. The Selva depends on this system for service to many centers that have no other system of transportation. The principal airport, having the largest movement of passengers and freight, is at Lima-Callao.

As previously noted, transportation systems have had appreciable effects on urban places in the last decades. Lima, center of the whole system of transportation and communication in Perú, has been perhaps most directly affected by the evolution of transportation systems. The physical size of this city has grown from 402 hectares in 1862 to 882 in 1920 and finally to an estimated 15,000 hectares by 1961. This expansion was first made possible by three railroads, then by tramway lines, and finally, by several major avenues and roads that linked together all the districts of the city.[8] Another direct effect of transportation is the increasing centralization of Lima. Workers in nearby cities like Huacho and Ica, for example, tend to reside in Lima, and not where they are employed.

Sometimes urban places decline when roads that have served them are rerouted in another direction. This is particularly likely to happen if a town has depended heavily on a single road for the development of its economic activities. The completion of the Pan America Highway on the coast, for instance, diminished the importance of direct communication by sea between several small towns. The small port of Cerro Azul between Callao and Pisco, which depended on local service by sea, is one of the towns that has virtually no inhabitants today. Air transportation, to some extent, produced similar results in the Amazon region. On the one hand, it made possible the growth of new centers and the development of the region as a whole. On the other, towns like San Ramón in the center of Perú, which was a very important airbase twenty years ago, has since lost its importance due to the construction of new roads, like those between Lima and Pucallpa.

The indirect effects of transportation systems on the urban place

[8] See also Chapter 7, pp. 224-34

can be observed in the fate of colonization programs. Various colonization attempts have been undertaken in a number of regions of Perú during the last decades. The principal projects are Tournavista, Perú Vía and San Lorenzo. Tournavista, in the central Selva, was started by an American entrepreneur. A new city was built and portions of the Selva were cleared for settlement. A new road was started toward the already existing penetration roads. This project, however, has only been partially successful. Perú Vía, started in the late 1950s, was to be developed on an area of about 100,000 square kilometers, starting about 100 kilometers east of Lima, and roughly describing a square, with Cerro de Pasco near the northwest corner and Cuzco near the southwest corner. Studies were carried out to provide for an integrated development of natural resurces. A complete transportation system was considered, including the Central and Southern railroads of Perú. Unfortunately, there have been no further developments of this project. San Lorenzo is based on an immigration project in Piura. New terrain suitable for agriculture is being developed and a new city for more than 50,000 people has been planned. The program is presently under way. It is apparent that in the future the Peruvian government will have to undertake integrated planning of colonization projects which simultaneously takes into account the objectives of a particular project, the comparative suitability of locations for development as urban places, and the availability of transportation links for such sites.

REASONS FOR RURAL-URBAN MIGRATION IN PERÚ

The pattern of rural-urban migration in Perú is also, though less directly, related to the availability of transportation links to urban areas. The general case for rural-urban migration throughout Latin America also holds for Perú. The migration trend is generally from the rural mountain areas to important towns in the larger valleys of the Andes, from these to the coastal region, and finally to Lima. The centers that have traditionally received the greatest number of immigrants are: Lima, Arequipa, Trujillo, and to a lesser degree, Piura, Chiclayo, Ica and Tacna.[9] But whereas Arequipa, Trujillo

[9] John P. Cole, *Geografía Urbana del Perú*, Publicación de Instituto de Etnología y Arqueología, no. 10 (Lima: Universidad de San Marcos, 1955), p. 71.

and the other secondary urban centers on the coast often represent intermediary stopping-off places in the migration process, Lima represents the end of the chain. In this sense, it is possible to infer that most migrants to Lima have already become urban dwellers, prior to their arrival there.[10]

Chimbote and Pucallpa present two special cases in the phenomenon of internal migration. In 1963 Chimbote became the primary fishing port of the nation. The establishment of a steel industry and the boom of the fishing industry in the early 1960s created new job opportunities and better salaries.[11] The result was a population explosion during the last ten years, due primarily to an increasing number of internal migrations. By 1961, the total population of Chimbote was 59,990 as opposed to 4,243 in 1940. Today its population is estimated at above 100,000. Such rapid and uncontrolled urban growth over a short period of time has produced many problems which seriously affect life in this city. As presented in a study by César A. Solis, some of the most important problems were: (1) the intensification of an ethnic heterogeneity, with the predominance of a low cultural level; (2) absence of an urban community conscience; (3) an industrial growth unrelated to the urban community; (4) a rise in the cost of living; (5) a decrease in cultivable land in areas close to the city; (6) unplanned urban environment; (7) disorderly land use; (8) speculations in land and housing; (9) insufficient educational facilities; (10) scarce or defective public services; (11) air and water pollution.[12]

In contrast to Chimbote, Pucallpa is located in the Departamento of Loreto, between the Andes and the Amazon region. On most maps it was generally not shown as an urban center prior to the 1950s. However, Pucallpa was one of the fastest growing cities in Perú between the last two censuses, increasing from a population of

[10] The concept of city-oriented migration by stages was originally set forth by Ernest Ravenstein, "The Laws of Migration," *Journal of the Royal Statistical Society*, 48 (June 1885): 228.

[11] The fishing industry in Chimbote is one of the most important in the world. There are 33 large firms engaged in the industry, and together with the remaining 17 along the coast of the same departamento (Ancash), they add up to a total of 50. One of these firms held the first place in the world's fish flour production in 1962. Today there are over 450 vessels in the port, with a total crew of 6,000 fishermen. The inland population working in related activities is above 10,000.

[12] César A. Solis, *Fuentes de Migración al Puerto Industrial de Chimbote* (Lima: O.N.P.U., 1960).

2,386 in 1940 to 26,391 in 1961. This increase was again mainly due to the arrival of a large number of immigrants, but the attraction here was Pucallpa's strategic location as a point of communication with the Amazon region. Thus, migration to Pucallpa was to a large extent part of a colonization process. This was facilitated by the opening of the highway from Lima in 1943. As with Pucallpa, the geographic location of cities largely determines their functions and future growth. Favorable locations have produced continuous growth, as demonstrated by the principal centers of manufacturing and distribution, where economic development has attracted heavy migrations.[13]

In Perú, the rural dweller tends to migrate to the places to which people from his area have already migrated. The first migrants might have selected a particular urban place at random, but once established, the migratory trends continue. Rural migrants usually move to places where they think they will find a group with characteristics similar to their own, either close friends or at least other "paisanos" from their original area to help them during the period of adaptation. The volume and length of population movements are a positive function of city size, inversely proportional to the distance traveled by migrants. The correlation of expected values with the actual percentage of migrants from different parts of the country suggests that the volume of migration is directly proportional to the population size of the place of origin.[14] The existence of specific places of opportunities, facilities or services lacking in the native region often direct the migratory movement. In the general case, the distance traveled by migrants varies in the same ratio as the magnitude of the city which is their destination.[15] Other

[13] See Walter D. Harris, *et al.*, *Housing in Peru* (Washington, D.C.: Pan American Union, 1963), p. 9 for amplication of this point.

[14] The length of movements are also proven to be indirectly proportional to the distance from point of destination, as foreseen by W. Isard (*Methods of Regional Analysis*) in developing a formula to compute the attraction force exerted from a city. Though Ernest Ravenstein ("The Laws of Migration") and others have argued that the growth of the metropolis exercises a force of attraction out of proportion to its existing population, the evidence clearly shows that the volume and length of population movements to cities is a function of city size.

[15] Walter Isard, *Location and Space Economy* (New York: John Wiley and Sons, Inc., 1956).

empirical studies have indicated that the more urban a community is, the higher the percentage of long-distance in-migrants it attracts.[16]

Among the most important causes of migration, is the system of rural land ownership and its effect on where the Indian works. Two types of land ownership characterize the Peruvian highlands: the *latifundio* or large landholding belonging to the whites and mestizos, where the Indian lives as a "colono" or "jornalero"; and the small landholdings, simply referred to as *comunidades de indígenas* or Indian communities. The continuous rise of population density in the *comunidades* generates a division among the *comuneros*, who then take different routes: some move into the *haciendas* (farms); while others, abandoning their lands, move into the mines or take jobs in small local industries. The majority of Indians, however, migrate to the coast, where "the desert has no land to offer them and the cities receive a new burden of poverty..[17] The migration usually takes place by family, though often by stages. In many cases some of the migrating members of a family may return from time to time to their original rural home and a few years may pass by before an entire family moves permanently. The families in the highlands filter down to the coastal valleys after the planting of crops and then return to the Sierra at harvesting time. Many however, do not return. Where do these peasants go? Because it is difficult for them to find a proper home or job in their hometown, they gather along the periphery of the cities, and become squatters, contributing to the formation of the barriadas.

Perú, then, like most of the Latin American countries, has a large migration of population from rural to urban areas. They arrive in numbers that often exceed the absorbent capacities of cities, posing large burdens and problems. If one seeks the main causes of the migration, as shown by a study in 1956 on the movement of 17,426 families to Lima, these turn out to be primarily economic. When the heads of the families were asked to explain why they had

---

[16] Donald J. Bogree, "Migration and Distance," *American Sociological Review* 14 (1949): 242.

[17] J. Luis Bustamante, quoted by Pablo Berckholtz Salinas, *Barrios Marginales Aberración Social* (Lima, 1963), p. 40.

decided to establish a permanent residence in Lima, their answers were as follows:[18]

Reasons for migrating	No.	%
Economic	13,713	61.05
Social	5,133	22.85
Education	1,936	8.62
Military Service	766	3.41
Health	595	2.65
Housing	179	0.80
Other services	139	0.62

The in-migrating population that remains in the city faces many difficulties—the major one being employment. The migrants differ in their evaluation of their new situations. Some at least, feel that they "lived better in the Sierra." Nevertheless, they all stay in the city and do not try to return to their lands. If this flow of rural population to crowded urban centers is to be arrested, the improvement of rural living conditions is essential. Only if working and living conditions in the country become more attractive will the magnetic pull of the urban centers be diminished.

Urbanization in Chile

The Republic of Chile extends along the southern half of the western coast of South America occupying a narrow strip of land measuring about 4,400 kilometers in length and 742,000 square kilometers in area. The national territory averages about 174 kilometers in width, although at some points it is less than 40 kilometers. As in Perú, the total country population is very unevenly distributed. However, the major proportion of the population of Chile is concentrated in the central third of the Republic, more than nine-tenths of the people inhabiting the area between Copiapó and Puerto Montt and almost two-thirds, the area between Valparaíso and Concepción. This concentration has been the result of both geographic and ethnic factors. The deserts of the north and the inhospitable archipelago of the south have discouraged and prevented settlement, whereas the upper Central Valley and several of the

[18] José Matos Mar, *Urbanización en America Latina*, ed. Philip M. Hauser (UNESCO, 1961).

transverse valleys to the north possess fertile soils as well as a health-ful and favorable climate. The aversion of the early settlers to the forested areas of the south with their damp, cold winters so like those of northern Europe and the attractions of central Chile with an environment similar to the Spanish homeland made this region the heartland of Chile.

Population density in Chile as a whole is comparatively low, Chile ranking thirteenth among the twenty Latin American coun-tries.[19] Densities in the four most northern and the three most southern provinces vary from 0.8 persons per square kilometer in Aisén to 21.2 persons per square kilometer in Coquimbo. It is sig-nificant that these seven provinces account for 76.3 percent of the total land area of the country. The highest densities occur in the central region of the country and center around the Santiago, Valparaíso and Concepción areas. Only in Santiago can density patterns in the range of more than 1,000 persons per square kilo-meter be found. Density focus is concentrated along a central spine running north and south from Santiago, with major concentrations running between Santiago and Concepción. This density pattern has an historical precedent, as can be seen on table 4.5 by com-paring the densities for the period between 1930 and 1958 of the different regions of the country.

TABLE 4.5

CHILE: POPULATION DENSITY BY REGIONS

REGION	PROVINCES	(PERSONS PER SQUARE MILE)			
		1930	1940	1952	1958
Total: Chile		15.0	17.5	20.7	25.8
Northern	Tarapacá and Antofagasta	4.1	3.6	4.1	5.2
North-Central	Atacama and Coquimbo	5.7	7.3	7.5	9.2
Central	Aconcagua through Nuble	66.1	78.8	96.9	120.5
South-Central	Concepción through Cautín	42.5	49.2	54.6	68.0
Lake	Valdivia through Llanquihue	17.6	22.3	26.4	33.0
Austral	Chiloe through Magallanes	1.6	1.8	1.8	2.4

SOURCE: M. L. Bohan and M. Pomeranz, *Investment in Chile* (Washington, D.C.: U.S. Department of Commerce, 1960), table 19, p. 39.

[19] See Chapter 2, map 2.1, p. 40.

Only a few general conclusions can be drawn from table 4.5 since these densities are based on the average density of each comuna, rather than on the density of each individual city as it is related to the rural-urban fringe. Since the data on individual cities is not immediately available, one must depend more heavily on analysis of other variables—employment opportunities, potential for economic expansion, transport facilities—to explain the patterns of urbanization. What is important to observe is a general tendency toward centralization, with a high proportion of the population concentrating around the comunas surrounding Santiago, Valparaíso and Concepción. Less intense density patterns occur in a linear fashion along the coast so that it may be inferred that the coastal port cities are to a large degree responsible for these patterns.

HISTORICAL LOCATION OF URBAN PLACES

The historical location of urban places in Chile may be divided into six distinctive periods: (1) Pre-Columbian; (2) Spanish Conquest; (3) Spanish Colony; (4) Spanish Colonial Reconstruction; (5) Independence; and (6) Republican. The particular conditions of each period determined the location and function of the cities founded during that time. With some variations due to local conditions, these periods characterize the history of all the Andean nations.

During the second half of the fifteenth century (Pre-Columbian Period), the Inca Empire extended south from Perú into the north and central parts of Chile, up to the Maule River. Beyond these limits lived the Araucanos, a tribe of Indian warriors who later played a major role in the long and difficult attempt to settle this area of the country. The Inca domination was characterized by a strong administrative organization created to facilitate the exploitation of gold. Thus the cities such as Andacollo, Punitaqui, Marga-Marga and Tiltil,[20] founded during this period, were often located close to extraction sites in rivers. Colonies of farmers were also established down in the central valleys. The cities Limache, Coihaique, and Pomaire created there were later refounded by the Spanish conquerors. The most important Inca road extended through the Atacama Desert into the Mapocho Valley, where the capital of the country is now located.

[20] Francisco Frias V., *Historia de Chile*, I, (Santiago: Editorial Nascimiento, 1947), p. 15.

As in the rest of South America, two main features characterized the Spanish conquest during the sixteenth century: the search for treasures of ancient civilizations, and the expansion of the Christian faith and Western culture. In contrast to Perú, there was no important culture in Chile before the Spanish conquest. The invasion of the conquerors from the north was made through the natural path that the two Andean chains permitted and was continued in a southward direction. One city after another was founded, in a linear pattern. The foundation of cities was in every case determined by a very rigorous set of laws, *Leyes de Indias,* dictated by the Spanish Crown.[21] These laws gave specific instructions as to where and how cities were to be located in the American colonies. The most favored location was generally along the margins of a river and the site was divided into square blocks 400 feet to the side, with streets 35 feet wide. Each block was in turn divided into four equal parts (solares), and each one given to a different owner. The central square was left as an open plaza (plaza de armas or plaza mayor) around which the principal official buildings, the government palace, town hall and cathedral were built.[22] The Spanish movement was only arrested at the area of Arauco, by the same Araucanos who had stopped the Incas before.

Between 1541 and 1553, Pedro de Valdivia founded eight cities and four fortifications. Among them were the three first-rank cities in Chile today: Santiago, the capital; Valparaíso, created as a port to connect the capital with Perú and close enough to the mines of Marga-Marga; and Concepción, close to the Bio-Bio River and within the area of Arauco. Other important cities founded during this time were: La Serena, a port and gold mining area; La Imperial (today Carahue); Valdivia, a gold mining area; and Villarrica and Angol. The forts of Arauco, Tucapel, Purén and Los Confines were built to consolidate the conquest in the dangerous southern area. Between 1558 and 1594 the cities of Canete, Osorno, Castro, Chillán, Nombre de Jesús, Rey don Felipe and Santa Cruz were founded. Their major function at the time was to reinforce the conquest of the Arauco and to incorporate the southern lands into the colony.

---

[21] See Dan Stanislawski, "Early Spanish Town Planning in the New World," *The Geographical Review* 37 (1947): 94–105.

[22] See discussion of common elements in the structure of Latin American cities, Chapter 8.

Most of these cities later developed as agricultural centers for the valleys of the rivers to which they were attached.

The decline of the Spanish Empire under the rule of the last Hapsburgs in the seventeenth century was reflected in an era of poor administration in the American colonies.[23] In Chile, questionable governors, Indian rebellions, and frequent earthquakes discouraged further settlements. Only the city of Talca and the fort of Corral, near Valdivia, were founded during this period.

In contrast to the previous century, the eighteenth century was marked by a period of administrative progress in Chile for which a succession of efficient governors was responsible. More than thirty cities were created or reconstructed in the central part of the country and their linear location pattern was thus consolidated (see fig. 4.1). A chief goal of the new government policy was the attempt to concentrate the growing population in agricultural, mining and commercial centers throughout the country. The influential farmers (hacendados) were to donate the land for these settlements and to move their residences to the small towns that were deliberately created for that purpose. San Felipe, Los Andes, Los Angeles, Cauquenes, Linares, Parral, San Fernando, Talca, Melipilla, Rancagua and Curicó were founded as agricultural centers: Copiapó, Vallenar, Illapel, Combarbalá and San José de Maipó as mining centers. Quirihue, Coelemú, La Florida, Casablanca, Petorca and La Ligua, Rere, Yumbel and Tucapel el Nuevo, new small residence towns were founded as frontier cities. The ports of Constitución and Ancud were also founded during this period.

The period of the Wars of Independence (1800–1830) was characterized by a slowdown of the process of settlement in the country. Only three cities were founded, all during the dictatorship of O'Higgins: Vicuña, La Unión and San Fernando.

The subsequent years brought an era of significant prosperity to the country following the discovery of several rich mining deposits: coal in the south; silver, gold, copper and nitrates in the north. The northern cities and camps of Chanarcillo, Taltal, Tocopilla, Chañaral, Antofagasta, Zapiga, Negreiros, Huarás, Pampa Negra and La Noria were created for the exploitation of mines. In the coal mining area of the south were founded the cities of Lirquén,

[23] Frias V., *Historia*, p. 105.

Coronel, Lota and Lebu. Almost all of these cities are defined today by their primary extractive function. Only Antofagasta and Tocopilla, which serve as ports for the shipment of minerals, have become more diversified in economic activity. The introduction of the railroad further connected these two cities with the rest of the country.

In 1851, the first railroad in Chile was operated between the city of Copiapó (silver mining area) and the port of Caldera. By the end of the century, several railroads linked the mining fields with the ports in the north. In the south, the railroad followed the existing pattern of cities connecting all the country except the extreme south.

Another factor influenced the settlement pattern in the extreme south. This was the need to create fortified cities to complete the incorporation of the Arauco. For this purpose, German immigrants were brought to the cities of Puerto Montt, Mulchén, Temuco, Nueva Imperial, Lautaro, Curacautín, Pucón and Chaima.

Also in this period, the city of Viña del Mar was created as a neighborhood of Valparaíso, and, at the extreme south, the port of Punta Arenas. Situated in the Magallanes Strait, Punta Arenas was strategically located in an area of intense navigation and trade in the period antedating the opening of the Panama Canal.

The twentieth century has not been an important period for the foundation of new centers. Only the cities of Chuquicamata (copper mines) and Calama in the north, and Puerto Aisén in the south are worthy of mention. Contemporary efforts seem to have been concentrated more on improving existing centers with the building of railroads, roads, and public utilities, than on creating new ones. The trend toward centralization has reinforced this tendency. However, it is probable that under the existing regional plans, new centers will be created in the more underdeveloped areas of the country.

CLASSIFICATION OF URBAN PLACES ACCORDING TO POPULATION SIZE

The trend toward urbanization in Chile has been especially marked during recent decades. The national census of 1940 was the first to report a greater urban than rural population. Urban population increased from 52.4% in 1940 to 54.8% in 1950 and 63.7% in 1960. Significantly, the three provinces of Santiago, Valparaíso and Concepción alone accounted for 55.2% of the nation's urban population in 1960. So important are these provinces that if they were eliminated, the rural population would exceed the urban population in Chile.

In table 4.6 cities with a population above 20,000 inhabitants are ranked according to the census of 1960. For comparison, population figures for 1952 are also given. (See Appendix, table 2 for ranking of cities over 5,000 inhabitants, 1960).

TABLE 4.6

CHILE: CITIES OF OVER 20,000 INHABITANTS

1960 RANK	CITY	POPULATION, 1960	POPULATION, 1952
1	Santiago	1,983,945	1,423,623
2	Valparaíso	384,324 [a]	315,506 [a]
3	Concepción-Talcahuano	314,412	220,391
4	Antofagasta	87,860	62,272
5	Temuco	72,132	51,497
6	Talca	67,463	55,059
7	Chillán	66,771	52,576
8	Valdivia	61,334	45,128
9	Osorno	54,693	40,120
10	Rancagua	53,318	39,972
11	Punta Arenas	51,200	34,440
12	Iquique	50,665	39,576
13	Lota	48,693	45,411
14	Puente Alto	43,557	32,599
15	Arica	43,334	18,147
16	Puerto Montt	41,681	28,944
17	La Serena	40,854	37,618
18	San Antonio	39,619	18,394
19	Los Angeles	35,511	25,071
20	Coronel	33,870	17,372
21	Coquimbo	33,794	24,962
22	Curicó	32,562	26,773
23	Copiapó	30,123	19,535
24	Quillota	29,447	22,640
25	Linares	27,562	19,624
26	Tomé	26,942	18,228
27	Quilpué	26,588	26,066
28	Calama	26,116	12,955
29	Chuquicamata	24,798	—
30	San Fernando	21,779	17,598
31	Tocopilla	21,580	19,353
32	Los Andes	20,448	19,162

SOURCES: "Resumén del País," *XII Censo General de Población y Vivienda, 1952* (Santiago: Dirección General de Estadística, Chile, 1956). *Entidade de Población 1960* (Santiago: Dirección de Estadística y Censos, Republicaíde Chile, 1962). NOTE: *a.* Includes Viña del Mar.

As might be expected, the growth of urban places in Chile is the result of a number of interrelated dynamic variables. Some of these —employment opportunities, potential for economic expansion, transport facilities—will be discussed in the following sections. As noted above, Chile has a relatively high degree of centralism: more than 25% of the people live in Santiago (1,983,945); Valparaíso, the next largest urban complex, contains only a fifth as many people (384,324); and between 1952 and 1960 Santiago has grown 39% as compared to the 26% growth of the country as a whole.

TABLE 4.7

CHILE: POPULATION GROWTH BY SIZE OF CITY

SIZE OF CITY IN 1960	POPULATION (IN THOUSANDS)		
	1940	1952	1960
More than 1,000,000 (Santiago)	952	1,423	1,983
100,000 – 1,000,000	362	424	517
50,000 – 100,000	379	441	570
20,000 – 50,000	378	517	718
10,000 – 20,000	189	247	333
Urban towns with less than 10,000 [a]	376	594	845
Rural areas [a]	2,388	2,360	2,485
Total population	5,024	5,933	7,375
All towns with less than 10,000 [a]	2,764	2,954	3,330

SIZE OF CITY IN 1960	ANNUAL RATE OF GROWTH (%)		
	1940–1952	1952–1960	1940–1960
More than 1,000,000 (Santiago)	2.9	4.3	3.5
100,000 – 1,000,000	1.3	2.5	1.8
50,000 – 100,000	1.3	3.2	2.0
20,000 – 50,000	2.6	4.1	3.2
10,000 – 20,000	2.2	3.8	2.8
Urban towns with less than 10,000 [a]	3.8	4.4	4.1
Rural areas [a]	−0.1	0.6	0.2
Total population	1.4	2.7	1.9
All towns with less than 10,000 [a]	0.5	1.5	0.9

SOURCE: Herrick, *Migration and Development in Chile*, table 3.3, p. 31. © 1965 The M.I.T. Press.
NOTE: *a*. Urban population by census definition (See Chapter 2, fn. 6).

Table 4.7 contrasts the growth of Santiago with that of smaller urban places in Chile. It may be observed that among places with more than 10,000 people, Santiago grew faster than urban places of any other size. The other two centers with a population above 100,000, Valparaíso and Concepción-Talcahuano, however, grew at a lower rate than the national rate of population increase.

Between 1952 and 1960 the growth of population in Chile and the resulting intensification of urban agglomerates can be distinguished by three characteristic processes. In the first, the total population of the urban places[24] grew proportionately to the growth of the total provincial population for the same period. A proportional increase was also shown in the percent of total population living in the principal city of some provinces. However, the urban population within most of the principal cities remained almost totally constant or varied by a maximum of one percent in the twenty-year period. It may be inferred from this that while the total population grew in absolute terms, the role of the principal provincial city as a primate urban place remained relatively unchanged. Although other urban places within a province underwent a dynamic growth, the keynote here was the static and perhaps transitory role of the principal city. This process was characteristic of the provinces of Aconcagua, Colchagua and Maule, with their respective principal cities of San Felipe, San Fernando and Cauquenes.

The second process also involved provincial population growth, but the pattern of distribution varied, with a change in the importance of the provincial primate city. In this case, the total population, the percent of total population in urban places, the total population in the principal city and the percent of urban population in the principal city, all increased significantly over the twenty year period. As a result, it may be inferred that the role of the principal provincial city as primate urban place was strengthened; and to a large degree, increased urbanization was centered in this city. Linkages between the principal city and other urban places generally became more pronounced, with the principal city acting as the center focus of the province. This pattern of increasing dominance of the principal city was found in the provinces of Nuble, Coquimbo, Magallanes, Chiloé, Malleco and Cautín, the principal cities of which are, respectively, Chillán, La Serena, Punta Arenas, Ancud, Angol and Temuco.

The third process was characterized by a growth of the total

[24] As used here, the term urban place indicates a settlement containing 5,000 or more inhabitants in 1960.

population and of the percent of total population in urban places and a significant decline of the percentages of total population and urban population in the principal provincial cities. During the twenty-year period, the primate role of the principal provincial city was highly reduced. There was a simultaneous gain in importance of the links among the urban centers other than the primate cities. The result was the formation of a very complex structure of communication links within these particular provinces. The most important of these were the provinces of Tarapacá, Antofagasta, Atacama, Valparaíso, Santiago, Curicó, Talca, Linares, Concepción, Arauco, Bio-Bio, Valdivia, Osorno, Puerto Montt, and Puerto Aisén. This has been perhaps the most significant development in the overall process of urbanization in Chile between 1940 and 1960. The high proportion of provinces affected—15 out of 25—indicates the growing importance of centers, but most important, an increasing interrelationship of linkage networks among cities springing up around the principal primate cities.

Five ranks of cities are spatially located on figure 4.1 according to the following population distribution:

Rank	Population	Number of Cities
I	100,000 & over	3
II	50,000 – 99,999	9
III	20,000 – 49,999	21
IV	10,000 – 19,999	24
V	5,000 – 9,999	35

In 1960 there were 35 fifth-rank urban places, accounting for a total population of 237,713. This figure represented 3.1% of the country's total population, or 4.8% of the total urban population. Urban places in the fourth rank were 24 in number, accounting for 336,647 inhabitants (4.4% of the total population or 6.8% of the total urban population). The third-rank urban places were close in number to the fourth-rank group (21). They accounted for a total population of 673,791, representing 8.8% and 13.8% of the total population and total urban populations, respectively. There were only 9 urban places in the second rank, but they accounted for a total population of 565,436, representing 7.4% of the country's population or 11.6% of the urban population (see Appendix, table 2).

Greater Santiago is the primate city of Chile. As in the case of Perú, urban primacy in Chile remained more or less constant during the 1952–60 intercensal period:

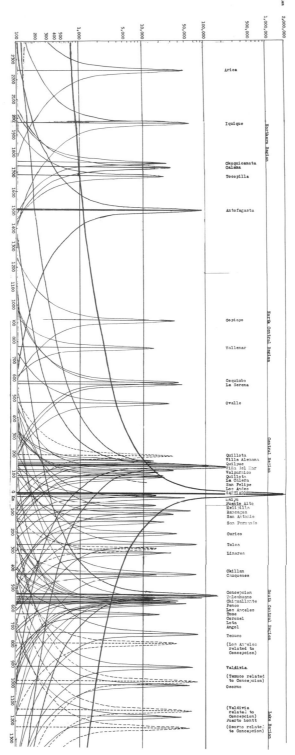

FIG. 4.1 *Chile: Ranking of Urban Places. Ratio of Urban Sphere of Influence of Santiago on Urban Places with more than 10,000 Inhabitants.*

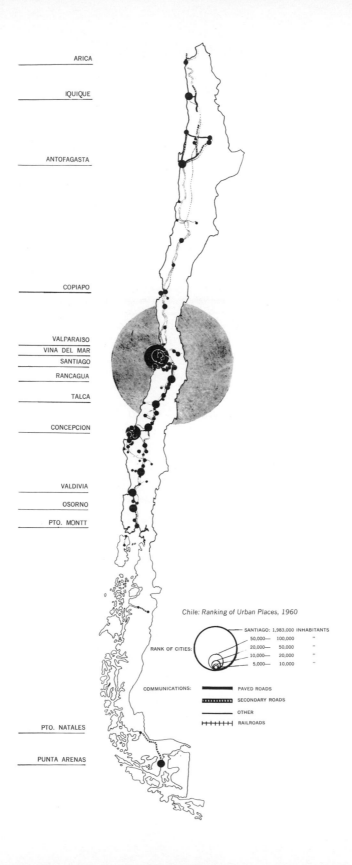

ARICA

IQUIQUE

ANTOFAGASTA

COPIAPO

VALPARAISO
VINA DEL MAR
SANTIAGO
RANCAGUA
TALCA

CONCEPCION

VALDIVIA
OSORNO
PTO. MONTT

PTO. NATALES

PUNTA ARENAS

Chile: Ranking of Urban Places, 1960

SANTIAGO: 1,983,000 INHABITANTS
50,000—   100,000   "
20,000—   50,000   "
RANK OF CITIES:
10,000—   20,000   "
5,000—   10,000   "

COMMUNICATIONS: PAVED ROADS

                         SECONDARY ROADS

                         OTHER

                         RAILROADS

	Largest City (Santiago)	*Second City* (Valparaíso)	*Third City* (Concepción-Talcahuano)
1952	100%	22%	15%
1960	100%	19%	16%

However, the proportional differences between the first, second and third largest cities are less pronounced. Figure 4.1 indicates the dominance of Santiago over all other cities with more than 10,000 inhabitants (the Austral Region not included). The ratio of urban sphere of influence was determined for each city by dividing its total population by its respective distance in kilometers from Santiago. There appears to be a direct relationship between ratio of influence and population size and an inverse relationship between ratio of influence and distance. It may be observed that Valparaíso and Concepción are the two most compact urban agglomerates closest to Santiago. The slightly higher influence of Santiago on Valparaíso is primarily the effect of its proximity. The increasing influence of the Concepción-Talcahuano nucleus is shown on the graph by the dotted lines which relate this city to other cities in the Central and Lake Regions. Greater Santiago contains 1,983,945 people, which represent 41% of the total urban population of the country. The second largest city, Valparaíso, had 384,324 people in 1960 (including Viña del Mar) or 7.9% of the total urban dwellers in Chile. The third metropolitan complex of the nation, Concepción-Talcahuano, contained 314,412 inhabitants or 6.5% of the total urban population. In summary, these three cities accounted for a population of 2,682,-681 in 1960, representing 55% of the total urban population.

URBAN PLACES CLASSIFIED ACCORDING TO BASIC ECONOMIC ACTIVITY

According to their economic base activity, urban places in Chile may be classified as: (a) industrial centers, (b) market centers, (c) extractive centers, and (d) dormitory centers. Industrial centers are those that contain important industrial activities within the context of the country as a whole (a large number of individual units and a large labor force). In general such centers are characterized by a large population, high densities, advanced transportation systems and a high rate of rural in-migration. Within this type of urban place, one may distinguish between diversified centers (with more than two principal types of manufacture), Santiago, Valparaíso, Concepción-Talcahuano, Antofagasta, Valdivia; and nondiversified centers (with only one or two types of manufacture)—Arica, Iquique, Chuquicamata, La Serena, Coquimbo, Talca, Osorno, Puerto Montt, Punta Arenas. Market centers serve primarily as the trading areas of agricultural regions, varying in size and importance according to each region. They are characteristically located in the agricultural zone of the country, between the provinces of Aconcagua and Llanquihue, and, as indicated earlier, generally date from the eighteenth century, when agriculture replaced the search for gold as the primary activity. These centers generally rely heavily on railroads for transportation, have moderate or low densities and a large labor force in the primary sector—Vallenar, Ovalle, Illapel, Quillota, Rancagua, San Fernando, Curicó, Linares, Chillán, Los Angeles, Angol, Temuco. Extractive centers are those devoted directly or indirectly (shipping, production of energy) to mining. They are mostly located in the northern zone of the country, with a large labor force also in the primary sector—Tocopilla, Chañaral, Potrerillos, Copiapó, Coronel, Lota. Dormitory centers cluster around large industrial centers, serving mainly as residential areas—Calama (near Chuquicamata), Viña del Mar (near Valparaíso), Puente Alto (near Santiago).

Obviously, the location of primary resources, transportation networks and concentrations of labor have influenced the location of the major manufacturing centers in Chile. Antofagasta is the main industrial center and port of the northern region, which has historically been the major mining area in Chile. Major nitrate fields are found in the inner slopes of the coastal mountains, in the provinces of Tarapacá and Antofagasta. The exploitation of nitrates played a major role in the economy of Chile before World War I, but is now of relatively little importance due to the discovery of chemical substitutes abroad. The first focus of exploitation in the past century was located in the areas surrounding the city of Iquique, the main port through which the mineral was exported. Today, chemical industries of subproducts of nitrate are located there, but during the present century the bulk of the extraction and transformation of this resource was transferred to the fields of Antofagasta. In the new location, mechanized plants have been installed which send their materials to the exterior through the port of Tocopilla.

The most important copper mines of the country are in Chuquicamata. In this typical mining city is concentrated 50% of the total copper production of Chile. It has a total population of 24,798

(1960), of which 30% is directly employed in the extraction of copper. Land transportation connects Chuquicamata with Antofagasta and Tocopilla. Calama serves the mining city as a dormitory center.

Arica is a free port and gateway to Perú. Its importance as a communication center is heightened by its location on the Pan American Highway and the railroad that runs north into Perú, to Tacna. The Northern Region is the third largest fishing zone of the country, with an annual production of 33,800 tons (1957). Thirteen industrial plants which process the catch are distributed among the ports of Arica, Iquique and Antofagasta. This industry is the beginning of efforts to diversify the economy of the north.

The industrial resources of the North Central Region are primarily mineral. In the past, the exploitation of the copper mines of Potrerillos constituted one of the main contributions to the economy of the country; but now these mines are almost completely exhausted. However, a new field has been discovered a few kilometers from this site and its exploitation is now under way. A road running east-west connects Potrerillos with Chañaral on the coast.

The iron fields near La Serena and Coquimbo, two third-rank cities on the coast, monopolize practically the whole iron ore production of the country. Although most of the iron ore is exported, some is used to supply Hauchipato, the steel mill located in Concepción.

In the provinces of Aconcagua, Valparaíso, Santiago and O'Higgins, there is also some copper mining though to a lesser degree than in the northern regions. A large field is located in El Teniente, near the city of Rancagua, where the offices and dockyards are located. Other important nonmetallic mineral fields are dispersed throughout this region. The cement industry in the city of La Calera (18,134 inhabitants in 1960), for example, has acquired a new importance.

But the most important economic activity of the Central Region is the manufacturing industry. Political and economic centralization, favorable market conditions—namely, population concentration and transportation facilities, water resources, and natural resources—all contribute to the high level of industrial development. This pattern of centralization is especially marked in the provinces of Santiago and Valparaíso, where 70% of the total industrial production of the country is concentrated. Santiago alone accounts for 54%

of the production, 60% of the total industrial labor force in the country, and 53% of total industrial units (see table 4.8).

The valleys of this region play a major role in the localization of industry because of their access to water and hydroelectric power. The Aconcagua Valley is perhaps the best example. This zone is particularly well served by hydroelectric power. Its industry is primarily engaged in light manufacturing. A large number of small plants are devoted to the production of consumer goods, mainly textiles, food and clothing. With the exception of the construction industry and the important dockyards for the railroads in San Fernando (21,779 inhabitants), there is no equipment industry as such. Santiago is the site of 60% of the textile industry, with 25,000 workers engaged in this activity. Textile industries are also concentrated in the cities of Viña del Mar and Quillota (29,447 inhabitants). Fish canning industries are important in the ports of San Antonio and Valparaíso accomplishing 12% of the total production of the country. The oil refinery in Concón near Valparaíso has been responsible for numerous industries processing by-products of petroleum.

In the South Central Region one may distinguish two major urban systems, reflecting the chief industrial and agricultural areas respectively. The first is the cluster around Concepción-Talcahuano, which connects the satellite coal mining towns of Lirquén, Lota, Curanilahue, Pilpilco and Lebú. The second system follows a linear pattern in the central agricultural areas and falls on the longitudinal spine described by the Pan American Highway. The cities of Los Angeles (35,511 inhabitants) and Temuco (72,132 inhabitants) are the principal nodal centers of this system.

The area of Concepción has been characterized by a rapid growth, the result of the increasing industrial diversification which has taken place in recent decades. The only steel manufacturing in the country is located in Huachipato. The favorable factors for the establishment of this industry were the availability of coal in nearby areas, good port facilities, plentiful water resources (Bio-Bio River) and a large labor force concentrated in Concepción. Around this industry, numerous secondary activities have developed, exploiting the various resources of the region. Huachipato supplies the entire steel needs of the country. It exerts a powerful attraction for a large labor force which in turn offers a valuable market for the consumption of the agricultural products of Bio-Bio and Mallocó. Coal mining in the surrounding area has existed since the past century, when it was the main source of power for the country. Coal exploitation led to the growth of many mining towns such as Lirquén, Coronel, Lota and Curanilahue. Timber industry has also been developed in the region and, subsequently, cellulose and paper industries. Textile industries exist in Tomé and Chiguayante, where the wool from Punta Arenas is processed. Both of these cities form part of the urban system around Concepción-Talcahuano.

The bulk of industry in the Lake Region is an offshoot of agriculture or the exploitation of the forests. The only exceptions are the diversified industries located in Valdivia, a second-rank city (61,334 inhabitants) which serves as port for the region. Valdivia and Puerto Montt (41,681 inhabitants) are more or less equidistant from Osorno, another second-rank city (54,693 inhabitants). These three urban places are interconnected by the Pan American Highway in a linear pattern which is a continuation of the longitudinal system of the South Central Region. The forest resources of the region are vast, with more than half of the usable areas located near Valdivia. This city developed as a major industrial center after German colonists were brought to this area during the last century. The major activities are meat packing and canning. Osorno has a large output of dairy products and frozen meat. Sugar industries are located at Llanquihue, between Osorno and Puerto Montt.

Cattle raising is the activity that dominates the economy of the Austral Region. It is concentrated in the extreme south, having the port city of Punta Arenas (51,200 inhabitants) as its major center.[25] The rest of the economic life is essentially complementary to this activity. Frozen meat industries are established in areas surrounding Punta Arenas, but take second place to the wool industry.

The exploitation of the oil resources near Punta Arenas creates some diversification in this area. The refinery in Mantiales serves the local needs but the bulk of the production is shipped to Concón (5,381 inhabitants).

[25] Punta Arenas is the world's southernmost city. It lies 1,688 nautical miles southwest of Buenos Aires, and 6,146 nautical miles south of New York. (See Bohan and Pomeranz, *Investment*, p. 36.)

TRANSPORTATION LINKAGES: HIGHWAYS, RAILWAYS,
AIR TRANSPORT, PORTS

Road links in Chile are generated from the major longitudinal
Pan American Highway (see fig. 4.1). This road traverses the
country and comes down to the sea at Antofagasta and Valdivia. It
extends from the Peruvian border to Puerto Montt, a distance of
approximately 3,300 kilometers.

The Pan American Highway is the only north-south route totally
traversing the country and as a result it takes on increase significance
as an indicator of links among urban concentrations. The road is
generally paved, either with hard surface materials or gravel except
for two major breaks totaling about 340 kilometers. These unpaved
breaks occur between Mulchén and Lautaro. This pattern of paving
in effect delimits three major linked regions: a northern region
stretching between Vallenar and Arica; a central region stretching
between La Serena and Mulchén, and a southern region between
Lautaro and Puerto Montt. The provinces of Aisén and Magallanes
are not penetrated to any appreciable extent by a road network.

In the northern region there is a characteristic pattern of
secondary roads that indicates the relative importance of the urban
centers there. This pattern is a triangular subsystem connecting the
mines of Chuquicamata with the ports of Tocopilla and Antofagasta.
However, it is important to note that the north-south connection is
still chiefly maintained by the Pan American Highway.

Contrasted strongly with this single triangular subsystem is the
linkage pattern of the central region. Between La Serena and
Mulchén, the Pan American Highway is crossed many times by the
complex network of roads interconnecting urban places. This secondary road system is, however, generally unpaved, with the only
improved highways occurring between Santiago and the Valparaíso
and San Antonio coastal stretches.[26] The country's major road connects with Argentina just above Santiago at Llay-Llay and travels
east through San Felipe and Los Andes.

The southern region also has a relatively complex network of secondary roads overlaid on the major north-south route. But unlike the

[26] As in the case of Lima and Callao, Santiago and San Antonio constitute an
urban-pair—a port city connected to a first-rank city in the hinterland (See Chapter
7, pp. 203-06).

central portion, there are no improved secondary systems of any noticeable consequence.

Urban-place links—as indicated by the road network described above—seem to be primarily dependent on the Pan American Highway. Secondary connections in the northern region run mainly east-west with no major interconnections. In the central and southern regions, secondary networks are increasingly important with the central region having the major areas of improved roads.

The air network can be classified into two major categories: international and internal. There are four international airports in the country: Los Cerrillos in Santiago, Cerro Moreno in Antofagasta, Chacalluta in Arica, and Chabunco in Punta Arenas. The facilities at Santiago and Antofagasta are capable of accommodating jet flights. Other major paved facilities with scheduled flights exist at Iquique, Vallenar, La Serena, Calama, Potrerillos, Tocopilla and Quintero. Connections among these points are apparent, but what is significant is the large number of small unpaved airports that fall into a linear pattern along the country. Although information concerning flight pattern and volume is not available, it is apparent from the spatial pattern and locations of these facilities that they are of prime importance in augmenting the road system.

Historically, foreign capital influenced the growth of railroad lines in Chile, particularly in the north. Their construction followed closely the pattern common in Latin America—foreign financing of railroads designed to carry export products to the port cities. The need to export nitrate products, for instance, explains the railroad network around such ports as Iquique, Tocopilla, Caleta, Coloso and Taltal. Railroad networks around Chañaral, Caldera, Huasco, Coquimbo and Los Vilos were used to move copper and other minerals. Like the highway system, in this area the railroad linkages run characteristically in an east-west rather than north-south direction. In the central and southern regions, the railroad lines, generally running parallel to the Pan American Highway, have cross-links running again east-west to port cities. The major network pattern connects the Talcahuano-Concepción-Lebu area. Freight and passenger traffic have increased only slightly since World War II. Annual passenger traffic in 1951 was 26,829 and by 1958, this figure had increased to only 28,792.[27] This is probably explained by the

[27] Bohan and Pomeranz, *Investment*, p. 197.

increase of highway traffic during the same period. In general, the linkage patterns apparent in the location of railroad lines tend to reinforce those of the major highways and follow closely the linear pattern of urbanization in Chile.

Port activity has been extremely important in the growth of urban places in Chile, particularly if one considers the long coast line of the country. There are no natural harbors in northern Chile. In the central region, Talcahuano and Corral only have partially protected harbors and Valparaíso is partly protected by a promontory to the south. The ports are therefore mostly artificial, protected by constructed breakwaters. This construction has facilitated the location of ports in relation to the linkage system of land transport; and the growth of the port cities has depended on the traffic generated by the mining and natural resource activity occurring in the Andean chain. The five leading ports—Valparaíso, Tocopilla, Cruz Grande, Talcahuano and San Antonio—handle almost 60 percent of the total tonnage of the nation.

Valparaíso and San Antonio are the principal general cargo ports serving the most highly developed central region of the country. At one time Valparaíso was not only the commercial capital of Chile but the most important Pacific port in the Western hemisphere. As late as the middle 1930s many of the country's principal firms had their head offices in this city. However, the growing importance of government in the economic life of the country and the shifting emphasis from foreign trade to domestic manufacturing were the two principal reasons for the eclipse of Valparaíso. It is still Chile's second most important industrial and commercial center, although Concepción is increasingly gaining in importance. The 21% relative growth in population of Valparaíso between 1952 and 1960 may be contrasted with the 42% relative growth of Concepción during the same period. Perhaps a more immediate factor contributing to the decline of Valparaíso may be found in the dynamic growth of the port of San Antonio, which is 46 miles closer to Santiago. In the last decade San Antonio grew from a population of 18,394 to 39,619, representing a relative growth of 115%. Only the northern port of Arica surpassed the rapid growth of San Antonio. Between 1952 and 1960 Arica underwent a relative growth of 138%, the highest of any other urban center. In 1952 Arica had a population of 18,147, but the figure had climbed to 43,334 by 1960 owing, in part to the development of a free port. The city is the terminus of the Arica-La Paz

Railway and it is also connected by air and highway with Perú and points south in Chile. Prior to the establishment of a free port, Arica's commercial life depended on the transit trade with Bolivia and with Tacna in Perú and on its role as the supply center for the small but fertile Lluta and Azapa Valleys, where agricultural products are produced. As a free port it has built up an important retail trade catering to customers in Perú, Bolivia and Chile. It has also been able to attract a number of industries, the most important being fish meal plants.

Tocopilla and Iquique are two major nitrate ports. Other minerals flow from Cruz Grande, Antofagasta, Lota and Coronel. The smaller ports are the so-called *cabotaje* type. These ports provide internal coastal linkages between subdominant port cities. The close interconnection between the small and larger ports takes full advantage of the important land connections and the location of major industrial and agricultural areas. Spatially, the port system reinforces the east-west patterns of land travel.

REASONS FOR RURAL-URBAN MIGRATION IN CHILE

Chile is no exception to the rural-urban migration phenomenon in Latin America. During the present century, the percentage of the total population in the Central and Lake Regions barely held its own and that in the Northern and North Central Regions decreased. These changes have been due almost exclusively to internal migratory movements. Between 1950 and 1960, 592,389 rural migrants actually moved to the cities. But in Chile, as in the rest of Latin America, not all regions received an equal proportion of the migrants. The reasons for rural-urban migration in Chile are generally those outlined for Latin America as a whole in the preceding chapter, although in this particular case it seems that opportunities in industrial employment have most often provided the major impetus for the migrations.

The manufacturing industry in 1961 was responsible for the greatest contribution to the national income. During the last few decades, industry has relocated in places where available labor is concentrated, reinforcing the growth of cities. The large industrial centers of the country, Santiago, Valparaíso, Concepción-Talcahuano and Antofagasta, concentrate over 35% of the total population of the country and over 50% of the urban population. Within the provinces of Aconcagua, Valparaíso and Santiago is concentrated 65% of the industrial units of the country, employing 73% of the total industrial labor force in the country (see table 4.8).

TABLE 4.8

CHILE: INDUSTRIAL UNITS AND EMPLOYMENT
BY REGIONS AND PROVINCES

REGIONS & PROVINCES	INDUSTRIAL UNITS	%	EMPLOYMENT	%
Northern Region	*203*	*3.46*	*4,258*	*2.04*
Tarapacá	75	1.28	1,589	0.76
Antofagasta	128	2.18	2,669	1.28
North Central Region	*145*	*2.47*	*2,088*	*1.00*
Coquimbo	50	0.85	432	0.21
Atacama	95	1.62	1,656	0.79
Central Region	*4,349*	*74.20*	*162,835*	*77.81*
Aconcagua	81	1.38	2,011	0.96
Valparaíso	598	10.20	24,866	11.90
Santiago	3,156	53.85	126,401	60.48
O'Higgins	107	1.83	1,894	0.91
Colchagua	41	0.70	819	0.39
Curicó	47	0.80	612	0.29
Talca	121	2.06	3,623	1.73
Maule	34	0.41	201	0.10
Linares	61	1.04	923	0.44
Nuble	113	1.93	1,485	0.71
South Central Region	*674*	*11.50*	*28,416*	*13.60*
Concepción	334	5.70	22,167	10.61
Arauco	13	0.22	133	0.06
Bio-Bio	63	1.07	1,725	0.83
Malleco	62	1.06	1,348	0.64
Cautín	202	3.45	3,043	1.46
Lake Region	*383*	*6.53*	*9,355*	*4.47*
Valdivia	164	2.80	5,475	2.62
Osorno	124	2.11	2,214	1.06
Llanquihue	95	1.62	1,666	0.79
Austral Region	*108*	*1.84*	*2,041*	*0.98*
Chiloé	17	0.29	140	0.07
Aisén	13	0.22	140	0.07
Magallanes	78	1.33	1,761	0.84
Total, Country	*5,862*	*100.00*	*208,993*	*100.00*

SOURCE: Dirección de Estadística y Censos, *Censo Industrial* (1957), adjusted by Corfa, *Geografía Económica de Chile* (Santiago, 1962) 3:194–95.

In 1962 Greater Santiago reported 125,000 people active in manufacturing, or 27% of the labor force of the city. Concepción had approximately 13,500 employed in manufacturing, representing

22.4% of the labor force. Valparaíso provided 27,300 jobs, accounting for 20.7% of the economically active labor force. Antofagasta had considerably fewer people active in manufacturing (3,800), but still reported 15.6% of the labor force active in that sector. The importance of the service sector as a complementary branch of industry should also be kept in mind as an attraction force in rural-urban migrations. This tertiary sector, in fact, has been growing at a faster rate than any other branch of industry and annually provides more jobs than manufacturing. Greater Santiago, for example, has more than 66% of its labor force engaged in the service sector, while the average for Concepción, Valparaíso and Antofagasta is very close to 69% of their labor force.

The actual size of the migration to Greater Santiago may be assessed from a labor force survey carried out by the Institute of Economics of the University of Chile in June, 1963. Migrants were defined simply as those not born in the area where they live, as opposed to the natives who were identified as those born in the area where they now reside. It was established that migrants constituted 37% of the population of Greater Santiago; and the survey showed that of a labor force of 778,000 workers, more than half (53%) were migrants.[28]

Table 4.9 shows that in 1952 the largest number of migrants came from the central third of the country. The census of that year counted 1,755,000 people living in Santiago province, of which 567,000 (32.3%) were natives of other provinces. Of the 567,000 migrants, 89.3% were born in the eighteen other central provinces, 9.7% in the three northern provinces, and 1.0% in the three southern provinces. This pattern of migration can be explained within the framework of the regional development characteristics of Chile during the intercensal period, 1940–1952. If one examines the railroad connections to Santiago, for instance, it may be observed that a railway runs as far north as Iquique, located in the northernmost province. However, no railway systems connect Santiago with the southern third of the country. Since potential migrants from the southern provinces could only reach Santiago directly by airplane or boat, it may be inferred that the high transportation costs generally discouraged migrations from this area. For the same reason,

[28] Herrick, *Migration and Development*, p. 46.

TABLE 4.9

CHILE: REGIONAL CONTRIBUTIONS TO MIGRATION TO
SANTIAGO PROVINCE, 1952

REGION	POPULATION	NATIVES LIVING IN SANTIAGO IN 1952
Three northern provinces[a]	367,700	54,876
Eighteen central provinces[b]	4,029,700	506,375
Three southern provinces[c]	182,100	5,747
Total	4,579,500	566,998

	PERCENT OF CHILE'S POPULATION LIVING OUTSIDE SANTIAGO	PERCENT OF ALL MIGRANTS TO SANTIAGO
Three northern provinces	8.0	9.7
Eighteen central provinces	88.0	89.3
Three southern provinces	4.0	1.0
Total	100.0%	100.0%

SOURCE: Herrick, *Migration and Development*, table 4.3, p. 49. © 1965 The M.I.T. Press.
NOTES:
  a. Tarapacá, Antofagasta and Atacama
  b. Excluding Santiago province
  c. Chiloé, Aisén and Magallanes

the more efficient transportation systems (roads, railroads) connecting Santiago with the central provinces facilitated a larger migratory movement.

Combined with the differences in transport facilities, the relative growth of employment opportunities, potentials for economic expansion and differences in population density seem to be even more important in explaining the migratory movement from the far north and far south. Between 1940 and 1952, the northern provinces lost 38% of the copper work force.[29] At that time the economy of the southern provinces was largely based on forest, fish and wool and the possibilities of expansion seemed to be greater. Moreover, these provinces only had half as many people to become potential migrants.

[29] Ibid., p. 48.

The question of whether the rural residents moved directly to Santiago from the rural areas or whether they moved to the capital by stages from other smaller urban places is answered by two recent surveys made in Santiago.[30] Preliminary results from one of these surveys carried out by the Latin American Demographic Center showed that 65% of the migrants lived in towns of more than 5,000 inhabitants prior to their final journey to Santiago. The other survey was carried out by the Institute of Economics, and showed that 63% of the migrants were actually born in towns having more than 10,000 inhabitants in 1952. This supports the earlier suggestion that migrants to the largest city tend to come largely from smaller cities rather than directly from the countryside (see Chapter 3, fn. 8.)

An important urbanization phenomenon frequently associated with the internal migratory movement is the growing agglomerations of low-income families in the outskirts of Greater Santiago and the other large urban places in Chile. These peripheral settlements are known as *callampas* and are the equivalent of the barriadas in Perú. Their most significant proliferation occurred during the last two decades, and they continue to spread.[31] Callampa José María Caro in Santiago, for example, has more than 100,000 people, making it larger than the fourth city of Chile, Antofagasta. The type of urban growth that has taken place and the policies that have influenced it are now undergoing study by the Corporación de Vivienda (CORVI) and other public and private institutions.

In 1959, CORVI conducted a survey to obtain an estimate on the origin and conditions of 17,500 callampa dwellings distributed in 122 settlements in Greater Santiago.[32] The results showed that only 25% of the members of the 276 households that were interviewed were born inside Greater Santiago. The remaining 75% of the households were found to be wholly or partly of migrant origin. Among the adult respondents who were of migrant origin two-thirds had lived elsewhere in Santiago before coming to the settlement in which they lived at the time of the inquiry. Many of these had migrated singly, lived for a while with relatives or friends, and moved to a callampa after bringing their families or forming a

---

[30] Ibid., pp. 51–52.

[31] See table 7.2 and the case study of barriadas in Lima, Chapter 7.

[32] Survey carried out by the *Servicio Social de la Oficina de Autoconstrucción de la Corporación de la Vivienda* (CORVI), with the collaboration of the *Servicio Nacional de Salud* and the *Intendencia de Santiago*. (See ECLA, *Urbanization in Latin America*, E/CN 12/662 (1963), p. 12.)

family in the city. More than 60% of the migrant respondents moved directly from their places of origin to Santiago, while nearly 30% made at least one stop along the way in a smaller urban place.

Most of the provinces of Chile are represented in the migrant part of the callampa population, but more than 80% came from the central group of provinces limited by Coquimbo to the north and Concepción to the south. Eleven percent came from Santiago Province outside Greater Santiago; 10 percent came from Nuble; 9 percent each came from Colchagua, Cautín and O'Higgins (no other province contributed more than 6 percent). The percentages for the provinces other than Santiago are quite similar to the percentage for immigrants living in Santiago Province, including the metropolitan area, recorded by the 1952 census.

The average growth of the total population in Greater Santiago, Valparaíso, Concepción and Antofagasta was approximately 36.0% for the period, 1952–1960. This change can largely be attributed to migrations to the urban areas. And it is interesting to note that parallel to the in-migratory movement, there has been a pattern of remigration in the same cities. But this movement took place from the central part of the cities to the outlying regions, still within the metropolitan areas. The explanation may be found in the fact that industry is becoming increasingly a suburban activity in many Chilean cities. Due to a number of ecological and physical limitations, it is becoming more profitable to locate the various manufacturing activities away from the older, traditional city center. It is not unlikely that this trend will continue, with the result that there will be an even larger migration from the city centers to the surrounding regions.

5

Urban Systems in a Regional Context: The Central American Case[1]

THE evolution of a people having some common social and political characteristics is usually directly associated with the number and size of cities within their political territory. In the case of Central America, however, such common characteristics have developed despite the absence of numerous and large cities, and, moreover, have developed across political boundaries. In this area it is the regional context that has been significant because the high density of regional population has outweighed the fact that there is only one city that approaches the half-million mark. El Salvador, for example, with 332 inhabitants per square mile, has the second highest population density in the hemisphere.

While the relationship of size, function, and flow among cities can define the characteristics of an urban system, the physiographic characteristics of each urban site exercise a strong influence on the development of cities in newly developing regions or in countries where exploitation of natural resources is a prime economic activity.

The Central American isthmus is made up of three natural regions stretched across five political divisions, and what makes this area unique is that these three regions are characterized by greater homogeneity than is found within any one of the five countries across which they cut.

[1] Honduras, El Salvador, and Guatemala have been selected as the major examples, though there are occasional references to Costa Rica, Nicaragua, and Panamá (see map 1.1). See Appendix, table 3 for a comparison of some related indices of economic and social development of Honduras, El Salvador and Guatemala. I am indebted to Mario E. Martin whose "Urban Systems in Central America" serves as a basis for this chapter.

The most important element in the physiography of this area is the mountainous region running the length of the isthmus; the remainder of the territory is divided into two coastal areas, the north Caribbean lowlands and the Pacific lowlands. The two coastal regions have proven very suitable for the two crops that have played an important role in economic development and in the formation of cities, bananas and coffee. Since the establishment of banana plantations in the early 1900s and the large-scale production of coffee beginning around 1880, the economic balance and population stability of these regions have been influenced by the growth and decline of these two major exports on the world market.

Climatic influences in part determined the early settlement pattern; in selecting sites for important cities the Spaniards showed a preference for the cooler highlands. Even today more than half of the population still lives in the highland valleys, depending basically upon agricultural production. The fact that only one major city, San Pedro Sula, is located in the humid coastal area and that all five capitals are located inland suggest the importance of climatic considerations as locational criteria in the foundation of cities (see map 5.1). But even more important in shaping the final pattern of population settlement in northern Central America have been the preexisting settlement patterns dating back to prehistoric times. These were based on a direct response to the fertility of the soil, and in turn determined the strategic location of towns by the Spaniards for purposes of conquest and colonization. The Guatemalan highlands and the Pacific slopes of El Salvador were densely populated regions under the Meso-American cultures: "Within and adjacent to the volcanic axis (of Central America) are found some of the most fertile tropical highlands and lowlands of the Americas: chiefly for that reason this area for a millennium has been densely populated."[2]

The Spanish founding of towns began in Central México, where the heart of the Meso-American culture had been conquered in 1519. Attracted by promising descriptions of wealth and large centers of culture, the Spaniards advanced along the logical route

[2] R. C. West, "Surface Configuration and Associated Geology of Middle America" in *Handbook of Middle American Indians,* eds. R. Wauchope and R. C. West (Austin: University of Texas Press, 1964): 74.

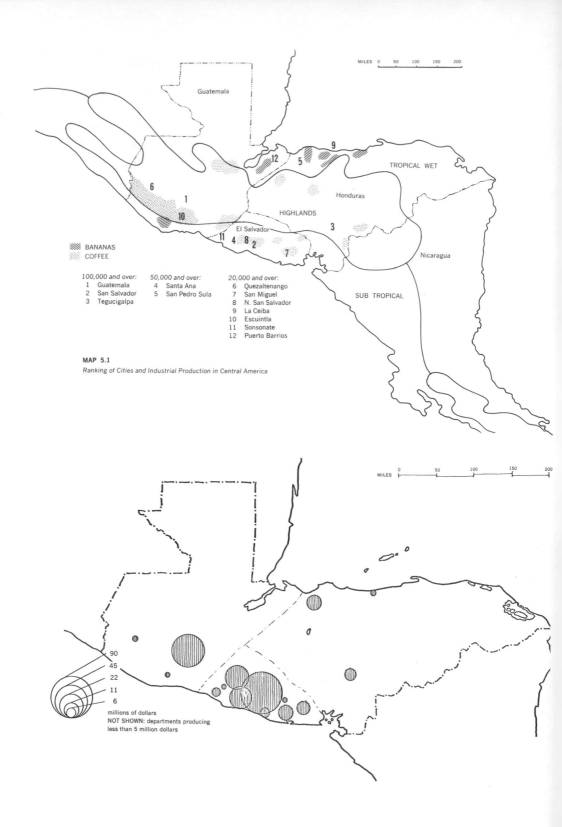

MILES 0 50 100 150 200

Guatemala

TROPICAL WET

Honduras

HIGHLANDS

El Salvador

Nicaragua

SUB TROPICAL

BANANAS
COFFEE

100,000 and over:	50,000 and over:	20,000 and over:
1 Guatemala	4 Santa Ana	6 Quezaltenango
2 San Salvador	5 San Pedro Sula	7 San Miguel
3 Tegucigalpa		8 N. San Salvador
		9 La Ceiba
		10 Escuintla
		11 Sonsonate
		12 Puerto Barrios

MAP 5.1

Ranking of Cities and Industrial Production in Central America

MILES 0   50   100   150   200

90
45
22
11
6

millions of dollars
NOT SHOWN: departments producing
less than 5 million dollars

through the Mexican highlands into Guatemala. There were no cities or large ceremonial complexes functioning in the area at the time, the lowland Maya centers having already been abandoned for new urban centers in northern Yucatán. Therefore in this case the location of the present-day cities did not follow a previous urban settlement pattern, but instead underscored the dispersed but well-populated rural pattern over the highland region. Thus, the first Spanish city, meant to be the capital of the new territories, was founded "near the center of all the country."[3] Despite some instability due to natural disasters that caused migrations to nearby sites twice between 1524 and 1773, the general location of the Spanish headquarters and administrative capital was unequivocally determined.

A second colonization movement became necessary in view of threatening unrest within the second most important Indian culture in the area, and in 1525 San Salvador was founded in the midst of their territory.[4] The third important center, planned as an administrative center was to be founded "half-way between the oceans"[5] according to the instructions given the founder of Valladolid de Comayagua, later the capital of Honduras, in 1529.[6] Except for some considerations given to site conditions including proximity to water, available agricultural land, and general topographic suitability the specific locations of these three centers, eventually becoming the most important cities in the area, were determined by the Spanish ad hoc town planners on the basis of the former native agricultural settlement pattern and the strategic needs of colonization and conquest.

There were early settlements on the coasts but, unlike ports such as Cartagena, Lima-Callao, Buenos Aires and Montevideo in South America, the port settlements in Central American did not assume administrative functions and took considerable time to develop into

[3] C. L. Jones, *Guatemala, Past and Present* (Minneapolis: University of Minnesota Press, 1940), p. 9.

[4] Larde y Larín, *El Salvador: Historia de sus Pueblos, Villas y Ciudades* (San Salvador: Ministerio de Cultura, 1957), p. 400.

[5] W. E. Curtis, *The Capitals of Spanish America* (New York: Harper & Bros., 1888), p. 115.

[6] The seat of the Honduran government was moved from Comayagua to Tegucigalpa, a rival city in the regional political warfare, in 1880. Comayagua subsequently dropped from first place in population in 1880 to eighth place in 1961.

important urban places. Significantly, no administrative city was located specifically with a regard to soil or other resource exploitation by the Spaniards. Thus, in general, when the original expectations about natural or accumulated wealth proved false, these cities gradually took on the function which gave them their rationale, namely, administration. Since the large agricultural potential was mostly exploited on a subsistence basis, particularly after the conquest discouraged native trade, the port settlements did not become essential as was the case in many other parts of the New World that had minerals and useful crops to export to the Old World. The Central American territory was, in effect, so shallow and contained so few known exportable resources that the importance of the maritime fringe was not realized. Eventually trade did develop, based on the export of cocoa, cochineal and textiles, but the destinations and the volume of this trade were such that its most important routes were by land to México and from there by boat to Cuba and Spain.

The end result of the pattern of colonial settlement was a system of cities located mostly on the highlands, tied together by an administrative organization and relatively unconcerned with foreign trade.

Population Growth and Density

In Central America, the present growth rate of the population is more than 3% per year. This rate, which is nearly double that of the industrialized countries and is higher than the growth rate in México and South America, is attributable in large measure to the reduction of the death rate (see table 5.1).

The rate of urbanization, however, has not been precisely determined due to the lack of a standard definition of the term urban. The countries under consideration have applied the classification of urban to settlements that range from 133 to 573,000 inhabitants. In Honduras where 23.3 percent of the population was considered urban the classification for the 1961 census was applied to places with a minimum population of 1,000 inhabitants which possessed some basic urban services such as primary schools, telephone or telegraph service, utilities such as electricity and running water, and transportation access. Administrative function was not con-

TABLE 5.1

AARI IN CENTRAL AMERICA
COMPARED TO OTHER WORLD REGIONS
(percentage)

COUNTRIES	1920–40	1940–50	1950–59
Costa Rica	1.95	2.59	3.87
El Salvador	1.69	1.39	3.38
Nicaragua	1.39	2.54	3.34
Honduras	2.92	2.23	3.32
Guatemala	2.66	2.36	2.98
Panamá	1.65	2.54	2.82
Central America TOTAL	2.12	2.20	3.20
México	1.57	2.69	2.87
South America	1.97	2.12	2.45
United States	1.09	1.39	1.73

SOURCE: ECLA, *Human Resources of Central America, Panamá and México, 1950–1980, in Relation to Some Aspects of Economic Development* (New York: United Nations, 1962), p. 4.

sidered in the criteria. In El Salvador, however, no urban services were required for the 1961 census but the center, which varied from 156 to 349,374 inhabitants did have to serve as a municipal center. The criteria for the 1964 Guatemalan census were identical to El Salvador except that centers varied from 133 to 572,934 inhabitants. Here 33.6 percent of the population was considered urban by census definition compared with 38.5 percent in El Salvador.[7]

It is interesting to note that in a high percentage of the cases, urban places fail to fulfill other conditions which, for purposes of a study of urban systems, should be considered intrinsic to the functions of a city. One such condition is the existence of transportation connections with the rest of the cities; another is the existence of secondary and tertiary economic activities.

The dynamics of regional population movements suggest a more reliable explanation of the relative importance of urban centers.

[7] Census data for Honduras from *Cifras Definitivas de Población y Viviendas en Cabeceras Municipales y en Aldeas y Caserios, April, 1961* (Dirección General de Estadística y Censos, Honduras: Tegucigalpa, March 1963); for El Salvador from *Tercer Censo Nacional de Población, 1961* (Dirección General de Estadística y Censos, El Salvador: San Salvador, 1962); for Guatemala from *Trimestre Estadístico* (Dirección General de Estadística, Guatemala City, Guatemala, 1964).

Analyzing statistical data on population growth by department (natural and migratory combined) indicates a clear intensification of population density in two basic areas: the Pacific coastal areas where the majority of the population has always lived; and the Caribbean coastal plains. These are the regions which, because of soil and topographic factors, have been found to be excellent for the production of bananas and coffee. Except for these two regions, the rest of the territory has remained very much as it was when settled in the sixteenth century. In effect, the departments of Izabel, Atlántida, Cortés, Yoro and Santa Bárbara along the north coast of the area have shown quite marked percentage increases (see Appendix, table 4); on the Pacific side, La Unión and Escuintla show comparable, although lower, rates of increase (see Appendix, tables 5 and 6). The reasons for the larger population shifts are to be found in the employment opportunities implicit in large-scale banana and coffee production. Covering large portions of the Caribbean coastland as they do, the banana plantations have built whole towns for their personnel which constitute the increase in population of previously small cities like Tela, Progreso, and La Lima.

One result of these large migratory currents has been the development of at least one new economic region, with higher per capita income than and relatively isolated from the rest of the country. This kind of regional identity is to be found along the north coasts of both Honduras and Guatemala, and is marked by a basically expert-oriented economy to which new population and technological elements have contributed during the approximately sixty years of the uninterrupted operations of the banana industry. On the Pacific coast and the mountain slopes, coffee production attracted foreign investment and trade operations from about 1910 to 1939 oriented predominantly toward markets in Europe and the United States.

The first period of substantial growth of the port cities came as a consequence of the export of bananas and coffee and the development of transportation facilities to move the natural products to processing locations or shipping piers. The ports of San José, Acajutla and Amapala on the Pacific, and Puerto Castilla on the Caribbean became the gateways to the area from 1900 until about 1935, when air transportation assumed more importance. Puerto Castilla rose and fell with the productivity of the region that surrounded it; when the banana company stopped production in the

Aguán Valley, the port lost its raison d'etre and has since remained without transport facilities. With banana exports making up close to 50 percent of the national export total in Honduras and close to 15 percent in Guatemala, and with coffee comprising around 70 percent of total exports in Guatemala and around 75 percent in El Salvador, the potential for economic and population growth of the banana and coffee regions should be a relatively influential factor in future population concentration.

A comparison of population growth by departments and the growth of cities indicates an inverse relationship: the departments with the highest growth in the last sixty years have generally not developed large urban centers, despite increasing density; the capital cities, despite moderate growth in their respective departments, have registered increases up to 900 percent in sixty years (see table 5.2[8]).

[8] Based on Appendix, tables 4, 5 and 6.

TABLE 5.2

HONDURAS, EL SALVADOR AND GUATEMALA:
SELECTED CUMULATIVE PERCENTAGE GROWTH

CITY AND DEPARTMENT	URBAN GROWTH %	AREA GROWTH %	PERIOD
San Salvador	900		
SAN SALVADOR		350	1901–1961
Guatemala	800		
GUATEMALA		530	1893–1964
Tegucigalpa	700		
FRANCISCO MORAZÁN		370	1901–1961
San Pedro Sula	800		
CORTÉS		950	1901–1961
La Ceiba	350		
ATLÁNTIDA		1100	1901–1961
Santa Ana	230		
SANTA ANA		275	1901–1961
Honduras		375	1901–1961
El Salvador		329	1901–1961
Guatemala		314	1893–1964

In short, the population movement has followed two trends: regional area increase, associated with banana and coffee production, without corresponding urban concentration; and city growth, in the capitals, without a marked increase in settled areas.

City Size, Rank and Function

Empirical observations have supported the idea of systems of cities based on a predictable relationship in population sizes. A worldwide ranking of the cities within each country has produced two basic models: either rank-size[9] regularity; or primacy.[10] Both, in effect, express the tendency for cities to arrive at a hierarchical pattern of population sizes, with one largest city and a descending order of sizes down to the last village or hamlet. Although primacy has been notoriously prevalent in the underdeveloped countries, attempts at correlation of the indices of economic development and primate cities have yielded negative results.[11] More specifically, according to a recent worldwide survey, primacy seems to be characteristic of those small countries with low income per capita, dependence upon exports, a colonial history, an agricultural economy, and a fast rate of population growth.[12]

[9] The concept of rank-size, originated by G. K. Zipf, develops a mathematical relationship between rank and size, by means of a graphical representation consisting of a straight line plotted on double logarithmic paper. Deviations from the model are readily perceptible by plotting the rank and size of all the cities, or of those above a certain size, for example 10,000 inhabitants (see rank-size graph 5.1). See also Berry and Garrison, "Alternate Explanations of Rank-Size Relationship," in *Readings in Urban Geography*, eds. Mayer and Kohn (Chicago: University of Chicago Press, 1959), p. 232.

[10] The so-called "law of primacy" was first suggested by Mark Jefferson, "The Law of the Primate City," as follows:

All over the world it is the law of the Capitals that the largest city shall be supereminent, and not merely in size, but in national influence. Once a city is larger than any other in its country, this mere fact gives it an impetus to grow that cannot be affected by any other city, and it draws away from all of them in character as well as in size. . . . It becomes the primate city.

[11] B. J. L. Berry, "City Size Distributions and Economic Development," in *Regional Development and Planning*, eds. Friedmann and Alonso (Cambridge, Mass.: The M.I.T. Press, 1964).

[12] A. S. Linsky, "Some Generalizations Concerning Primate Cities," *Annals of the Association of American Geographers* 55 (September 1965).

Central America seems to possess all of these characteristics apparently associated with the development of primate cities. Against this background, the rank-size curves of Honduras, El Salvador and Guatemala will be observed both in their present state and as they have changed through the last forty to fifty years. The main concern in this exploration is the assumption that one of the more important reasons for urban growth is the present size and corresponding rank each city holds in the whole national system (see Appendix, table 7). Until the mid-century, national economic and spatial frameworks imposed strict limitations on independent urban growth. The situation began to change following the creation of the Central American Common Market in 1953. This is exerting an important influence on development in this region.

In Zipf's theoretical formulation, the relationships between the sizes of the first, second and third cities are 100–50–33 respectively. Honduras, El Salvador and Guatemala show variations ranging from an almost perfect rank-size distribution to clear primacy with a ratio of 100–40–17 for Honduras, 100–24–13 for El Salvador, and 100–8–5 for Guatemala.[13]

The overall trend in the rank-size graphs for Honduras, El Salvador, and Guatemala indicates a gradual emergence of the capital city with varying degrees of follow-up by the second and third cities in each country's urban system. Thus, in Honduras, San Pedro Sula emerges in a position close to the theoretical ideal size of the rank-size model, while Quezaltenango in Guatemala has only recently begun to grow after half a century of being less than one-tenth the size of the primate city (see rank-size graphs 5.1, 5.2, 5.3, and Bibliography, respective census publication).

The relative importance of a city's administrative function in providing a basic employment source for the urban population is the underlying factor in the top-heavy development of the hierarchy of cities. Only when other economic activities have concentrated elsewhere and provided a significant number of jobs has it been possible to have a nonprimate urban system, as has been the case in Honduras.

Beginning with the evolution of the administrative hierarchy

[13] Data for Honduras and El Salvador from 1961 census, for Guatemala from 1964 census. Census figures for 1965 show a ratio of 100–50 for Honduras (see Appendix, table 7 on which these ratios are based).

during colonial times, there has been a consistent correlation between highest administrative function and largest population in the cities of Central America. Guatemala is the epitome of the primate city; it has fulfilled the classical conditions set by Jefferson both with respect to the total Central American area during the colonial period and with respect to the country of Guatemala after independence. Despite earthquakes and floods which twice completely destroyed the city, Guatemala was—from its foundation until independence in 1821—the preeminent city in the Central American region both in size and sphere of influence.[14]

It was in Guatemala that the most important political, ecclesiastical, educational and economic activities were conducted for here was located the only important university to be found between México and Lima, a university which drew the outstanding intellectuals of the area and provided a forum for advanced political opinion. When independence was declared in Guatemala, the rest of the territory was then notified, post facto. The order of hierarchy descended to the provincial capitals of San Salvador and Camayagua, to become the capitals of independent countries after 1821, and certainly after the dissolution of the Central American Federation in 1838. Subsequently each of the five countries broke off almost all relations with the former capital city of Guatemala and began to

---

[14] An indication of the relative importance of Central American cities in the colonial period is given by the following ranking of "prices" paid the Spanish Crown for the individual personal privilege of exercising the municipal authority (under Royal delegation of authority) in 1611 [F. de P. Garcia Pelaez, *Memorias para la Historia del Antiguo Reino de Guatemala* (Guatemala: Biblioteca Payo de Revera, 1943), p. 222.]:

Guatemala City	76,764 (pesos)
San Salvador (provincial capital)	22,875
San Miguel	12,376
Chiapa (now in México)	10,614
Granada (Nicaragua)	10,122
León de Nicaragua	9,825
Sonsonate	9,300
Gracias (Honduras; seat of court)	6,050
Valladolid de Comayagua (prov. cap.)	5,325
San Vicente	5,200
Realejo (Nicaragua)	4,350
Segovia (Nicaragua)	3,395
Cartago (Costa Rica)	2,820
Truxillo (Honduran port)	2,035
Xeres (Choluteca, Honduras)	+716
San Pedro Sula	465
Olancho (Honduras)	175

develop a true national capital of its own, with the multiple institutions and prestige symbols befitting the new status of nationhood. Thus, a multiplication of the bureaucratic organization and of the centralized operations of national governments and economies resulted in the creation of independent primate cities in each of the five countries, and within their respective countries. The five primate cities concentrated the outstanding elements of political and economic life. The inhabitants of the capitals enjoyed exclusively the few available facilities for the pursuit of culture, politics and business; to this day, except for one department of economics which has operated in the second city of Honduras, all the departments of all the universities are located in the capital cities, the end result being the draining of new talent and enterprise from the rest of the country with a consequent concentration in the capitals. The urban system of this region thus evolved into five independent, primacy-prone systems, as can be seen in the rank-size distribution for each country in graphs 5.1, 5.2, and 5.3. The extreme primacy evident in the case of Guatemala can be explained in part by the function that this capital city fulfilled during colonial times; it was then the primate city for a large territory and therefore concentrated population far out of proportion to the size of the country itself. The second- and third-ranking Guatemalan cities, on the other hand, were strictly limited in influence to their local regional and national context; they were not influential in Central America as a whole. This has been a factor in the great gap in size and importance between Guatemala City and the other cities in the country.

But, in general, in the evolution of the systems under independence, especially in the latter part of the last century and the early 1900s, the political administrative centers became the higher-ranking cities of their urban systems in direct relation to the economic importance of their function. The rank-size graph for Honduras (5.1), for example, shows a fairly even population size in ranks 2, 3, 4 and 5; there seems to have been little growth differential among these larger cities which were, not surprisingly, regional administrative centers within the national territory. The same thing occurred in El Salvador, where the two regional centers— eastern and western—followed the capital in size. To this day, government employment as an important sector of the urban economic base is a decisive factor in the capital city continuing to

GRAPH 5.1

Honduras: Rank-Size of Cities

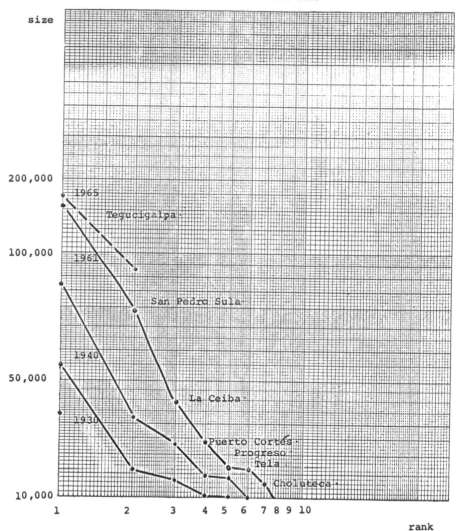

outstrip the other centers in growth. Public administration is, in effect, the traditional impetus to city-building activity in Central America.

From colonial times, the administrative operations of the central government have employed a considerable portion of the communities' economically active population.[15] Data on the evolution

[15] F. V. Solorzano, *Evolución Económica de Guatemala* (Guatemala: Ministerio de Educación Pública, 1963), p. 104.

of this type of economic activity are not readily available; however, an analysis of the national budget figures for the 1962 fiscal year in Honduras yields some evidence on the importance of the government payroll (national only, not municipal) in the economic life of the capital city, Tegucigalpa.[16]

[16] *Presupuesto General de Gastos* (Tegucigalpa: Ministerio de Economía y Hacienda, 1962).

GRAPH 5.2

El Salvador: Rank-Size of Cities

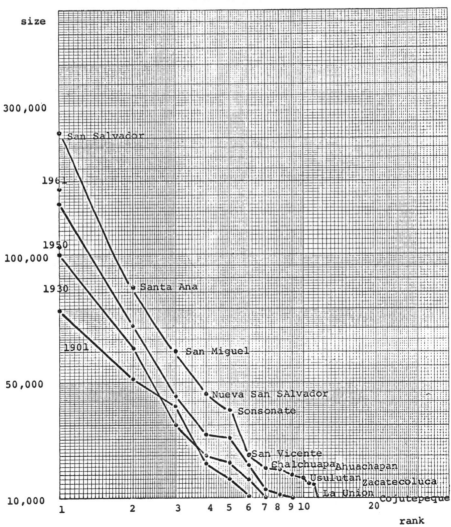

GRAPH 5.3

Guatemala: Rank-Size of Cities

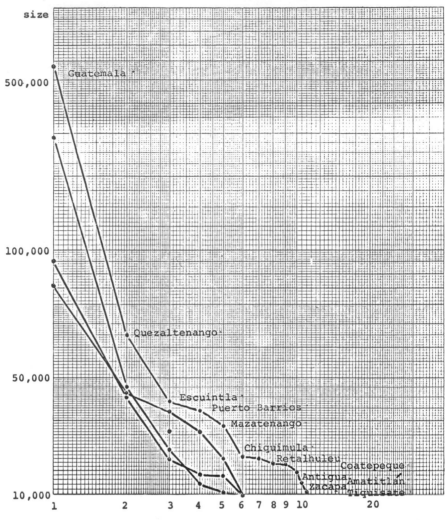

As the seat of the overwhelming majority of central government operations, Tegucigalpa is the pump which circulates the revenues and services that tie the government to its people. Like most national capitals, Tegucigalpa contains the three branches of government and the majority of the personnel of the various ministries. The basic distinction of Tegucigalpa is that, in the absence of industry and related primary economic activities, the government payroll has been the sole economic base for the core of the local population. Its importance has diminished as industry and trade have risen to such a degree as to compete with public administration in the number of people employed. Nevertheless, of the $50 million budget, $18 million was spent in payrolls and $32 million in capital expenditures. Of the payroll figure of $18 million, 55% was spent in the capital city as pay to 7,600 employees, or one-half the total of the personnel of the national government. This means that fully 35,000 people were directly dependent on the government payroll (four dependants is common as an average). This is in effect basic employment, or employment performed for nonlocal needs, since the national government serves all the people in the country.[17] Following the basic-nonbasic concept, the ratio would normally vary from 1 to 2; that is, there would be one or two jobs supported by the needs of the basic or export employees. The total employment generated by government operations, basic and nonbasic, would then run from 15,200 to 22,000 jobs. Consequently, there would then be from 75,000 to 100,000 local inhabitants whose livelihood would derive from the government payroll. This was, in effect, from 50 to 66% of the total population of Tegucigalpa at the time of budget expenditures in 1962.

Although the employment figures for 1961 show a comparable number of industrial jobs (5,500) and a typically high number of tertiary service jobs, qualitatively, government and industrial employment tend to be the most effective indicators of economic base, since other service employment is notorious for its part-time or temporary nature, and may be considered, then, disguised unemployment.

The evolution of this urban economic base can only be inferred from related data. Since the ratio of national government consumption to gross national product has remained essentially static for at least ten years, from 9 to 12%, depending on the country,[18] one can assume the number of employees and effective payroll to have remained approximately the same. With increased industrial employment and production, the share of the economic base contributed by the government payroll can be assumed to have decreased. The trend has more likely than not been toward a reduction in the eco-

[17] J. W. Alexander, "The Basic-Nonbasic Concept of Urban Economic Functions" in *Readings in Urban Geography.*

[18] ECLA, *The Process of Industrialization in Latin America,* Statistical Annex (New York: United Nations, 1966), p. 52.

nomic importance of the administrative function of the cities and a consequent diversification of the economic base.

In the second-rank cities there has more often been a dynamic growth of secondary activities, since there the administrative function has never had the importance it has had in the capital cities. The example of San Pedro Sula is all the more important, then, since that city's population growth has increased at an unusually fast rate without the economic base that has propelled population growth in the capital city. Here is a case of city growth which does not conform to the traditional pattern and which may indicate a greater future potential than even that of the capital city, in spite of the present difference in population.

Transportation and Functional Diversification

At the present time, among the many changes taking place in Central America one of the most important is the specialization of urban functions. This can to a large extent be attributed to the achievement of an efficient complementarity in production which favors specialization, in spite of the natural barriers that have always isolated regions and cities from one another. Given the varying degrees of national transportation integration within each of the three countries under study, the area is a good test for the hypothesis that, "The least developed countries are least specialized and urban areas have fewer specialized functions and are tied least into an integrated economic system by an efficient transportation network."[19] Directly related to this hypothesis is the assumption that a country well integrated through transportation is likely to develop a rank-size distribution of cities, instead of primacy. This would seem to be a logical conclusion, but as will become evident later in this discussion, this has not taken place in any of the three countries under discussion.

The forces that brought about the construction of surface transport systems were, on the one hand, the exportation of bananas and coffee on both coasts; and on the other hand, centralized govern-

[19] B. L. J. Berry, "Urbanization and Basic Patterns of Development," in *Urban Systems and Economic Development*, ed. F. R. Pitts (Eugene: University of Oregon, 1962).

ment activity which determined large infrastructure investments radiating outward from the capital. Exporting crops led to the establishment of a pattern of railroads which eventually covered extensive portions of the Caribbean lowlands in Honduras and Guatemala and the mountain slopes on the Pacific. The ports became terminal points and customs centers for incoming merchandise, but the larger part of the investment was undertaken to make possible the shipment of the produce to the United States and European markets. At the time of the expansion of the foreign companies in the area—the early 1900s and, on the Pacific, the late 1800s—the railroad, given the state of transportation technology at that time, was the natural choice as the form of transportation. There was even a project to build an interoceanic railroad in Honduras, as a substitute for the construction of a canal.

The first railroad in the area opened the Pacific coffee lands south of Guatemala in 1880; it reached the capital only after the Guatemalan government paid for the extra section between Escuintla and the capital, in 1884.[20] The Honduran isthmus project, an obvious interoceanic route, was begun, but it ran into financial difficulties and was abandoned sixty miles inland; lack of economic justification was also a factor, in view of the competition offered by the Panama Canal and the lack of exportable resources in the Honduran highlands. This was as close as Tegucigalpa has ever come to having railroad connections with any part of the country. El Salvador and Guatemala were linked by the only international railroad line ever built in Central America, running from Puerto Barrios to Acajutla and La Unión and connecting the two capitals and the most important ports, both on the Caribbean and on the Pacific.

The development of the railroad network, although primarily undertaken to permit the export of coffee and bananas, served to involve the capital cities of Guatemala and El Salvador in natural product transformation, which later became the backbone of local industry. In the case of Honduras, however, only the north coast benefited from the railroad and port facilities, thus developing a strong, economically independent base for industrial and trade relations with its own region and with foreign markets. Tegucigalpa was not integrated into this relatively powerful economic develop-

[20] Solorzano, *Evolución Económica de Guatemala*, p. 363.

ment, government activity continuing to be its only economic activity of major importance.

It was natural that efforts by the government to develop transportation infrastructure started from the capital and were intended to reinforce the centralized operation of the national government. The telegraph and telephone systems radiated from the capital and functioned principally for the official needs of administration and emergency communications. The first roads were built out from the capital and barely reached the more important nearby administrative centers; the effort to integrate the relatively prosperous north coast with the rest of the country has been too much for limited national resources, so that the interoceanic road, although a recurrent idyllic dream, has not been built to this day.

Important changes were effected by the construction of the Inter-American Highway between 1930 and 1942; the first of the three countries to finish its share being El Salvador, which thereby integrated its entire small territory in a double transport pattern. The density of population, the proximity of its cities and the rapid communication among them resulted in the best-integrated urban system in Central America.[21] By contrast, the Honduran system is still fragmented, and many of its cities are still outward-oriented in terms of trade and transportation. Furthermore, the Inter-American Highway, although intended to connect all the capitals, did not reach the Honduran capital. Unless some further consideration is given to the relocation of the highway, Tegucigalpa will be left outside the main transport route through Central America—a disadvantage in many ways, not the least of which will be its inability to share in the tourist trade, which is developing rapidly at the present time (see map 5.2).

As a substitute for the lack of internal transport routes, Honduras developed an intense air transport system starting in 1930 and reaching a peak of 121,527 passengers in 1957.[22] Although there was not one single paved highway in the country, there were as many as thirty airfields with frequent passenger and high-value cargo service

[21] Interurban passenger movement between San Salvador and Santa Tecla, 8 miles apart, was 487,900 passengers by electric trolley alone in 1921. *Anuario Estadístico* (San Salvador, Dirección General de Estadística y Censos, El Salvador, 1924), p. 59. Highways, 1963, on map 5.2 from ECLA, "Possibilities of Integrated Industrial Development" (New York: United Nations, 1964).

[22] ECLA, *Análises y Proyecciones del Desarrollo Económico*, vol 11, *El Desarrollo Económico de Honduras* (México, 1960), p. 100.

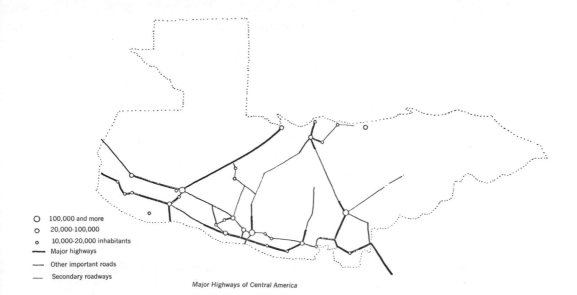

O   100,000 and more
o   20,000-100,000
o   10,000-20,000 inhabitants
—— Major highways
— Other important roads
–·– Secondary roadways

Major Highways of Central America

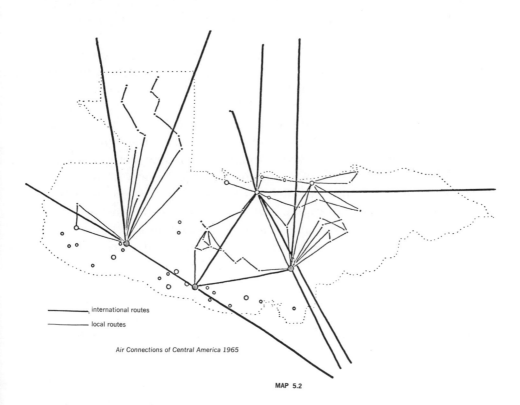

—— international routes
— local routes

Air Connections of Central America 1965

MAP 5.2

to the capital city. The whole system was so centralized that in most cases one could not go between second-rank cities without being routed through the capital. Although this development in itself took some pressure off the demands for highway communication, it provided no adequate substitute for the interchange of natural and heavy manufactured products. The more accessible cities from abroad have always been the capitals. This was clearly the case in the international airline system in the 1930s until about the middle of the 1950s, when decisions to decentralize airline operations began to do away with the centralized pattern based on capital cities and led to the building of a multichannel system which reinforces second-rank cities and opened direct air communication with foreign countries. Tourism, ease of access for foreign businessmen, and increased facility to "go shopping" in cities in the United States are some results of this freer air transport system; the cities, therefore, are no longer tied to their capitals in the exchange of goods and people (see map 5.2).

The urban systems have developed partly in response to the building of transportation systems. The whole rank-size distribution of cities shows the direct influence of accessibility: for example, the near-perfect agreement to the ideal Jeffersonian rank-size distribution found in the Honduran system can be explained by the lack of communication between the second and first cities; they grew independently through their own unrelated economic activities (although, indirectly, the banana production tax helped support the national budget by approximately 50%, and therefore provided the economic base for the capital). If there had been easy, or even reasonably efficient communication by road or railroad, the capital city would probably have arrested the development of the second city and would have retained primacy, as it has in El Salvador and Guatemala. In brief, the rank-size distribution in Honduras developed in spite of and because of the lack of interurban communication. In El Salvador, the contrary has occurred: primacy is developing in the framework of well-integrated urban and transportation systems.

Now, with the new integration movement and the need to facilitate transportation among regions and cities, a new framework of spatial interrelationships is emerging. Trade flows somewhat freely among countries; gone are the customs barriers and roadblocks, and the unfinished roads in border areas. Secondly, new "integration" roads are being built to connect especially fertile agricultural areas with the cities. Not only do these areas become consumers of industrial products, but they also supply cities with increasingly larger amounts of agricultural produce. Thirdly, distances are diminishing, and the relatively shorter travel time between cities is making "shopping trips" easier between countries. This will mean an increase in those activities that naturally locate in urban centers, such as commerce, professional services, and industry.

Assuming a general policy of continuing improvement of the existing Central American integration roads and the opening of the new border crossings for facilitating the export of natural production, the regional nodes, or cities from which the transportation networks originate will be more strongly affected due to an increased accessibility. Guatemala and San Salvador, located as they are along the corridor of the Inter-American Highway linking Central America from end to end, will be especially favored under such circumstances. The bulk of the movement can be expected to continue along the Pacific coast, with branch routes leading north to the Caribbean ports.

With the high degree of accessibility afforded the cities in El Salvador as a consequence of early transportation development and with the additional advantage of being along the main corridor spanning all of Central America, one would expect the degree of urban specialization there to be higher than in Honduras and Guatemala, according to the hypothesis previously advanced. And if this is the case, it carries special import for the future evolution of urban function in Latin America because of the tendency for people to identify urban centers with a certain range of services and to direct their pattern of movement accordingly so as to satisfy their needs for these services.[23]

The knowledge that a certain hierarchy already exists in the kinds of services offered by the larger cities in the area of study will indicate varied growth potentials and possibly an intensification of the hierarchical differences due to the increased mobility of goods and people brought about by the Common Market.

[23] This concept of a hierarchy of services, and the corresponding hierarchy of cities according to their functions is based on the central place theory of Christaller. See B. J. L. Berry and W. L. Garrison, "Alternate Explanations of Urban Rank-Size Relationship" in Mayer and Kohn, *Readings*.

One measure of the service hierarchy is found in the listings of the telephone yellow pages (1963–64). Guatemala lists highly specialized services, for example, "business consultants" and "translators and interpreters." San Salvador lists a narrower range of such services, but features such highly specialized quaternary activities as "investment advisory services." Both of these cities offer wholesale services such as "hospital equipment and supply," "hardware, wholesale" and "grocery, wholesale." Tegucigalpa, on the other hand, besides having substantially fewer listings does not include anything but basic services and goods. Although population size may lead to the conclusion that the hierarchy among the three larger cities is Guatemala first, San Salvador second and Tegucigalpa third, it becomes apparent that in terms of the hierarchy of services offered, the difference between the first two is small, while the difference between the first two and the third is much greater than the mere population figures would lead one to expect.

One obvious conclusion is that San Salvador, with all its high-ranking urban services and its excellent accessibility, is drawing trade from quite a wide region, which probably includes Tegucigalpa itself. Between Guatemala and San Salvador there is complementary exchange, and their respective attraction is probably determined more by accessibility and national cohesiveness than by their relatively greater supply of services or goods.

The existence of businesses which require a wide territorial range, such as complete department stores (Sears, in the case of San Salvador), also indicates a higher hierarchy of urban function. In the same category are certain branch offices of leading banks (First National City Bank in San Salvador and Bank of America in Guatemala). If they need them at all, Tegucigalpa and the population centers between it and San Salvador are likely to avail themselves of the services provided by these firms in San Salvador.

The classifications of employment by the national censuses into primary, secondary and tertiary groups provide a less refined indicator of diversification, and this information, as explained previously, is only available for departments; it does, however, show important differences according to the degree of urban concentration.

Of all the departments in Honduras and El Salvador, the employment profile of San Salvador is by far the most service-oriented. Following San Salvador in percentage of tertiary service employment are Francisco Morazán (Tegucigalpa) and Cortés (San Pedro

Sula). This is, then, a direct reflection of the degree of urban concentration in each department, and additionally suggests the existence of service employment as an indicator of urban specialization.

Taking into consideration the difference in population between San Salvador and Guatemala, the factor which has influenced the relatively high degree of urban specialization in San Salvador has been the integration provided by the transport system. Guatemala, by comparison, is not as well integrated with the rest of its territory; Honduras is the least integrated, as has already been suggested.

New factors have been brought to bear on the evolution of the systems of cities in the area through the conditions of freer inter-urban mobility and wider urban attraction that have evolved out of the policies of the Common Market. While during the period of limited trade and strong political centralization the systems followed the pattern of the administrative hierarchy, now with the increased economic importance of other urban activities and with an increased tendency toward urban specialization, the systems are tending to organize along the lines of a service hierarchy instead of an administrative one. The emphasis now is on a hierarchy of trade centers, presently appearing to be led by San Salvador and Guatemala in the first rank, Tegucigalpa and San Pedro Sula in the second rank, and the regional national centers in third rank.

Lacking a complete network of good highways within the area and the facility to travel to much larger cities in the United States by air, so-called intervening opportunities have been introduced into the pattern of interurban travel in the whole Central American area. It is still more expedient to fly from San Pedro Sula to Miami or New Orleans for specialized medical services, or even for shopping, than it is to fly to San Salvador. However, as average incomes increase and highway transportation improves, it is more than likely that there will be a substantial increase in the numbers of shoppers and migrants to the Central American cities, thereby reinforcing the hierarchical structure of service centers within the area.

Emerging Spatial Pattern

The spatial relations of urban systems in a developed country, especially one with a long tradition of rural settlement, tend to conform to the central-place model. The areas where this model has been tested—southern Germany, southern England and south-western Wisconsin[24]—are basically agricultural regions without the dynamic characteristics associated with growing industrial centers. Although the concept of hierarchy of cities as service centers can be a structural model for the spatial operation of commerce, community facilities and services, the more dynamic industrial spatial distribution tends to depart from a hierarchical pattern and to maintain a more fluid interrelation among regions or centers.[25]

Since the urban change implied in the operation of the Common Market is also directly related to industrialization, as indicated by the rise in total production in the last ten years (see Appendix, table 8), the spatial distribution of the industrial activity will have an important influence on new migration in search of employment, and consequently on the size of cities. The determination of those cities which contain key location factors for industry will provide the elements of the industrial locational pattern over the area of study. Industrial employment is a very critical element in the growth of cities due to the leverage or intrinsic basic quality it has with respect to the urban economic base.

Perroux, in his writings on the "poles of growth," has studied and described the evolution of industrial complexes. The applicability of his model to newly developing economies has been explored by other regional scientists, notably Friedmann.[26] The concept is related to the operation of the two sectors of the national economy, the urban and the rural. Alternate ways of expressing this duality are to describe them as the industrial versus the agricultural economy, or the surplus versus the subsistence economy. Spatially, the model has a definite separation of the basic elements: the center is the urban economy and the periphery is the rural, agricultural, subsistence economy.

The appearance of the regional differences corresponding to the duality which is implicit in the "poles of growth" concept are already perceptible in the operation of the Central American Common

[24] J. E. Brush and H. E. Bracey, "Rural Service Centers in Southwestern Wisconsin and Southern England" in Mayer and Kohn, *Readings*, pp. 210–17.

[25] Isard, *Methods*, Appendix to Chapter 6.

[26] See F. Perroux, "Consideraciones en Torno a la Noción de 'Polo de Crecimiento,'" *Cuadernos de la Sociedad Venezolana de Planificación*, 2 (June-July 1963), and John Friedmann, "Regional Economic Policy for Developing Areas" in *Papers and Proceedings of the Regional Science Association* 11 (Philadelphia, 1963).

Market. Although the quantitative differences between the imports and the exports between Honduras and El Salvador are small (see Appendix table 8), the qualitative differences are important: Honduras has consistently been exporting agricultural products to El Salvador while importing manufactured goods from it.

There is an obvious disadvantage—similar to the well-known situation of the terms of trade in underdeveloped countries—in that the industrial country accumulates greater profits by importing raw materials and transforming them into manufactured goods, which it then sells at a profit to the agricultural country. This has direct consequences for urban development, since light, market-oriented industrial operation is at present not likely to concentrate in large industrial complexes; however, certain concentrations of heavier, more stable operations are apparent in the larger cities in El Salvador.[27]

To obtain a clearer picture of the spatial distribution of the industrial activities as a whole, three measures of spatial concentration will be explored: the present relative size of industrial production, based on department data; the market and employment potential as deduced from the population potential of the major urbanized regions; and important industrial location advantages.

The data on industrial production, on table 5.3 based on departments, provide the ranking of total dollar values. (See also map 5.1.) The first two departments on this table, San Salvador and La Libertad are contiguous and actually form one geographic unit of industrial activity, their two main cities being only eight miles apart. It would be more realistic to consider the two departments as one urban region, which would raise its combined production to 132.4 million dollars and 45 percent of the total national production of El Salvador. Clearly, this is the strongest industrial complex in the whole area of study; second place would fall to Guatemala, third to Santa Ana, fourth to San Pedro Sula and fifth to Tegucigalpa. It is therefore clear that the population size of the cities themselves bears little relationship to the industrial potential of the immediate urban hinterland.

---

[27] Although Central America as a whole had about 6 percent employment in metals, machinery, electrical and transport industries in 1962, El Salvador had 9 percent. See ECLA, *Process of Industrialization*, p. 52.

TABLE 5.3

RANKING OF TOTAL DOLLAR VALUES OF INDUSTRIAL PRODUCTION

DEPARTMENT, YEAR MAJOR CITY	TOTAL IND. PROD. (MILS.)	PROD. PER CAPITA	% OF NAT. IND. PROD.
SAN SALVADOR, 1961 (San Salvador)	$90.0	$190	30%
LA LIBERTAD, 1961 (Nueva San Salvador)	42.4	200	15%
SANTA ANA, 1961 (Santa Ana)	39.9	130	14%
GUATEMALA, 1958 (Guatemala)	67.7	111	68%
FRANCISCO MORAZÁN, 1962 (Tegucigalpa)	21.6	70	32%
CORTÉS, 1962 (San Pedro Sula)	30.4	150	45%

SOURCES: Data for El Salvador from Tercer Censo Industrial y Comercial (San Salvador: Dirección General de Estadística y Censos, 1962); for Guatemala from *Trimestre Estadístico* (Guatemala: Dirección General de Estadística, 1964); for Honduras from *Primer Compendio Estadístico, Honduras* (Tegucigalpa: Consejo Nacional de Economía, 1964).

An indirect measure of the possible external economies and the economies of scale that an urban location may offer future industries is found in the present value of industrial production. It is an acceptable assumption that the volume of present production is a better indicator of industrial growth potential than the population figures for the city or department.

The second measure readily available in the statistical data is the effective population concentration within a certain time-distance, which in this case can be taken as one hour's ride by highway from the center of the city. This measure is essential for the determination of the market potential and labor supply of any given center. It could be expressed as primary trade area or labor shed, in the terms of urban geography.

By determining the distance that highway conditions permit to be covered in one hour, a travel radius was drawn to include a number of municipal units; then the total population was determined. Twenty-seven percent of the total population of El Salvador, or

752,600 inhabitants lived within one hour's travel from San Salvador, 25 percent of Guatemala's population, or 1,118,000 inhabitants lived within one hour's travel from Guatemala, 12 percent (230,000 inhabitants) of Honduras' population lived within one hour's travel from Tegucigalpa and 224,000 inhabitants (10 percent of Honduras' population lived within one hour's travel from San Pedro Sula.

For the evaluation of market potential, some measure of income levels or effective purchasing power is necessary; in this discussion it may suffice to say that, if anything, income levels tend to reinforce the differences in population potential, since the larger cities —especially San Salvador with its higher percentage of industrial employment—are certain to have higher average incomes than the smaller industrializing regions of Tegucigalpa and San Pedro Sula. (A comparison shown on table 5.3 will show variations in the same direction.)

Thirdly, an evaluation of the more obvious advantages in location, against the background of the previous discussion of transportation, will further define the urbanized regions tending to become poles of growth within the three countries. The important question is: How well does the existing transportation infrastructure serve the new industrial economic activity of the cities? The answer varies. In Guatemala the main industrial center coincides with the largest market and labor supply; the transport network is relatively extensive and effectively connects the strategic cities—the ports on both oceans, the larger urban markets, and many of the potential tourist attractions in the central region. In El Salvador, the infrastructure has always coincided with the markets and labor supply, and in general minimizes the cost of movement from port to plant and from plant to markets. Besides, San Salvador has its own port eighteen miles away and is well served by railroad. In Honduras, the better-developed infrastructure (the banana plantation railroads) corresponds to the relatively limited market and labor supply of the north coast, whose ports, considerably distant from the market in the rest of Honduras, are currently disconnected from the rest of the Central American market. In general, the industrializing urban areas of the north coast are somewhat peripheral to the larger market potential of the Pacific coast centers. The best locational advantages for market-oriented industries are found in the larger cities of El Salvador and Guatemala.

Industries such as glass factories, cellulose and chemical fertilizer plants, and steel mills, proposed under the Common Market program being new and natural-resource oriented, will tend to locate according to their requirements for raw materials. These will require a different set of conditions than the market-oriented industries, and may create moderate urban migration to cities other than the six largest in population.

It can be concluded that the emergence of industrial poles of growth in the study area will be as follows: first, the San Salvador–Santa Tecla–La Libertad region; second, Guatemala; third, Santa Ana; fourth, San Pedro Sula–Puerto Cortés; and fifth, Tegucigalpa. The pattern as it emerges is made up of at least four major urban industrial centers, two on the Pacific side (San Salvador and Guatemala), one on the Atlantic side (San Pedro Sula), and one in Tegucigalpa. Growth is most likely to concentrate at these focal points, relegating the remainder of the territory largely to a peripheral, hinterland position. Before the formation of the Common Market, dynamic growth centered exclusively in the capital cities; now growth is being determined by industrial activity and the potential for further growth. This pattern will tend to intensify, reducing the importance of the traditional government administrative function and the prevailing hierarchy of the past.

The urban systems in Central America, then, have gone through three stages of development: (1) the colonial period when the hierarchy of cities followed the administrative hierarchy of colonial authority; (2) the independence period during which each country developed its own hierarchy based on the political administrative system, beginning with a primate city and, as other important economic activities arose—specifically coffee and banana production—giving way to a regional pattern based on sources of employment other than government payrolls; and (3) the Common Market period, from about 1955 on, with the systems tending to integrate on the basis of a complementarity service hierarchy between regions into an industrial and urban services pattern which operates for the whole of Central America.

The emerging hierarchy is expected to follow the pattern of the regional poles of growth, with the more industrialized cities attracting larger numbers of migrants, leaving the less industrialized areas in a disadvantageous position for economic growth. The potential for growth of any city is going to be determined by its capacity to develop basic types of employment, in direct competition with five or six important urban regions which have taken the lead in developing the future industrial complexes.

Spatially, this means that, unless consideration is given to future infrastructure investment and to industrial location inducements, the trend will accentuate the duality between the urban industrial regions and the rural agricultural ones, producing a critical migration pattern toward the industrializing cities. Depletion of potentially productive natural regions will undermine balanced regional development.

The Inter-American Highway which connects the more important industrial centers and the larger market areas, and the Interoceanic Highway connecting it with the Honduran north coast will be two main axes of spatial development. The accessibility afforded by these two main routes will be an important factor in the growth of smaller cities; while the large cities will tend to concentrate the man-made elements for economic growth and expanding thereby the services and economic activities comprising their economic bases, the smaller cities can utilize natural advantages in the development of their local economic bases. Obvious possibilities exist for resorts, tourist centers, ports, break-of-bulk points, and even for future staging areas for the colonization of previously unexploited regions like the Mosquitia and Peten.

Tegucigalpa, Honduras. Photo by author.

Although the capital cities all share a certain advantage of concentrating important economic and political functions, the difference in growth potential has been clearly indicated in the foregoing comparisons. Since it is evident that the administrative function is providing a decreasing share of the economic base of the capitals, and since some of the capitals are not as well-endowed or developed to undertake an efficient industrial function, it becomes necessary to give some thought to a general policy of inducing the development of other, nonindustrial activities to complement the economic base of the less privileged capitals. A possibility which is suggested as the Central American administrative governmental system grows is to locate future area-wide services in Tegucigalpa, a role for which its central location ideally qualifies it, and the addition of such services would in turn help balance the economy of the city. The other capitals also offer special advantages. San Salvador would make a suitable headquarters for commercial and industrial service firms, as well as serving as the main regional Pacific gateway city. Guatemala offers special locational and natural advantges for becoming the tourist headquarters for northern Central America because of its excellent climate, its extremely archaeologically rich hinterland, and its gateway position for air travel.

Good port sites in Cortés on the northern coast of Honduras could, with improvements, become the gateway to Central America for goods from Europe and the United States, and the area has the additional advantages of natural beaches, fishing and archaeological sites. Finally, the southern Honduran region seems especially appropriate for transportation service facilities: a port, a break-of-bulk point, a good geographical location for industrial assembly operations which require facilities for handling large volume and a central location in relation to Central American markets. This region is the actual geometric center of the area, and sits astride the main longitudinal transport route, the Inter-American Highway.

A regional development policy based on these considerations and on more detailed technical feasibility studies will become an important tool for securing balanced regional development. With the expansion of the goals of the Common Market to include coordinated national development policies, greater possibilities will be offered for the urban and regional development of Central America.

6

The Growth of Metropolitan Areas in Latin America

THE development of large metro-cities has become a worldwide phenomenon. Demographic studies have shown that during the last hundred years the number of world inhabitants has doubled, but during the same period, the number of people living in urban areas has quintupled. A high proportion of this increase in world urban population is to be found in metropolises.

Industrial development and the subsequent rural-urban immigration are usually credited with being responsible for metropolitan expansion. Innovations in transportation or the centralization of political and administrative organization are also often regarded as playing a part in this process. The multiplicity of opportunities which the interaction of a large population promotes seems to be the basic advantage offered by metropolitan life, a fact that is to some extent independent of economic level of development.

In Latin America during the last twenty years, Santiago de Chile has doubled its population, Bogotá more than doubled, México City almost trebled, São Paulo trebled, and Lima more than trebled. It will be noted that there are wide differences in climate, degree of urbanization, population size and economic level among these growing metropolitan areas.

The metropolitan areas of advanced countries have been the major concern of urban studies over many decades and increasingly refined techniques of research and a profusion of explanatory theories have been developed. Until recently, the metropolitan areas in Latin America remained virtually unknown, and only now is modern planning technology being applied to the analysis of the most basic problems of urban-metro relationships in such places as Bogota, São Paulo, and México City among others.

A study that has been particularly helpful in making possible international comparisons among metropolitan areas is that undertaken by the Institute of International Studies at the University of California in Berkeley. We will use the definition of a metropolitan area (M.A.) adopted by the Institute for its project:

> An area with 100,000 inhabitants or more, containing at least one city (or continuous urban area) with 50,000 inhabitants or more and those administrative divisions contiguous to the city (or to the contiguous urban area) which meet certain requirements as to metropolitan character.

These "certain requirements" are:

> (a) that such division have more than 65% of its labor force working in economic activities other than agriculture (farming, hunting and fishing);
> (b) that it be contiguous to the city or other divisions already included in the M.A. according to (a);
> (c) that if one division does not meet requirements of (a) but is completely surrounded by divisions that do, it is included;
> (d) that if one division meets requirements of (a) and (b) but is too far (defined in each case with regard to available transportation, etc.) it is not included;
> (e) that if one division falls between two cities, the dividing line determining in which of the two M.A.'s it is included is arrived at by drawing a line based on the lowest point of the industrial or density gradient from each city;
> (f) that in cases where information on employment is not available, the criterion of density is used instead: (1) if the division is contiguous to the central city and has ½ or more of its density, it is included; (2) if one division is contiguous to another division already included in the M.A. and has ½ of the density of the immediate inner ring of divisions, or two times the density of the immediate outer ring of divisions, it is included.[1]

Since we did not make the analysis of divisions, done by the Institute of International Studies for 1950, but were able only to obtain data for the divisions already included in that study, *it is very likely that*

---

[1] International Urban Research, Institute of International Studies, University of California, Berkeley published in *The World's Metropolitan Areas* (Berkeley: University of California Press, 1959). Originally published by the University of California Press; reprinted by permission of The Regents of the University of California. In: "Tendencias de Localización y Crecimiento de la Población Urbana Latinoamericana," appendix, pp. 1–22. For this chapter, any reference to the years 1950 or 1960 is based on individual country censuses taken between 1947–1953 and 1960–1964. For actual census dates and figures see tables 6.4–6.10 and Appendix, tables 7 and 9, as well as *The World's Metropolitan Areas* and table 2.1 (see also maps 6.1–6.5, table 6.2 and 6.3).

there are more metropolitan areas than the ones listed, and that other divisions should be included with the M.A.'s existing in 1950. The procedure here used, consisted of:

(a) Taking the M.A. identified for 1950 by the Institute of International Studies, University of California, Berkeley, and listing all the divisions included in each one; then computing the new figures for the censuses of around 1960 and obtaining the new totals. As stated before, we did not have the necessary information to decide whether new divisions contiguous to those listed for 1950 would meet the requirements.
(b) Including all the cities of more than 100,000 population in 1960. Again, the surrounding divisions of these cities were not included nor of those of more than 50,000 population. Hence, their M.A. may well be larger than the population here listed.

1950 and 1960 Ranking of Metropolitan Areas

Table 6.1 presents the ranking of the metropolitan areas in Latin America for 1950 and 1960, according to the Institute of International Studies' definition. Five ranks were determined, selected at random for practical purposes: I, 2,000,000 & over; II, 1,000,000–2,000,000; III, 500,000–1,000,000; IV, 250,000–500,000; V, 100,000–250,000. But a classification of metropolitan areas according to population size clearly implies more than a number distinction: *it implies a relationship between population and urban function.* As a metropolitan area grows in size, it is evident that the urban settlement becomes more complex, more differentiated, and increasingly multi-functional.[2] For our purposes at this point, however, the problem in question is posed by a comparison of metropolitan population and the ranking from the largest to the smallest metropolitan area according to size for every country in Latin America. When these ranks were assigned in table 6.1, a regular relationship emerged; there are few first-rank metropolitan areas in Latin America, and the number increases, as the ranks decrease in size; for example, in 1960, there were only 4 metropolitan areas in the first rank, 7 in the second rank, 14 in the third rank, 20 in the fourth rank and 59 in the fifth rank. Several important observations should be made. The 1960 ranking gives a total of 104 cities with over 100,000 popula-

[2] Mayer and Kohn, *Readings*, p. 127. See also Bibliography, respective entries for census data for each Latin American country.

tion. Comparing this number to the 73 metropolitan areas with populations over 100,000 in 1950, we see an increase of 42% in a span of 10 years—another indicator of the total population growth which Latin American cities are undergoing today. Considering the different ranks separately, however, it can be observed that only the fifth rank reflects the total number increase of metropolitan areas. Cities with a population of between 100,000 and 250,000 totaled only 44 in 1950, but a 34% increase accounted for the 59 in 1960. Only the third-rank cities with 500,000 to 1,000,000 population and the second-rank cities with 1,000,000 to 2,000,000 population show a more dramatic increase in number. The five cities recorded in the third rank in 1950, Montevideo, Bogotá, Recife, Caracas and Rosario, had all skipped to the second rank by 1960; whereas 14 new cities took their place in the third rank, representing, in other words, an increase of 180% in number.

By 1960, there were still only 4 metropolitan areas with a population above 2 million, the same as in 1950: Buenos Aires, México City, Rio de Janeiro, and São Paulo. The order of rank was almost identical to that of 1950, with the exception of México City, which moved into second place over Rio de Janeiro with a difference of 125,000 population. The total population of the four cities for 1960 was 20,628,419, representing almost a doubling since 1950. The 1960 total, however, still represents about 30% of the total metropolitan population in Latin America, a similar proportion to the year 1950.

Three metropolitan areas filled the second rank in 1950, Santiago, Lima and La Habana. A case had to be made that Lima should be included in this group, since its total population by 1950 was most certainly above 1,000,000. The problem was due to the fact that Perú produced no census in 1950. The figures given here for Perú correspond to those of 1940 adjusted to 1950.

As would be expected Brazil, the most populous country in Latin America (1960: 70,309,000), leads the 1960 ranking list with twenty-six metropolitan areas or cities with a population above 100,-000. It should be noted that Brazil is the only country with two cities in the first rank, Rio de Janeiro and São Paulo. México follows closely with 22 metropolitan areas, but with 15 in the fifth rank. Only Colombia is close to this group with 17 metropolitan areas, and 13 in the fifth rank. Argentina, with 11 metropolitan areas, remained as in 1950. The remaining countries follow at a distance, with very few metropolitan areas: Venezuela 5, Cuba 4, Chile and Perú 3 each,

TABLE 6.1

LATIN AMERICA: RANKING OF METROPOLITAN AREAS, 1950, 1960

RANK	1950		1960	
	METROPOLITAN AREA	TOTAL POPULATION	METROPOLITAN AREA	TOTAL POPULATION
I. 2,000,000 & over	1. Buenos Aires	4,723,918	1. Buenos Aires	6,751,769
	2. Rio de Janeiro	3,052,012	2. México City	4,816,393
	3. México City	2,960,120	3. Rio de Janeiro	4,691,654
	4. São Paulo	2,448,938	4. São Paulo	4,368,603
		13,184,988		20,628,419
II. 1,000,000–2,000,000	5. Santiago	1,423,623	5. Santiago	1,983,945
	6. La Habana	1,240,369	6. Lima	1,845,910
	7. Lima	1,211,752 (est.)	7. La Habana	1,594,000
			8. Caracas	1,492,378
		3,875,744	9. Montevideo	1,202,890
			10. Bogotá	1,188,180
			11. Recife (Bra.)	1,064,345
				10,371,648
			12. Guadalajara (Me.)	977,779
			13. Cali (Col.)	812,810
			14. Medellín (Col.)	776,970
			15. Porto Alegre (Bra.)	745,430
III. 500,000–1,000,000	8. Caracas	790,456	16. Monterrey (Me.)	695,504
	9. Montevideo	768,413	17. Belo Horizonte (Bra.)	693,328
	10. Bogotá	715,250	18. Rosario (Ar.)	671,852
	11. Recife (Bra.)	692,498	19. Salvador (Bra.)	655,735
	12. Rosario (Ar.)	529,801	20. Cordoba (Ar.)	589,153
			21. Guatemala City	572,937
		3,496,418	22. Guayaquil (Ec.)	567,895

METROPOLITAN AREA	TOTAL POPULATION
23. Barranquilla (Col.)	521,070
24. Fortaleza (Bra.)	514,818
25. Quito	510,286
	9,305,567
26. Santo Domingo	477,000
27. Maracaibo (Ve.)	422,847
28. Belem (Bra.)	402,170
29. Valparaíso (Ch.)	384,324
30. Santos (Bra.)	383,751
31. La Paz	378,319
32. Curitiba (Bra.)	361,309
33. San Salvador	351,276
34. La Plata (Ar.)	330,310
35. Puebla (Me.)	328,243
36. San José	320,478
37. Concepción-Talcahuano (Ch.)	314,412
38. Asunción	305,160
39. Mendoza (Ar.)	304,563
40. Tucumán (Ar.)	287,004
41. Panama City	285,365
42. Ciudad Juarez (Me.)	276,995
43. Mexicali (Me.)	261,299
44. León (Me.)	260,633
45. Santa Fé (Ar.)	259,560
	6,695,018

RANK	METROPOLITAN AREA	TOTAL POPULATION
IV. 250,000–500,000		
	13. Medellín (Col.)	441,444
	14. Porto Alegre (Bra.)	433,977
	15. Salvador (Bra.)	417,235
	16. Guadalajara (Me.)	413,629
	17. Córdoba (Ar.)	386,828
	18. Monterrey (Me.)	367,663
	19. Belo Horizonte (Bra.)	352,724
	20. La Paz	346,130
	21. Valparaíso (Ch.)	315,506
	22. Barranquilla (Col.)	308,713
	23. La Plata (Ar.)	302,073
	24. Guatemala City	294,344
	25. Cali (Col.)	284,186
	26. Fortaleza (Bra.)	270,169
	27. Guayaquil (Ec.)	266,637
	28. Belem (Bra.)	254,949
	29. Puebla (Me.)	250,961
		5,707,168

No.	City	
46.	Bucaramanga (Col.)	250,550
47.	Port-au-Prince	240,000
48.	Managua	234,600
49.	Mar del Plata (Ar.)	224,571
50.	Tijuana (Me.)	222,534
51.	Arequipa (Pe.)	222,377
52.	Santiago de Cuba	219,800
53.	Campinas (Bra.)	219,303
54.	Barquisimeto (Ve.)	212,172
55.	Torreón (Me.)	203,153
56.	Pereira (Col.)	199,700
57.	Cartagena (Col.)	197,590
58.	Manizales (Col.)	186,910
59.	Chihuahua (Me.)	186,089
60.	Mérida (Me.)	183,701
61.	Juiz de Fora (Bra.)	182,481
62.	San Luis de Potosí (Me.)	176,624
63.	San Juán (Ar.)	174,595
64.	Paraná (Ar.)	174,272
65.	Maceio (Bra.)	170,134
66.	Tegucigalpa	164,941
67.	Valencia (Ve.)	163,600
68.	Natal (Bra.)	162,537
69.	Camaguey (Cu.)	162,400
70.	Ibágué (Col.)	160,400
71.	Veracruz (Me.)	159,912
72.	São Luis (Bra.)	159,628
73.	João Pessoa (Bra.)	155,117
74.	Manaus (Bra.)	154,040
75.	Tulua (Col.)	151,370
76.	Bahía Blanca (Ar.)	150,354
77.	Palmira (Col.)	148,510
78.	Cúcuta (Col.)	147,250
79.	Aguascalientes (Me.)	143,293
80.	Tampico (Me.)	136,258
81.	Goiania (Bra.)	132,577
82.	Hermosillo (Me.)	132,324
83.	Brasilia (Bra.)	130,968
84.	Pasto (Col.)	130,130

No.	City	
30.	Santos (Bra.)	248,449
31.	Santo Domingo	239,464
32.	Maracaibo (Ve.)	235,750
33.	Torreon (Me.)	231,673
34.	San Salvador	220,929
35.	Concepción-Talcahuano (Ch.)	220,391
36.	Mendoza (Ar.)	219,034
37.	Port-au-Prince	212,135
38.	Quito	206,634
39.	Asunción	206,212
40.	Santa Fé (Ar.)	203,555
41.	Tucumán (Ar.)	190,062
42.	Panama City	180,575
43.	Curitiba (Bra.)	166,384
44.	Santiago de Cuba	159,410
45.	Mérida (Me.)	159,150
46.	San José	157,343
47.	León (Me.)	155,238
48.	San Luis Potosí (Me.)	152,547
49.	Campinas (Bra.)	148,106
50.	Paraná (Ar.)	140,334
51.	Managua	137,685
52.	Tampico (Me.)	131,308
53.	Ciudad Juarez (Me.)	128,877
54.	Cartagena (Col.)	128,809
55.	Arequipa (Pe.)	126,989
56.	Juiz de Fora (Bra.)	126,201
57.	Manizales (Col.)	123,811
58.	Mar del Plata (Ar.)	122,059
59.	Bahía Blanca (Ar.)	121,895
60.	San Juan (Ar.)	120,980
61.	Maceio (Bra.)	119,785
62.	São Luis (Bra.)	119,326
63.	João Pessoa (Bra.)	118,434
64.	Aguascalientes (Me.)	116,547
65.	Barquisimeto (Ve.)	115,342
66.	Pereira (Col.)	112,466
67.	Chihuahua (Me.)	112,252
68.	Bucaramanga (Col.)	110,443
69.	Veracruz (Me.)	

	1950		1960	
RANK	METROPOLITAN AREA	TOTAL POPULATION	METROPOLITAN AREA	TOTAL POPULATION
V. 100,000–250,000 con't.	70. Camaguey (Cu.)	110,388	85. Villa de Guadalupe, Hidalgo (Me.)	127,368
	71. Natal (Bra.)	103,215	86. Matamoros (Me.)	122,680
	72. Valencia (Ve.)	101,790	87. Morelia (Me.)	121,964
	73. Tegucigalpa	99,948	88. Pelotas (Bra.)	121,280
			89. Durango (Me.)	118,506
			90. Campina Grande (Bra.)	116,226
			91. Ribeirao Preto (Bra.)	116,153
			92. Saltillo (Me.)	113,805
			93. Aracaju (Bra.)	112,516
			94. Nueva Laredo (Me.)	112,280
			95. Buenaventura (Col.)	110,660
			96. Maracai (Ve.)	110,500
			97. Monteria (Col.)	110,130
			98. Sorocaba (Bra.)	109,258
			99. Armeria (Col.)	107,150
			100. Santa Clara (Cu.)	105,600
			101. Sevilla (Col.)	104,460
			102. Olinda (Bra.)	100,545
			103. Trujillo (Pe.)	100,130
			104. Teresinha (Bra.)	100,006
		6,878,095		9,167,982

TOTALS

	1950		1960	
2,000,000 & over	4	13,184,988	4	20,628,419
1,000,000–2,000,000	3	3,875,744	7	10,371,648
500,000–1,000,000	5	3,496,418	14	9,305,567
250,000–500,000	17	5,707,168	20	6,695,018
100,000–250,000	44	6,878,095	59	9,167,982
	73	33,142,413	104	56,168,634

TOTALS BY COUNTRY OF RANKING CITIES, 1950, 1960

COUNTRY	1950 RANK					TOTAL NO. OF CITIES	1960 RANK					TOTAL NO. OF CITIES
	I	II	III	IV	V		I	II	III	IV	V	
ARGENTINA	1		1	2	7	11	1		2	4	4	11
BOLIVIA					1	1				1		1
BRAZIL	2		1	5	8	16	2	1	4	3	16	26
CHILE		1		1	1	3		1		2		3
COLOMBIA			1	3	4	8		1	3	2	13	17
COSTA RICA					1	1				1		1
CUBA		1			2	3		1			3	4
DOMINICAN REPUBLIC					1	1				1		1
ECUADOR				1	1	2			2			2
EL SALVADOR					1	1				1		1
GUATEMALA				1		1			1			1
HAITÍ					1	1					1	1
HONDURAS					1	1					1	1
MÉXICO	1			3	9	13	1		2	4	15	22
NICARAGUA					1	1					1	1
PANAMÁ					1	1				1		1
PARAGUAY					1	1				1		1
PERÚ		1			1	2		1			2	3
URUGUAY			1		1	2		1				1
VENEZUELA			1		3	4		1		1	3	5
TOTAL	4	3	5	17	44	73	4	7	14	20	59	104

Ecuador 2, all the rest 1. The order in number for 1950 was practically the same: Brazil 16, México 13, Argentina 11, Colombia 8, Venezuela 4, Cuba and Chile 3 each, Perú and Ecuador 2 each, all the rest 1.

In 1950, the metropolitan population in Latin America accounted for 21.2% of the total population. The geographical distribution is indicated on map 6.1. In terms of country percentages, the picture is radically different from the one shown by considering the metropolitan areas in each country separately. It will be noted, for example, that Argentina's metropolitan population accounts for 41% of the total country population and thus represents the country with the highest percent of population living in metropolitan areas. Second is Uruguay, with 35% of its population living in one single metropolitan area, Montevideo, the capital of the nation. Next in decreasing order are Chile (32%), Cuba (28%), Venezuela (25%), Panamá (24%), Costa Rica (20%), and México (20%). Brazil and Perú with 17% of its total population living in metropolitan areas is in ninth place after Colombia with 19%. The countries with the

TABLE 6.2

LATIN AMERICA: INCREASE OF POPULATION LIVING IN
CITIES OF 100,000 AND OVER, 1950–1960

COUNTRY	1950	1960	DIFFERENCE
BRAZIL	9,094,368	16,123,912	7,029,544
MÉXICO	5,306,373	9,877,337	4,570,964
COLOMBIA	2,196,265	5,303,840	3,107,585
ARGENTINA	7,087,292	9,918,003	2,830,711
VENEZUELA	1,244,543	2,401,491	1,156,954
PERÚ	1,340,561	2,168,417	827,856
CHILE	1,959,520	2,682,681	723,161
ECUADOR	478,772	1,078,181	599,409
CUBA	1,517,141	2,081,800	564,659
URUGUAY	768,413	1,202,890	434,477
GUATEMALA	294,344	572,937	278,593
DOMINICAN REP.	239,464	477,000	237,536
EL SALVADOR	220,929	351,276	130,347
COSTA RICA	159,150	320,478	161,328
PARAGUAY	206,634	305,160	98,526
PANAMÁ	190,062	285,365	95,303
NICARAGUA	140,334	234,600	94,266
HONDURAS	99,948	164,941	64,993
BOLIVIA	346,130	378,319	32,189
HAITÍ	216,170	240,000	23,830

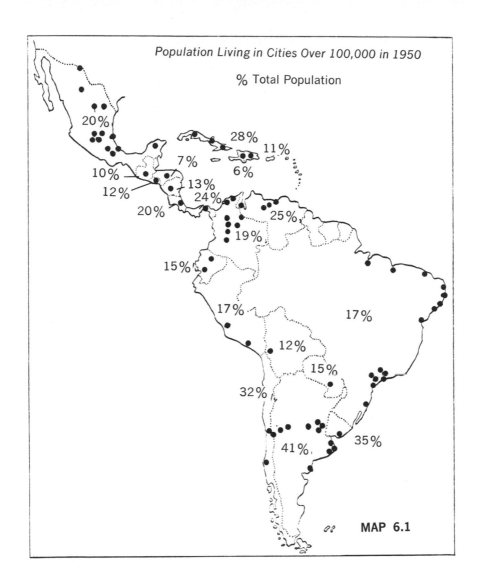

Population Living in Cities Over 100,000 in 1950

% Total Population

MAP 6.1

lowest percentages living in metropolitan areas were Guatemala (10%), Honduras (7%) and Haití (6%).

The total population in Latin America by 1960 was estimated to be 205,916,000. Out of this figure, 56,168,634 lived in metropolitan areas—that is, 27.4% of the total. This represents an increase of about 6%, when compared to the figures of 1950. Map 6.2 shows the percentages of population living in metropolitan areas in 1960 by countries. Uruguay, in this case, occupied the first place, with 48% of its total population living in Montevideo. Argentina, with

47% was a close second. The next four places in decreasing order were Chile (35%), Colombia (34%), Venezuela (33%) and Cuba (31%). As will be noted, Colombia which had placed eighth in 1950, presented a sharp increase of metropolitan population. Cuba, on the other hand, was displaced from a high fourth in 1950 to sixth place. Costa Rica (27%) and Panamá (27%) both dropped to seventh place. The countries with the lowest percentages of their total population living in cities over 100,000 population were again Bolivia (10%), Honduras (8%) and Haití (6%).

The population of Latin America living in cities over 100,000 population, seen as *percentages of the total urban population* in each country for 1960 is shown on map 6.3. Here, Costa Rica is found to have the highest percentage of urban population living in metro-

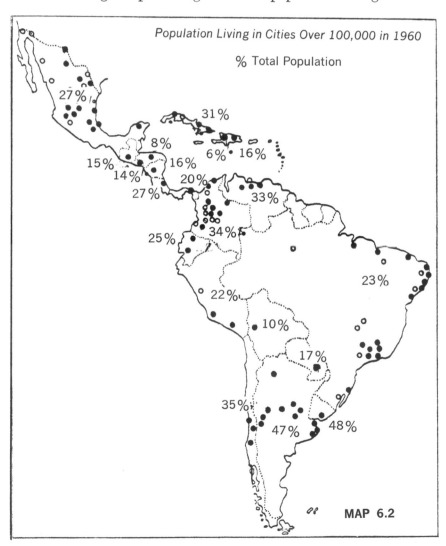

Population Living in Cities Over 100,000 in 1960

% Total Population

MAP 6.2

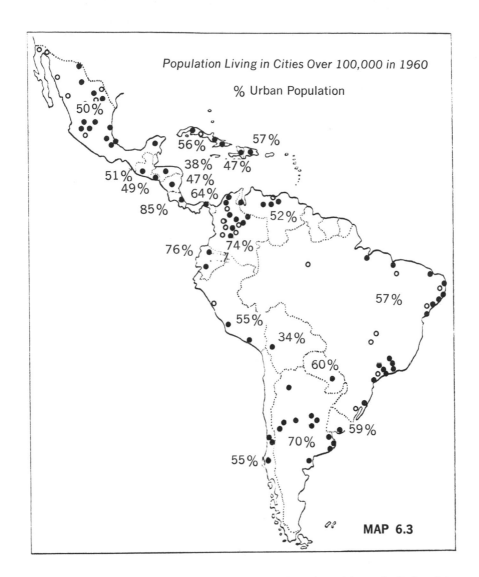

Population Living in Cities Over 100,000 in 1960

% Urban Population

50%

56%   57%

38% 47%

51%   47%
49%   64%

85%

76%   74%   52%

57%

55%

34%

60%

70%   59%

55%

MAP 6.3

politan areas (85%). Next come Ecuador (76%) and Colombia (74%), Argentina (70%), Paraguay (60%), Uruguay (59%) and Brazil (57%). Chile, Perú and Cuba form a middle group, each with about 56% of their urban population in metropolitan areas. Finally, in this case, El Salvador (49%), Honduras (38%) and Bolivia (34%) recorded the lowest percentages. By contrast, the 1950 picture was radically different. Costa Rica, with 69.0% of its urban population living in metropolitan areas, led, followed by Panamá (67%) and Argentina and Haití (64.0%). Next came Chile (59%) and Cuba (55%) and Perú (54%). Amazingly enough, by

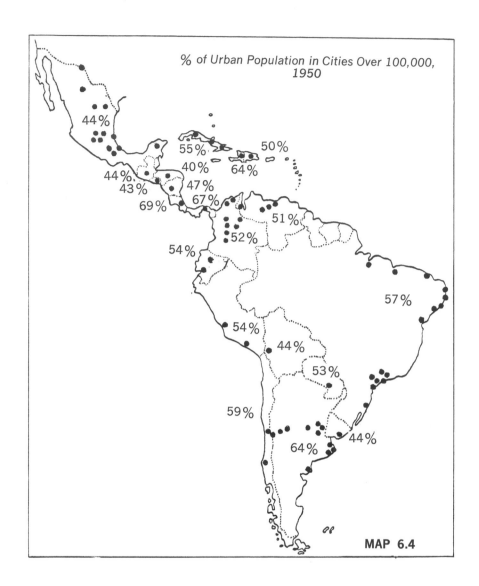

% of Urban Population in Cities Over 100,000, 1950

MAP 6.4

that time Colombia was only in ninth place with 52% of its urban population living in metropolitan areas. The lowest percentages recorded were those of Uruguay (44%), Bolivia (44.0%), El Salvador (43%) and Honduras (40%). The general percentage distribution for all the Latin American countries for 1950 is indicated on map 6.4.

The absolute numerical increases of population living in metropolitan areas of 100,000 and over between 1950 and 1960 are given on table 6.2.

Brazil, with an absolute increase of 7,029,544 inhabitants leads the list. México, Colombia and Argentina follow with increases of 4,570,964; 3,107,575 and 2,830,711, respectively. The lowest numerical increases were found to be those of Bolivia (32,189), and Haití (23,830).

Another indicator of metropolitan growth between 1950 and 1960 is found in Map 6.5, where the different percentages of total population increase in cities with over 100,000 population are given.

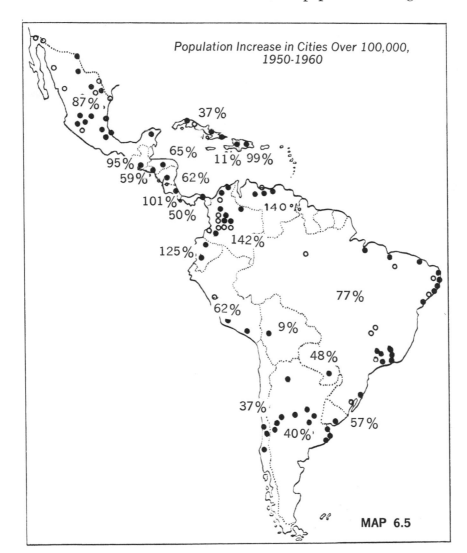

Population Increase in Cities Over 100,000, 1950-1960

MAP 6.5

As will be noted, the highest percentages in this case are those of Colombia (142%), Ecuador (125%) and Costa Rica (101%). Bolivia (9%), and Haití (11%), on the other hand, presented the lowest percentages of the total population increase in their metropolitan areas.

Primacy of Metropolitan Areas

All the countries of Latin America have at least one city, generally the administrative capital, that is disproportionally larger than the other cities and with a population that represents a large share of the country's total. As noted earlier, however, the significance of the primate city lies not only in its disproportionate size, but also in its being exceptionally expressive of the national capacity and feeling with respect to any other city in a country. Thus, as a rule, the major metropolitan area of a Latin American country is identified by its political capital. There are two exceptions: Ecuador and Brazil. In Ecuador, Guayaquil is the largest metropolitan area, whereas Quito is the capital. In the case of Brazil, which now has its specially built new capital of Brasilia, it is convenient to turn to Rio de Janeiro the former capital.

Table 6.3 contrasts the 1950 and 1960 primacy of the largest metropolitan area of each Latin American country, *in relation to the total country* population at the time. In 1950, the three largest cities —Buenos Aires, México City, and Rio de Janeiro—represented 27.5%, 11.2%, and 5.8%, respectively, of each country's total population. These percentages showed a relatively small increase by 1960—32.2%, 13.4%, and 6.7%, respectively. Only Buenos Aires accounted for an absolute percentage increase as high as 4.7%. However, it was the city of Montevideo, accounting for 35% of the nation's total population in 1950, that showed the highest percentage increase by 1960, by then possessing 48.3% of the country's total population. At a medium level, 40% of the primary cities shared percentages of between 10% and 15% of the country total population in 1950, with the exception of two pairs of primate cities, Rio de Janeiro 5.8%, São Paulo 4.7%, Guayaquil 8.3% and Quito 6.6%. Bogotá, Port-au-Prince and Tegucigalpa, with shares of only 6.1%, 6.4% and 7.0%, respectively of the country's total population,

TABLE 6.3

TOTAL AND URBAN PRIMACY OF METROPOLITAN AREAS IN LATIN AMERICA, 1950–1960

COUNTRY	LARGEST CITY	1950					1960					
		TOTAL POP. (x 1,000)	URBAN POP. (x 1,000)	POP. LARGEST CITY	LARGEST CITY AS % OF TOTAL URBAN	LARGEST CITY AS % OF URBAN	TOTAL POP. (x 1,000)	URBAN POP. (x 1,000)	POP. LARGEST CITY	LARGEST CITY AS % OF TOTAL URBAN	LARGEST CITY AS % OF URBAN	GROWTH OF LARGEST CITY (%)
ARGENTINA	Buenos Aires	17,189	11,038	4,723,918	27.5	43	20,956	14,161	6,751,759	32.2	48	43
BOLIVIA	La Paz	3,013	778	346,130	11.5	44	3,696	1,104	378,319	10.2	34	9
BRAZIL	Rio de Janeiro	52,178	16,083	3,052,012	5.8	19	70,309	28,329	4,691,654	6.7	17	54
	São Paulo	52,178	16,083	2,448,938	4.7	15	70,309	28,329	4,368,603	6.2	15	78
COLOMBIA	Bogotá	11,679	4,253	715,250	6.1	17	15,468	7,134	1,188,180	7.7	17	66
COSTA RICA	San José	801	232	159,150	19.9	69	1,206	377	320,478	26.6	85	101
CUBA	La Habana	5,508	2,753	1,240,369	22.5	45	6,797	3,816	1,594,000	23.5	42	29
DOMINICAN REP.	Santo Domingo	2,243	482	239,464	10.7	50	3,030	834	477,000	15.7	57	99
EL SALVADOR	San Salvador	1,868	515	220,929	11.8	43	2,490	721	351,276	14.1	49	59
ECUADOR	Guayaquil	3,197	878	266,637	8.3	30	4,317	1,423	567,895	13.2	40	113
	Quito	3,197	878	212,135	6.6	24	4,317	1,423	510,286	11.8	36	141
GUATEMALA	Guatemala City	2,805	674	294,344	10.5	44	3,765	1,124	572,937	15.2	51	95
HONDURAS	Tegucigalpa	1,428	249	99,948	7.0	40	1,950	432	164,941	8.5	38	65
HAITÍ	Port-au-Prince	3,380	340	216,170	6.4	64	4,140	513	240,000	5.8	47	11
MÉXICO	México City	26,366	12,144	2,960,120	11.2	24	36,018	19,741	4,816,393	13.4	24	63
NICARAGUA	Managua	1,060	297	140,334	13.2	47	1,477	502	234,600	15.9	47	67
PERÚ	Lima	7,969	2,498	1,211,752	15.2	49	10,025	3,904	1,845,910	18.4	47	52
PARAGUAY	Asunción	1,397	392	206,634	14.8	53	1,768	508	305,160	17.3	60	48
URUGUAY	Montevideo	2,195	1,734	768,413	35.0	44	2,490	2,030	1,202,890	48.3	59	57
VENEZUELA	Caracas	4,974	2,422	790,456	15.9	33	7,331	4,611	1,492,378	20.3	32	89
CHILE	Santiago	6,073	3,327	1,423,623	23.4	43	7,627	4,861	1,983,945	26.0	41	39
PANAMÁ	Panama City	797	282	190,062	23.8	67	1,055	447	285,365	27.1	64	50

remained at the lowest scale. It should be noted that these same three cities presented the lowest percentages in 1960— Bogotá, 7.7%; Port-au-Prince, 5.8%; Tegucigalpa, 8.5%, with the exception of Rio de Janeiro and São Paulo with 6.7% and 6.2%, respectively. But, whereas Bogotá shared an increase of 1.6% of the country's total population and Tegucigalpa an increase of 1.5%, Port-au-Prince experienced a decrease of 0.6% in its share of the country's total population. In 1960, Guatemala City, Santo Domingo, Managua, Asunción and Lima remained at a middle level, with shares of their country's total population of between 15.2% and 18.4%.

The general pattern of contrast between 1950 and 1960 is that of a progressive increase in the percentage of total country population residing in the primary cities. Only two cities, in fact, showed a decrease in their share of the percentage of total country population. These were Port-au-Prince (as pointed out above) and La Paz. In 1950, La Paz accounted for 11.5% of the total population in Bolivia. By 1960 its population share had been reduced to 10.2%.

When the *population figures of the primate cities* in Latin America are viewed in relation to the *total urban population* in each country, the percentages vary radically. Table 6.3 also presents the 1950 and 1960 tabulations of urban primacy per country. The percentages, in, every case, are considerably higher. With the exception of São Paulo, which in 1950 accounted for only 15% and Rio de Janeiro (19%), of the total urban population in the country, all the cities represented shares of total urban population of between 17% and 69%. The lowest percentage shares for that year were found to be those of Bogotá (17%), Quito (24%) and Mexico City (24%). The highest percentages, in turn, were those of Panamá City 67% and San José, 69%.

In terms of gains and losses in percentages expressive of the primate city population as a share of the total urban population, the picture for 1960 was very irregular. The highest percentage was again that of San José, 85%; but this time Panamá City experienced a drop to 64%. The other high percentages were those of Asunción of 60% and Montevideo, 59%, as compared to 53% and 44% in 1950. Santo Domingo accounted for 57% of the total urban population in the country and presented an absolute increase of 7% with respect to 1950, Panamá underwent an absolute decrease of 3%

in the ten-year period. Managua with 47% retained its 1950 percentage during the subsequent ten years.

As indicated earlier in this study, the urban population in Latin America is growing at a faster rate than the total population. However, as noted, this is not due to an external national migration, or natural increase in urban population, but rather to an internal migration of population from the rural areas to the cities, as well as to the excess of births over deaths in the country as a whole. The urban population explosion has changed cities almost completely. Table 6.3 indicates the dramatic population growth experienced by the primate metro-cities between 1950 and 1960. During that ten-year period, Quito and Guayaquil underwent the most spectacular growth (141% and 113%). Next on the list were San José (101.0%), Santo Domingo (99%), Guatemala City (95%), Caracas (89%), São Paulo (78%), with very high percentages of growth. The only low percentages were those of La Paz (9%), and Port-au-Prince (11%).

Studies of Seven Metro-Cities

New preliminary data and estimates by CELADE indicate that by 1980 Latin America will have a population of 350 million.[3] The estimates also suggest that slightly more than 60 percent, or 218 million, will reside in urban areas. Considering 1965 data, this would mean an increase of 100 million per population or 85.5 percent over the next 15 years.

According to 1960 census information, there were ten cities, including Havana, with populations exceeding 1 million. CELADE's estimate for 1980 indicates that by then there will be 28 cities including Havana with more than a million inhabitants each. Of these at least 7 will probably have a population exceeding 4 million.[4] These large metro-cities will possess characteristics similar to those of the large metropolitan centers normally identified with highly urbanized and developed countries elsewhere in the world—but with one tragic difference. The average per capita income of the

[3] CELADE, *Urban Development in Latin America* (Santiago: United Nations, 1969).
[4] Ibid., p. 44, table 7.

lesser developed countries will probably have risen by about only 20% during the same period, thus widening the already existing economic gap between Latin American countries on the one hand, and the United States and Europe on the other.

While problems in definition prevent outright comparison, recent evidence suggests that the smaller urban places—from 20,000 to 100,000—are also experiencing rapid growth. However, as previously mentioned, the sparsity of data on smaller urban places and the availability of reliable data on the larger ones makes it convenient to limit this discussion to the latter.

As might be expected, the growth of metropolitan areas in Latin America, both in absolute terms and in degree of intensity, has been the result of a number of interrelated dynamic variables acting upon the population context. It is not our purpose here to describe all of these variables, but rather to focus (to the extent made possible by available data) on the actual physical pattern of urbanization as manifested by the present tendencies of population growth and distribution.

Seven case studies have been selected to present the general pattern of recent Latin American metropolitan growth. (See Appendix, table 9 for statistics on additional Latin American cities.) The first three, of Buenos Aires, México City, and São Paulo, represent first-rank metro-cities (population of over 2 million). The next three, of Santiago, Lima, and Caracas, represent second-rank metro-cities (population of over 1 million). The last case study, of Panama City, represents a fifth-rank metro-city (population of over 100,000). Together they cover a cross-section of different types and sizes of Latin American metro-cities.

BUENOS AIRES

Although Buenos Aires is not located at the geographical center of Argentina, it is located at the center of the most populated area of the country. However, Buenos Aires did not always have this central position; in its early years it was only a terminal point on the route that connected it with Lima, Perú and Potosí, Bolivia. Consequently, the population of the country was located entirely along this route which became and remains today the main artery of the city—Rivadavia Avenue, formerly Camino de los Reinos del Norte (Road to the Northern Kingdoms). In the early years of the

Republic, communication between the northern Argentinian cities and Lima was cut off, thus strengthening the ties between the internal cities and Buenos Aires. This route or communication spine was also reinforced by the fact that Buenos Aires had become the main point of entrance and exit for the entire country.

Today the port of Buenos Aires is the setting for a large part of the nation's export and import activities, with the consequence that almost each region or city in Argentina is directly connected with the capital by three main road systems: one system extending to the north in the direction of Córdoba and Rosario; another to the western interior in the direction of Mendoza; and a third to the south in the direction of Bahía Blanca and Patagónia (see map 6.6).[5] In addition, by virtue of Buenos Aires' position as the center

[5] SOURCE: Maps 6.6, 6.8 from James, *Latin America*, p. 338.

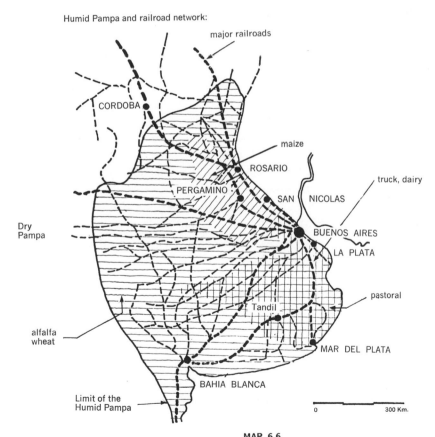

MAP 6.6

Geographical Location of Buenos Aires

of the administrative system for the whole country, and its decisive role in planning and development of the routes of communication for the entire country its significance is greater than it would be if based on economic power alone.

The growth of Buenos Aires as a metro-city started with the exploitation of the humid Pampa, a plain extending more than 400 miles westward from Buenos Aires. Its main production is wheat, maize and alfalfa. The agricultural development of the Pampa resulted in the building of a network of railroads toward Buenos Aires that later, when the city grew, was used as a means of transportation for commuters. Buenos Aires is located on the edge of the Pampa, on a plateau that reaches a maximum altitude of 300 feet and encompasses an area of approximately 400 miles inland from the coast. The growth of the city has been encouraged by this almost flat land area. Starting from the original settlement on the coast, the city has not had any difficulty in growing westward. The Pampa plateau ends in a cliff varying in height from 24 to 60 feet, facing the La Plata River which establishes a natural boundary for the city. In the southern part of the city there are flat areas between the cliff and the river, with the result that the city has expanded along the plateau, which is not affected by the flood threat to the nearby lowlands. However, in the central district, the problem of flooding has been overcome through the establishment and development of the port facilities.

The local routes in Buenos Aires evolved largely for the use of the surrounding facilities. Resorts have been built to the north of the city, along the La Plata River, and have attracted high-income residents. Another important route has been created with the construction of an airport at Ezeiza. The expressway in that direction has stimulated greater development and urbanization of the area, exemplified by the construction of a popular resort on that route. The southern part of the city has grown along the routes leading to the capital of the province of Buenos Aires, La Plata City.

Metropolitan Buenos Aires consists of the Capital Federal District and 18 partidos (districts) of the province of Buenos Aires (see table 6.4). When La Plata was established as the provincial capital, it was located about 30 miles south of Buenos Aires; but now the area in between is in a process of conurbation. The route that connects Buenos Aires–La Plata also connects with Mar del Plata, a sea resort located further south.

TABLE 6.4

BUENOS AIRES: POPULATION GROWTH OF DISTRICTS

INTEGRANTS	TOTAL: 1947 [a]	TOTAL: 1960 [b]
1. Buenos Aires	2,982,580 (1) [c]	2,966,816
2. La Matanza	98,471 (9)	402,642
3. Lanus	244,473 (4)	381,561
4. Moron	110,344 (8)	344,041
5. Avellaneda	273,839 (2)	329,626
6. Quilmes	123,132 (7)	318,144
7. General San Martín	269,514 (3)	279,213
8. Lomas de Zamora	127,880 (6)	275,219
9. Tres de Febrero [d]	—	262,119
10. Vicente López	149,958 (5)	250,823
11. San Isidro	90,086 (10)	196,188
12. General Sarmiento	46,413 (12)	167,753
13. Almirante Brown	39,700 (14)	135,202
14. Merlo	19,865 (15)	99,635
15. Tigre	58,348 (11)	88,220
16. San Fernando	44,666 (13)	84,388
17. Esteban Echevarría	19,068 (16)	69,296
18. Moreno	15,101 (17)	59,083
19. Florencio Varela	10,480 (18)	41,845
	4,723,918	6,751,769

SOURCES:
 a. "Censo de Población 1947," *VI Censo General de la Nacion*, vol. I (Buenos Aires: Dirección Nacional de Estadística y Censos, Argentina, 1957).
 b. Censos de Población 1960, Resultados Provisionales por Departamentos y/o Partidos (Buenos Aires: Dirección Nacional de Estadística y Censos, 1960–61).
NOTES:
 c. Numbers in parentheses indicate rank
 d. Included in San Martín in the census.

In the present layout of metropolitan Buenos Aires certain homogeneous areas can be identified. One of these is the port district, located in the lowlands between the center city and the La Plata River. Some industries are closely related to the port facilities, such as the thermoelectric plants which receive coal from abroad.

The central district presents a compact character, due to the fact that it keeps the traditional street pattern. The major industrial concentrations within this area are to be found around the railroad stations. On the periphery of the central district new residential developments have been built, with new street patterns. One important residential area runs just from the center in a northerly direction, along the La Plata River. The major public and private open spaces are generally confined to the northern section of Buenos Aires.

Buenos Aires is the largest first-rank metro-city in Latin America. Between 1947 and 1960 its population grew from 4,723,918 to 6,751,769—a total growth of 43%. The central district with 2,966,816 inhabitants still contains more than 30% of the total metropolitan population. However, as may be observed in table 6.4, this distribution changed with a population decrease of 15,764 compared to the previous census. By contrast, most of the peripheral districts experienced absolute population gains. This is shown by the extreme case of La Matanza which underwent a growth of more than 300% between 1947 and 1960; the present tendency of growth thus seems to indicate a rapid increase of density in a westward direction away from the central district.

MÉXICO CITY

Like most of the metro-cities of Latin America, México City has exhibited a shift from a very slow growth over a long period of time to a rapid growth during the last few decades. To understand the present configuration of México's first metro-city, it is useful to think in terms of the major periods of its development.

Tenochtitlán was founded on islands of the sea of Texcoco. At Cortés' arrival, 1519, the Aztec capital "had more than 50,000 houses with three main avenues two spear-lengths in width and many narrow canals resembling Venice."[6] The conquistadores almost completely destroyed Tenochtitlán, but many of the new administrative buildings laid out around the Zócalo or plaza mayor occupied the same position as the Aztec royal buildings. During the next three centuries México City grew slowly from 30,000 inhabitants (after the conquest) to more than 100,000. By the nineteenth century it had become the largest city in the Western Hemisphere. In 1900 its population was above 300,000; and by 1921, at the end of the Revolution, this figure had passed the 600,000 mark.

Through the nineteenth century, the city grew primarily westward. At that time the urbanized area occupied only one-half mile to the west. Further eastward expansion was blocked until the be-

[6] Norman S. Hayner, "Mexico City: Its Growth and Configuration," *The American Journal of Sociology* 50 (July 1944-May 1945): 296.

ginning of the present century by Lake Texcoco. The lake was then partially drained by a gigantic canal and tunnel project, but new residential neighborhoods to the east were discouraged by the alkaline character of the reclaimed soil.

Between 1880 and 1900 México City grew in a northward and eastward direction, up to the limits then determined by the various railroad lines. For several years the railroad network remained a barrier to further urban growth. In addition, the channels and rivers crossed by very few bridges presented another barrier to development, until 1930. In that year, Calzada de Balbuena (Morazán) was the northern limit of the city. The colonial city which remained at the south, on the other hand, facilitated a linear growth in a southward direction.

By 1940, the new developments to the south and west of the colonial city formed the urban ring which included Tlatilco, Santa Julia, Tacuba, Tacubaya, Santa Fé and Mixcoac. This ring repre-

TABLE 6.5

MÉXICO CITY: POPULATION GROWTH OF INTEGRANTS

INTEGRANTS	TOTAL: 1950 [a]	TOTAL: 1960 [b]
Federal District:		
1. México	2,234,795 (1) [c]	2,832,133
Delegations:		
2. Gustavo A. Madero	204,833 (2)	579,180
3. Atzcapotzalco	187,864 (3)	370,724
4. Ixtapalapa	76,621 (5)	254,355
5. Obregón	93,176 (4)	220,011
6. Ixtacalco	33,945 (7)	198,904
7. Coyoacán	70,005 (6)	169,811
State of México		
Municipalities:		
8. Tlalnepantla	29,005 (9)	105,447
9. Naucalpan	29,876 (8)	85,828
	2,960,120	4,816,393

SOURCES:
a. *VII Censo General de Población, 6 Junio de 1950* (México, D. F.: Dirección General de Estadística, México, 1952).
b. *VIII Censo General de Población, 8 de Junio de 1960* (México, D. F.: Dirección General de Estadística, México, 1963).
NOTE:
c. Numbers in parentheses indicate rank.

sented an area approximately equal to two-thirds of the total metropolitan urban area. Future urban growth, to the present day, has
resulted in a compact urban complex radiating from the center city,
roughly in a circular shape (see map 6.7).

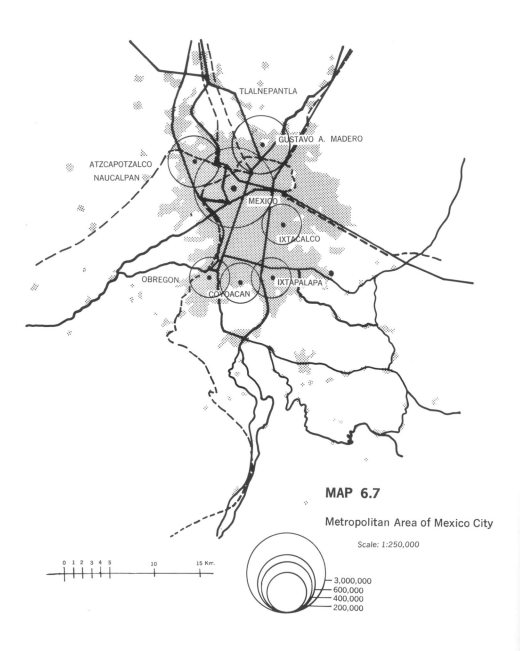

MAP 6.7

Metropolitan Area of Mexico City

Scale: 1:250,000

3,000,000
600,000
400,000
200,000

0 1 2 3 4 5   10   15 Km.

México City is among the first-rank metro-cities in Latin America, having grown from a population of 2,960,120 to one of 4,816,393 in the decade between 1950 and 1960. The Federal District contains more than 50% of the total metropolitan population (see table 6.5). However, the peripheral (subfederal districts) and the satellite municipalities are growing at a much faster rate than the Federal District. The extreme example is Ixtacalco, which underwent an absolute growth of more than 480% between 1950 and 1960. The present tendency of growth seems to indicate a rapid increase of density in the eastern peripheral delegations.

SÃO PAULO

São Paulo is not in a central position in relation to Brazil, but is located on a crossroad toward the interior (see map 6.8). Through the Paraiba Valley it is connected to Rio de Janeiro; and through the Mantiqueira Valley, it is connected to the Mato Grosso. These communication facilities have allowed the development of the region.

The main routes in the region are the one to Santos, the seaport of São Paulo, and the one to Campinas along the Tieté River. Most of the large coffee and cotton production of the region is exported over these routes. Other less important routes are the President Dutra Highway to Rio de Janeiro and the route that connects São Paulo with the southern states. The transportation network has followed mainly the flat areas of the valley.

Metropolitan São Paulo almost doubled its population, from 2,448,938 to 4,368,603 between 1950 and 1960 (see table 6.6). Several factors have accounted for this rapid growth. To the south of the central district, for example, in the direction of Santos, a corridor of growth has been formed following the three routes which connect the port with the inner city—the railroad, the old road that follows the railroad lines and the new road, Rodovia Anchieta. Man-made lakes to the south, which have provided new resort areas, have also promoted recent growth. But it is the sprawl of industry through the small towns surrounding São Paulo (Osasco, San Miguel Paulista, Itaquera, Santo André, Santo Amaro), that has perhaps been most important in the conurbation of these towns with the central district.

TABLE 6.6

SÃO PAULO: POPULATION GROWTH OF INTEGRANTS

INTEGRANTS	TOTAL: 1950[a]	TOTAL: 1960[b]
Municipalities and Districts:		
1. Sao Paulo	2,198,096 (1)[c]	3,825,351
São Paulo	2,120,149	
São Miguel Paulista	37,713	
Itaquera	14,886	
Guaianazes	10,057	
Parelheiros	7,141	
Parus	5,607	
Jaragua	2,543	
2. Santo André	127,032 (2)	245,147
Santo André	104,338	
Ribeirao Pires	10,955	
Maua	9,472	
Paranapiacaba	2,267	
3. São Caetano do Sul	59,832 (3)	114,421
São Caetano do Sul	59,832	
4. Guarulhos	34,683 (4)	101,273
Guarulhos	34,683	
5. São Bernardo do Campo	29,295 (5)	82,411
São Bernardo do Campo	24,899	
Diadema	3,023	
Riacho Grande	1,373	
	2,448,938	4,368,603

SOURCES:

a. Conselho Nacional de Estadística, Servicio Nacional de Recenseament, *VI Recenseamento do Brasil: Censo Demografico, 1 de Julho de 1950* (Rio de Janeiro: Instituto Brasileiro de Geografia e Estadística, 1951–55).

b. Censo Demografico (Rio de Janeiro: Servico Grafico do Instituto Brasileiro de Geografia Estadística, 1960).

NOTE:

c. Numbers in parentheses indicate rank.

The central district is the financial and industrial center of the whole metropolis. It retains very few elements from the early days of the city, having been completely transformed by the new routes laid along the valleys and the bridges over them. The industrial areas occupy a central position, reflecting the fact that industry is the main activity of São Paulo. The 26,822 factories operating in the metropolitan area, represent world-wide interests. The residential

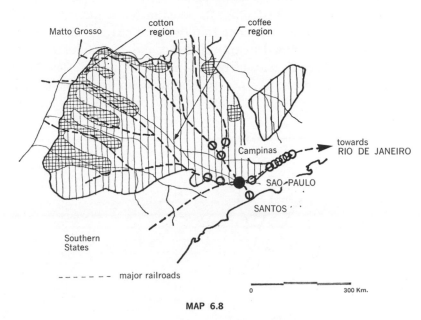

MAP 6.8

Geographical Location of São Paulo

areas of the Espigao Central belong to the high-income groups near the central district.

SANTIAGO

Santiago is located on a flat plateau in the Central Valley, surrounded by the Andean range and limited by the Maipo River to the south (see map 6.9). Railroad and highway linkages connect Santiago with the major seaports of Valparaíso and San Antonio and with practically every other important city in the country. The central urbanized area of the city is described by a railroad loop built during the nineteenth century, encircling an area of approximately 10 square miles. Within the metropolitan area, three major components are recognizable: 1) the central business district, 2) the center city, and 3) the outlying comunas.

The central business district is the regional and national center of the major government, financial and retail activities of the nation.

It extends over an area of 100 acres defined by the Mapocho River and Avenida Bernardo O'Higgins. Its location corresponds to that of the original Spanish settlement founded in 1541. In the center-city defined by the railroad loop, industrial and commercial establishments meet a high density of traditional courtyard houses. Most of this area was developed before 1930 and its limits coincide with those of the central comuna of Santiago. The outlying comunas are

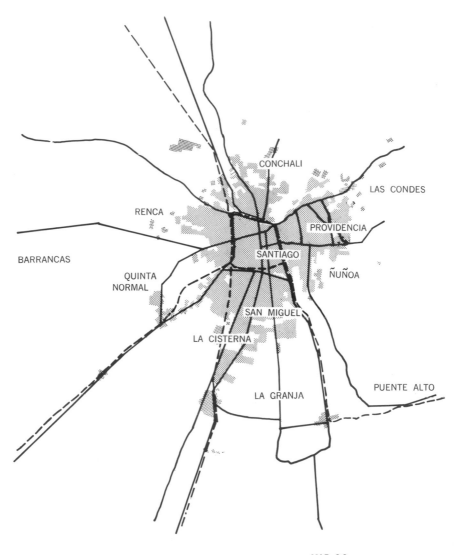

MAP 6.9

Metropolitan Area of Santiago

either urbanized areas contiguous to the center-city such as San Miguel, Ñuñoa, Providencia, or separate peripheral satellites, as is Puente Alto.

By the beginning of the present century, metropolitan Santiago had reached a population of 500,000, but the internal organization of the center-city retained the original gridiron pattern. The streets at the foot of the Santa Lucía hill were consolidated as the center-city core; and the residential areas extended the traditional pattern filling the area surrounded by the railroad loop. Between 1900 and 1930 Santiago's population reached the 800,000 mark; and the urban area extended beyond the city boundaries into the agricultural lands of the outlying comunas. Since 1930, there has been a large exodus of population from the center-city to the peripheral areas. This fact is illustrated by the central comuna of Santiago which underwent a decrease of population from 666,679 in 1952 to 646,522 in 1960 (see table 6.7). Today the eastern and southern comunas represent 60% of the total urban metropolitan area.

TABLE 6.7

SANTIAGO: POPULATION GROWTH OF COMUNAS

INTEGRANTS	TOTAL: 1952 [a]	TOTAL: 1960 [b]
Comunas:		
1. Santiago	666,679 (1) [c]	646,522
2. San Miguel	145,541 (2)	244,185
3. Ñuñoa	125,967 (3)	206,305
4. Conchalí	83,019 (5)	159,930
5. La Cisterna	58,830 (7)	154,668
6. Quinta Normal	123,571 (4)	150,560
7. Las Condes	38,852 (8)	86,236
8. Providencia	69,118 (6)	83,551
9. Barrancas	31,669 (10)	78,504
10. La Granja	17,147 (12)	68,408
11. Renca	30,631 (11)	53,640
12. Puente Alto	32,599 (9)	51,436
	1,423,623	1,983,945

SOURCES:
    a. "Resumen del País," *XII Censo General de Población y Vivienda, 24 de Abril de 1952,* vol. 1 (Santiago: Dirección General de Estadística, Chile, 1956).
    b. Entidades de Población 1960 (Santiago: Dirección de Estadística y Censos, Republica de Chile, 1962).
NOTE:
    c. Numbers in parentheses indicate rank.

The continuous decline of the central comuna as a residential area may be explained by the expansion of industry. The center-city accounts for 65% of the number of industrial establishments in the metropolitan area and 52% of the total labor force. The second most important industrial area is the railroad-oriented industrial belt immediately surrounding the central comuna, at Quinta Normal, San Miguel and Ñuñoa. This area accounts for 28% of the industrial establishments and 36% of the labor force. However, recent sanitary and zoning regulations are forcing the relocation of many of the center-city industrial establishments to outlying areas, along regional highways. It is estimated that between 1951 and 1958, about 40% of the industrial establishments in the center-city had already relocated along the Pan American Highway at Maipu, to the north of Santiago.[7]

LIMA

Lima is located on the central coast, more or less equidistant from the northern and southern borders and therefore in a central position relative to the coastal Pan American Highway. The capital also has a central position relative to the population distribution within the country; and like most cities on the Peruvian coast, it serves as a gateway for penetration of the highlands and the Amazon jungle. The most important economic elements within the region dominated by metropolitan Lima are the mines at Cerro de Pasco and the agricultural areas of the Mantaro Valley. The exploitation of their resources has been carried out through the transportation network that starts at Callao and penetrates the hinterland across the Rimac Valley (see map 6.10).[8] The Peruvian Central Railroad connects the Andean region with the coast. The central district is located on a relatively smooth plain cut by the Rimac River and surrounded by dry mountains without vegetation. It has developed mainly on the southern bank because of its relationship with the port of Callao—also located on the southern side of the river—and because for a long time the river was a physical barrier to urban growth. Future

[7] Official data, Ministry of Public Works, Chile.
[8] SOURCE: Map 6.10 *National Atlas of the World* (Washington, D.C.: National Geographic Society, 1963), p. 73.

developments continued in a southward direction due to the attraction of the sea resorts in Chorrillos, Barranco and Miraflores.

The original Spanish settlement was founded in the vicinity of the hills, but the city developed on the agricultural lands of the plain which offered better conditions than the desert lands surrounding the Rimac Valley. The agricultural lands extend to the north into the valley of the Chillón River. Only in recent years have the peripheral desert lands been occupied by low-income groups.[9]

Between 1940 and 1961 the metropolitan area of Lima underwent a growth of 186%, from a population of 645,172 to 1,845,910. Although the central district of Lima was still the most populated district in 1961, the population growth is more dramatically shown by the growth in the twenty-two peripheral districts (see table 6.8). Considering the first six most populated districts by order of rank, it is possible to outline the general pattern of metropolitan growth

[9] See case study on the barriadas in Lima, Chapter 7 of this book.

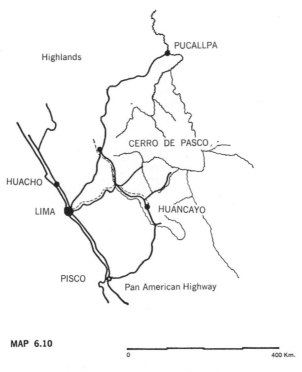

MAP 6.10

0   400 Km.

Geographical Location of Lima

during those two decades. A pronounced type of linear growth is apparent in a north-south direction, with a resulting tendency towards a semicircular form. In terms of percentages, the central district showed an increase of 25%, whereas La Victoria, Miraflores and Lince increased 271%, 94% and 221%, respectively. La Victoria, which ranked fourth in 1940 was the second most populated district, with 204,926 inhabitants, Callao underwent a growth of 132% and occupied third place. It should be noted that although

TABLE 6.8

LIMA: POPULATION GROWTH OF DISTRICTS

INTEGRANTS	TOTAL: 1940 [a]	TOTAL: 1961 [b]
Districts:		
1. Lima	269,738 (1) [c]	338,918
2. La Victoria	55,134 (4)	204,926
3. Callao	70,425 (2)	163,702
4. Rimac	57,154 (3)	144,320
5. Miraflores	45,489 (5)	88,446
6. Lince	25,636 (6)	82,393
7. Ate	10,602 (10)	78,578
8. Magdalena Vieja	5,859 (16)	68,560
9. Magdalena del Mar	16,057 (8)	55,737
10. Santiago de Surco	7,101 (14)	48,558
11. Bellavista	8,273 (12)	43,929
12. San José de Surco	18,625 (7)	42,449
13. Carabayllo	11,931 (9)	42,270
14. San Isidro	8,778 (11)	37,925
15. Lurigancho	7,472 (13)	32,561
16. Chorrillos	6,996 (15)	32,376
17. San Miguel	3,961 (17)	23,233
18. Pachacamac	3,597 (19)	11,726
19. Chaclacayo	1,109 (23)	9,363
20. Puente Piedra	2,544 (21)	8,370
21. Lurín	3,716 (18)	6,171
22. La Punta	3,589 (20)	5,909
23. Ancón	1,386 (22)	3,802
	645,172	1,845,910

SOURCES:
   a. *Censo Nacional de Población y Ocupación 1940*, vol. 1 *Resúmenes General* (Lima: Dirección Nacional de Estadística y Censos, Perú, 1944–1949).
   b. *Sexto Censo Nacional de Població 2 de Julio de 1961* (Lima: Dirección Nacional de Estadística y Censos, Perú, 1964).
NOTE:
   c. Numbers in parentheses indicate rank.

the city of Lima accounted for 41% of the total metropolitan population in 1940, its share was only 19% of the total in 1961. Moreover, the district of Lima had the lowest rate of increase of all the districts in the period between 1940 and 1961. This would seem to reflect the general tendency for a peripheral suburban growth.

CARACAS

The most populated areas of Venezuela form a corridor that goes from east to west following the mountain areas and enjoying a more temperate climate than the low tropical lands. This linear pattern of areas of higher population density has been reinforced in the last few years by the establishment of a highway network. Caracas has a central position in this linear pattern. But it must be observed that the continuous linear configuration did not have a historical precedent. Generally, what has distinguished Venezuela is the lack of interaction among regions. The nature of the economy of the regions—based on the exportation of oil—and great administrative and political centralization have been determining factors in the development of the general structure of the country.

Caracas differs from Buenos Aires or São Paulo because its growth is not due to the productiveness of the region surrounding the city but to that of regions which are quite removed from it, but which are nevertheless strongly dependent on the capital city for their administration. The main relationships of Caracas with the rest of the country are physically expressed in the routes toward Maracay-Valencia, in the route that connects with La Guaira and in the routes toward the eastern oil states. These main routes have not had a strong influence in directing the growth of the metropolis, chiefly because the hilly conditions of the site of Caracas are far stronger elements.

Caracas is located on a valley of the Caribbean coastal range at 2,400 feet above sea level and 9 miles from the Caribbean coast. The city was founded at the western end of the valley and its growth has followed the natural direction of the valley toward the east. Until 1950 this growth was characterized by the expansion of small independent settlements along the valley that were finally consolidated and now cover almost all the area of the flatlands. Since 1950 growth has been outside the main valley, in a southern direction.

TABLE 6.9

CARACAS: POPULATION GROWTH OF INTEGRANTS

INTEGRANTS	TOTAL: 1950 [a]	TOTAL: 1961 [b]
Distrito Federal [c]	709,602	1,257,515
Departamentos:		
Libertador (L)	623,713	1,116,245
Vargas (V)	85,889	141,270
Distrito:		
Sucre (Miranda) (S)	80,854	234,863
Parroquias:		
1. Sucre (L)	112,758 (1) [d]	202,990
2. Santa Rosalía (L)	74,276 (3)	139,726
3. El Valle (L)	38,312 (8)	110,616
4. El Recreo (L)	55,983 (4)	102,137
5. San Juan (L)	74,407 (2)	96,653
6. Petaré (S)	25,053 (14)	77,631
7. Maiquetia (V)	39,613 (7)	76,859
8. Catedral (L)	40,648 (6)	76,837
9. La Pastora (L)	54,860 (5)	75,125
10. La Vega (L)	19,501 (15)	64,545
11. Chacao (S)	25,788 (12)	64,006
12. Candelaria (L)	33,299 (11)	49,411
13. San José (L)	25,305 (13)	48,563
14. Baruta (S)	8,233 (21)	45,565
15. Leoncio Martínez (S)	16,930 (16)	44,412
16. Altagracia (L)	33,356 (10)	41,247
17. San Agustín (L)	36,818 (9)	40,162
18. Antimano (L)	12,117 (18)	37,440
19. La Guaira (V)	16,454 (17)	20,593
20. Carayaca (V)	11,681 (19)	16,239
21. Santa Teresa (L)	9,337 (20)	16,149
22. Macarao (Miranda)	2,737 (26)	14,644
23. Naiguata (V)	5,500 (23)	9,552
24. Macuto (V)	7,293 (22)	8,006
25. Caraballeda (V)	2,998 (25)	7,422
26. El Hatillo (S)	4,850 (24)	3,249
27. Caruao (V)	2,350 (27)	2,599
	790,456	1,492,378

SOURCES:

a. "Resumen General de la República, Parte A, Población," *Octavo Censo General de Población, 26 de Novembre de 1950* 12 (Caracas: Dirección Nacional de Estadística y Censos, Venezuela, 1957).

b. Noveno Censo General de Población, 1961 (Caracas: Dirección Nacional de Estadística y Censos, Venezuela, 1964).

NOTES:

c. Dept. Libertador + Dept. Vargas.

d. Numbers in parentheses indicate rank.

The basic linear structure of the Caracas landscape was accentuated by the grid of highways that emerged over the years. In the course of the last two decades, this structure became still more firmly engraved upon the landscape. Once the basic communication network was established, the central location of Caracas prevented major flows between the eastern and western halves of the country. Finally, all roads converged at the national metropolis and contributed to its growth.

The population of Caracas increased from 92,000 in 1920 to 709,602 in 1950, with the total population of the metropolitan area reaching 790,456 during the latter year. Between 1950 and 1961 the metropolitan population almost doubled, reaching the 1,492,378 mark (see table 6.9). A major reason for this rapid growth was the concentration of government revenue from oil at Caracas and the government's successful efforts to transform the physical appearance of the capital from a colonial town into a futuristic metropolis.

PANAMA CITY

Between 1930 and 1960, Panama City has increased its population four times, from an estimated 74,000 to 285,365. This last figure did not cover the population distribution over the same land area, however, for the simple reason that in 1930 most of the areas included in the 1960 census were practically deserted. But this fact does not distort the total picture of demographic growth.

In 1950, the limits of Panama City included only four corregimientos: San Felipe, El Chorrillo, Santa Ana and Calidonia. A special decree (*Acuerdo Municipal No. 70*) of June 23, 1960, expanded these limits and created nine other corregimientos, including Betanía, Bella Vista, Pueblo Nuevo, San Francisco, Parque Lefevre, Rio Abajo, San Miguelito, Juan Diaz and Pedregal. As a consequence of this, the 1950 limits of Calidonia, Juan Diaz, Pueblo Nuevo, Rio Abajo and San Francisco were modified. The old limits were retained, however, for San Felipe, El Chorrillo and Santa Ana (see map 6.11). For purposes of comparison, the population totals of 1950 for all corregimientos are here given in table 6.10 according to the limits established in 1960.

Between 1950 and 1960 the metropolitan area of Panama City increased its population about 50%. It is significant, however, that in the center-city, the corregimientos of San Felipe (18%), El

TABLE 6.10

PANAMA CITY: POPULATION GROWTH OF CORREGIMIENTOS

INTEGRANTS	TOTAL: 1950 [a]	TOTAL: 1960
District and Corregimientos:		
Panamá		
1. Calidonia	46,527 (1) [b]	53,794
2. Santa Ana	33,742 (2)	35,644
3. El Chorrillo	27,375 (3)	29,502
4. San Francisco	12,586 (4)	25,242
5. Rio Abajo	12,275 (5)	20,973
6. Parque Lefevre	5,305 (11)	18,540
7. Pueblo Nuevo	8,268 (8)	17,070
8. Betanía	7,160 (9)	15,758
9. Bella Vista	8,603 (7)	15,681
10. San Felipe	11,447 (6)	13,276
11. San Miguelito	918 (15)	12,975
12. Juan Diaz	3,736 (12)	7,736
13. Chilibre	5,466 (10)	7,659
14. Pedregal	3,498 (13)	7,249
15. Pácora	3,156 (14)	4,266
	190,062	285,365

SOURCE:

   a. "Población Urbana," *Quinto Censo le Población, 1950* 1 (Panama City: Dirección de Estadística Censo, Panama, 1956).

NOTE:

   b. Numbers in parentheses indicate rank.

Chorrillo (7.5%), Santa Ana (6%) and Calidonia (15%) only experienced a total average growth of about 12%. By contrast, the
northern corregimientos of Pueblo Nuevo, Rio Abajo and San
Francisco increased their total population by about 100% or more.
These differences of demographic increase reflect the general tendency of metropolitan growth in a northeastern direction. Internal
migrations from all parts of the country to the capital appear to be
a contributing factor. But San Felipe, El Chorrillo and Santa Ana,
which did not suffer any change in their limits in 1960, only registered a total average growth of 8.5% during the ten-year period.
This low increase in the center-city indicates a remigration from the
city to the newly developed suburbs. Immigration from the exterior,
on the other hand, has only occurred on a very small scale.

   A direct consequence of this large uncontrolled migration from

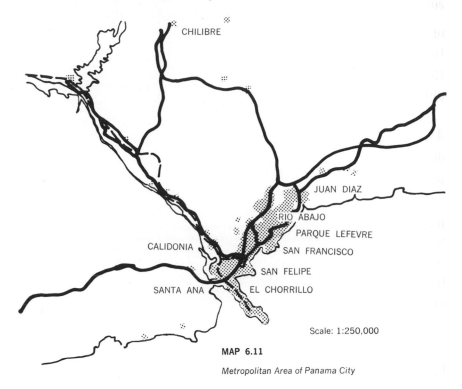

MAP 6.11

Metropolitan Area of Panama City

rural areas has been the creation of squatter settlements very close to the periphery of the center-city. The corregimientos which increased their population at the highest rates were San Miguelito and Parque Lefevre. San Miguelito is also the largest corregimiento, with an area of 5,000 hectares. Both corregimientos experienced intense urbanization, but especially San Miguelito, where government carried out an extensive program of public housing, aimed at the clearance of several squatter settlements. The corregimientos which showed the lowest increase—San Felipe, El Chorrillo and Santa Ana—will probably continue in the same way. The high cost of housing and the already high densities of these corregimientos (about 500 inhabitants per hectare) give little indication of future increase in density. The growth trend during the decade of 1950–1960 seems to corroborate this. In addition, it should be pointed out that the corregimientos with the least urban characteristics—San Miguelito, Juan Diaz and Pedregal—absorb 78% of the total area of the city, whereas they only account for 10% of the total population. The largest difference of population density is found between El Chorrillo with 602 inhabitants per hectare, and Juan Diaz, with only 2 inhabitants per hectare.

It appears that the two major critical areas in most of the Latin American metro-cities are the central districts and the peripheral areas. It is within these areas that the main urban changes due to metropolitan growth are taking place. The typical one- to two-story urban sprawl of the central district is being transformed by the new trend to vertical centralization; and the peripheral areas are being subjected to a rapid process of suburbanization. The process of suburbanization in Latin American metro-cities is being carried forward by low-income groups rather than by the affluent middle- and upper-income groups who live in the suburban areas of many North American and European cities. Its tremendous magnitude accounts for the fact that the areas with the highest densities are located on the periphery as will be seen in the following chapter.

7

Past and Present Influences on Latin American Urban Structure

In Latin America, most of the first-rank cities are situated on or near the coast. The notable exceptions are Bogotá and Mexico City. Their general location reflects a portoriented economy going back to the colonial period. In some cases a coastal city housing the administrative, marketing and residential capital was only a short distance from the port proper, such as Lima-Callao, and Santiago-San Antonio; in other cases an inner city and port were separated by a considerable distance, as with Quito-Guayaquil, and São Paulo-Santos. The latter can still be recognized today as distinctly separate urban pairs.[1] In the first group, however, as in the case of Lima-Callao, the inner city and port merged to form an integrated urban structure.

Another characteristic of many Latin American cities is the survival of a large population of indigenous origin, left more or less unaffected by the European colonization. This is manifested in the preservation of a series of old towns that constitute the basic urban systems in Central and Andean America.

In general, the urban structure of Latin America more readily invites comparison with North Africa and the Far East than with most North American cities. In the latter case, the relatively small indigenous population and the absence of preexisting towns led to the development of a civilization that was completely European in origin and divorced from the native past.

By contrast, the development in Latin America was shaped by

[1] The concept of urban pairs was first introduced by Pierre George, *La Ville* (Paris: Presses Universitaires de France, 1952), pp. 259–60.

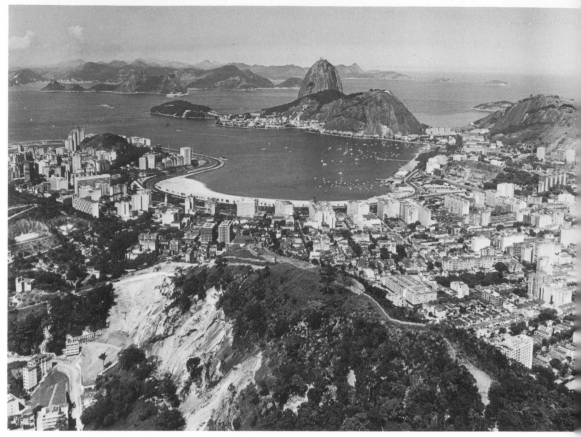

Rio de Janeiro, a city shaped dramatically by topography. ©
Manchete.

dual traditions: the Indian, more or less unaltered by colonization
after the sixteenth century; and the European commercial tradition,
with its emphasis on trade and speculation inspired by and oriented
toward the outside world. The result has been the development of
two coexisting urban systems. The first joins the old Indian towns
of Central America and the Andes; the second connects the commercial cities along the sea coasts that are products of the colonial
period and modern times.

The older Andean cities had a precolonial nucleus from which
industrial installations and working camps radiated in the course of
time. The cities that developed during the colonial period were
generally located near ports and were marked by a mixed type of
urbanization, combining monumental buildings (the product of
financial and commercial speculations) with neighborhoods housing
dockers and immigrants. In addition there are urban pairs, com-

posed of an old city and a port, as in the case of Caracas-La Guiara, and México City-Vera Cruz.

Among the first-rank Latin American cities, only one, located in the high plateaus, combines direct descent from the pre-Columbian tradition with the type of growth and urbanism characteristic of the modern city. This is México City, which as a consequence of its political functions and industrialization, had grown in population from about 900,000 inhabitants toward the end of the First World War to nearly 5 million by the 1960s. All other cities with over one million population are in the coastal regions and on the colonization fronts: Buenos Aires (over 6 million), Rio de Janeiro (over 4 million), and São Paulo (over 4 million), just to mention the first-rank metropolitan areas.

Latin American cities differ in their internal structure from European and North American cities in varying degrees. This is particularly true in the location of residential areas since many Latin American deviate from the generally accepted theories about urban

The center-city of Guatemala City, Guatemala. Photo by author.

form in this respect. The common theory has been that the structure of a city can be described as a circumference radiating from the center in a plane or surface with an arrangement of land uses changing gradually (usually along radial avenues) according to the intrinsic geometric values of the land toward the periphery.[2] In Latin American cities, this is not generally the case, since pronounced topographic discontinuities present real barriers to development. For example, Buenos Aires is on level land limited by the Rio de la Plata. Santiago is located in a valley surrounded by high mountains. Bogotá sits on a high plateau limited by a high steep mountain range to the east and the swamplands of the Bogotá River to the west. Rio de Janeiro extends along several valleys between numerous mountains and the Atlantic Ocean. It is clear that in every case the topography has had a controlling effect on the form and direction of city growth. The location of cities in the mountain valleys was favored by the more equable climate and the potable water from rivers in the valleys. Cities not situated on the ocean were invariably connected by road to the ocean ports, as in the case of São Paulo-Santos.

In the study of the urban shape of Latin American cities, it is useful to note that all or almost all of the cities founded with similar colonial specifications and possessing similar original core patterns have developed their shapes quite differently. According to their general shape, three major types of cities may be identified: (1) *circular cities*, São Paulo, Santiago, México City, Guatemala City; (2) *semicircular cities*, Buenos Aires, Montevideo, Lima, La Habana; and, (3) *linear cities*, Bogotá, Caracas, Panama City. Circular cities are generally found in the center of flat valleys, with major axial roads to the surrounding regions. Several of these cities, like México City and Santiago, originated from a cross shape. Linear cities such as Bogotá and Caracas have developed either next to narrow valleys or along coastal plains. Semicircular cities present at least three different subtypes: (1) the simple *semicircle*, such as Managua, which faces the waterfront where the center is located; (2) the *fan-shape* which are generally port cities, with one node of attraction, and penetration roads to the hinterland. Good examples are Buenos Aires, Montevideo, and La Habana; (3) the triangle, which

[2] Ernest W. Burgess, "The Growth of the City: An Introduction to a Research Project," *Publications of the American Sociological Society* 18 (1924): 85–97.

A residential area of Guatemala City, Guatemala. Photo by author.

is the opposite of the preceding types since the center is not near the waterfront, but in the hinterland. The city grows in the direction of the waterfront. Lima illustrates this type of growth.

All natural barriers greatly deform continuous order in the urban structure. It is possible to measure this phenomenon by drawing a circumference around the known center of the city, with a radius up to the periphery of its developed areas. Within the circumference all the undeveloped areas (i.e., areas that can be developed only at great cost or by squatter settlements) are discarded. The percentage of this area with respect to the total area of the circumference is then an approximate mean of the barriers of discontinuity for a uniform order of the model of the city. Excluding the sea, one finds that cities like Caracas, La Paz, Bogotá, and Lima, have more than 75% of their totally undeveloped areas within the existing natural barriers.

Other characteristic differences found in Latin American cities are the location of squatter settlements along the periphery, the absence of industry in the central areas, and the large variety of technologies applied in different sectors of a city. This last characteristic is often an expression of the marked differences in income, power and cultural values. Other Latin American urban characteristics, however, are similar to those of European and North American urban areas, namely, suburbanization of the middle and upper classes, resulting in the increasing use of the automobile and the congestion of the commercial core.

Several major forces producing the patterns just described can easily be identified, although one must bear in mind a complex group of various forces, each acting in a greater or lesser degree at the same time.

Influence of Population Growth and Peripheral Settlements on Urban Structure

The population growth of Latin America, with its increasing migration from rural areas to the cities, is dramatically shown in the proliferation of areas of precarious housing on the periphery of the urbanized areas or in zones within the urban texture that had previously remained unused. The increase of population density in the peripheral areas is due to a centrifugal movement of both low- and high-income groups away from the center of the city. The automobile has allowed the high-income groups to settle in the peripheral suburbs, taking advantage of the cheaper land there. This is also a familiar phenomenon in the cities of the United States. The significant difference in the case of Latin American cities, however, is the simultaneous migration of the low-income groups to the periphery.[3] Multiple reasons account for this movement of the population. Among these are: (a) the existence of land of little economic value, for either commercial or agricultural purposes on the outskirts of

[3] In Caracas, according to the 1961 census we find that the district of San Agustín, located in the center of the city, presents the lower rate of increase of population density per district. The rate of increase for the city is 92.5%; the rate for San Agustín, 9%. A similar phenomenon occurs in Lima, according to the 1961 census. The central district again has the lowest rate of increase of population density. These facts tend to indicate that cities are not growing through central slums but rather through the peripheral suburban sprawl.

the city (the case, for example, with the desert lands that surround Lima); (b) the availability of large spaces of public land on the periphery; (c) the existence of a large housing shortage[4] which has led to much overcrowding of the central areas, which allows little space for residential building in locations taken up for commercial and government use; (d) the fact that most of the low-income groups have come from rural areas and prefer the peripheral areas,

[4] In Latin America cities there is a tremendous gap between the increase of population and the availability of housing. For instance, Luis Dorich, in Hauser's *Urbanization in Latin America* (New York: International Documents Service, Columbia University, 1961), p. 281, notes that in Lima, between 1949 and 1956, 45,712 dwellings were built, while the population in the same period increased by 76,000 families. On the other hand, Harris and Hosse in *Housing in Perú*, p. 439, have pointed out that in Lima in 1960, less than four new dwellings per thousand inhabitants were built, while the city was growing at an annual rate of over 5%. Although these figures give us an idea of the housing need and supply in Lima alone, the situation is not much different from the other Latin American countries.

Bogotá, Colombia is located on a high plateau limited by a mountain range to the east and the swamp and Bogotá River to the west. Photo by author.

Panama City, a linear-shaped city. Photo by author.

where they at least have their own shelter and sometimes a small lot to cultivate.[5]

The movement of the low-income groups toward the periphery is more apparent in the cities that have had a high rate of population increase without industrialization. In Caracas and Lima, for instance, a high percentage of the total population lives in squatter settlements (see table 7.1), while in cities such as Buenos Aires or São Paulo the percentage is much lower. The location of squatter settlements in the periphery may sometimes be explained by the fact that natural barriers, the hills, swamps, flooded areas, bordering railroad lines or industrial areas, have prevented other types of development in these areas. In other cases original owners did not develop these peripheral areas in the deliberate hope that the value of the land would increase without any effort on their part. This

---

[5] In interviews done by the National Housing Corporation of Perú (Corporación Nacional de la Vivienda), people living in central slums of the city have shown a higher preference for living in the peripheral barriadas.

TABLE 7.1

LATIN AMERICA: PERCENTAGE OF POPULATION
RESIDING IN SQUATTER SETTLEMENTS

CITY	TYPE OF HOUSING	YEAR	POPULATION (%)
Rio de Janeiro	Favela	1961	38.0
Recife	Favela	1961	50.0
Guanabara	Favela	1960	10.2
Lima	Barriada	1961	21.0
Arequipa	Barriada	1961	40.0
Chimbote	Barriada	1961	70.0
México City	Colonia Proletaria	1952	24.9
Caracas	Rancho	1953	38.5

SOURCE: *Economic Study of Latin America* (New York: United Nations, 1963), pp. 168–69.

A small Central American City. Photo by author.

common type of speculation allowed large expanses of land to remain empty for many years thus becoming readily available for invasion by squatter populations. Peripheral settlements which have developed since 1930 in the majority of first-rank cities today represent between 10 and 50 percent of the newly developed areas in those cities.

In Rio de Janeiro, in little more than a decade (1947–1960) marginal settlements have grown from 17% to 38% of the total population (table 7.2). In Caracas, these settlements represent about 38% of the total population. In Lima, the growth of barriadas represents an unprecedented change in the structure of the city, extending it enormously, for one should properly consider these barriadas as an integral part of the city even though they are sometimes completely separated from the traditional city core and lack the most elementary urban and community services. The popular image of the city with a high density center becoming less dense toward the periphery until it disappears into rural terrain, has little validity, since the marginal populations now have densities almost as high as those of the center-city.

TABLE 7.2

LATIN AMERICA: INCREASE IN THE
NUMBER OF SQUATTER SETTLEMENTS

COUNTRY	YEAR	HOUSING	OCCUPANTS	POPULATION (%)
Chile	1952	130,000 [a]	645,000	10.9
	1960	196,000 [a]	1,044,000	14.2
Venezuela	1950	409,000 [b]	2,143,000	45.8
	1961	494,000 [b]	2,488,000	34.6
Honduras	1949	39,000 [c]		
	1961	56,000 [c]		
Brazil				
(Rio de Janeiro)	1947	Favelas	400,000	17.0
	1960	Favelas	900,000	38.0
(E. of Guanabara)	1950	58 Favelas	159,000	7.1
	1960	147 Favelas	337,000	10.2

SOURCE: *Economic Study of Latin America*, pp. 168–69.
NOTES:
  a. Pieza de conventillo, rancho, hut or callampa.
  b. Rancho.
  c. Houses with cane and straw walls.

Bogotá, Colombia, showing the downtown area. Courtesy USIS–Bogotá.

It has been calculated that some barriadas in Lima have densities of 400 inhabitants per hectare, compared with a density of 200 inhabitants per hectare in the city center. In Santiago, the callampa population reaches a density of 150 inhabitants per hectare, compared with some 200 inhabitants per hectare in the center-city.

The rapid growth of peripheral settlements has been aggravated by the fact that it has not been possible to provide adequate urban utilities in proportion to the needs of the new population. Poor provisional sanitary systems are constructed and often remain unchanged. A Santiago publication in 1966 referred to these problems in the following terms: "Because of lack of funds, only 75% of the urban area of Santiago has sewer service, and scarcely 50% has installations for rain water drainage . . . preference is given to the sewers; rain water drainage systems are left uninstalled." The problems of flooding and landslides in the favelas of Rio de Janeiro are well known. In 1963, México City had 40% of its population living

in zones without electricity, 150 colonias proletarias largely accounting for this deficit.[6] In Caracas, the super-blocks with densities of
620 inhabitants per hectare represented an attempt to consolidate
a standard of high densities in the periphery. But again no utilities
and transportation facilities were provided. As a result, the peripheral populations remained practically isolated and were never really
integrated into the structure of the city. The problem was intensified
since the majority of the population had to resort to more than two
means of public transportation in order to reach their jobs. It could
perhaps be argued that low-cost peripheral lands are the only ones
which can be acquired in large enough quantities to solve the housing problem for low-income populations. But unless communal
facilities and adequate means of transportation are provided, this
is not a real solution to the problem.

Industry presents a particular case in the allocation of peripheral
settlements. First, it should be remembered that industry has generally had only secondary importance in Latin American countries:
the primary economic activities of agriculture and mining still pre-

[6] See *Ercilla*, 27 April 1966; *Time*, 21 Jan. 1966, under Residential and *Visión*,
10 Dec. 1965, under Residential for articles on these subjects.

dominate over the secondary and tertiary activities, namely industry and services, in the employment structure. Industry has developed very slowly. For instance, Perú had the same percentage of total labor force engaged in industry both in 1950 and in 1960. Secondly, industry in Latin American countries is usually concentrated in one city, the capital, although in most of these cities there is a higher percentage of the city's total labor force engaged in the tertiary economic sector than in the secondary sector. In some cases, such as that of Lima, 75% of the total industrial labor force of the country is employed within this particular city. Only recently has industry started to become an important factor in the life of Latin American cities. Traditionally cities have been administrative and not industrial centers. This has influenced the location of industries within the cities, because industrial sites were developed after the cities had already been established and had grown—a pattern different from that in more developed countries, where people were originally attracted to the cities by the industries located in them. But in the last decades, the existing industrial zones of the large cities have expanded while many other such zones have sprung up in new sectors on the periphery. But the advantage of locating in-

Guatemala City, showing the central park, National Palace left, and the cathedral, right.

dustries near the peripheral populations which is predominantly comprised of workers is in every case reduced by the lack of adequate means of transportation.

In some cases, very specific needs determine the allocation of peripheral settlements; for example, university centers have become a focus of residential density on the periphery of México City, Bogotá, Caracas, Santiago. Similarly, the locations of stadiums generate and focus density patterns. In some instances, as in Caracas, it is not strange to find populations of scattered squatter towns within sectors of high-income housing—both in excellent new residential areas in the center of the city and in areas of older housing. This discontinuity of urban dwelling is, indeed, largely a reflection of a whole range of different types of discontinuities—natural, economic, social and technological—which give physical form to the city. The following case study of the barriadas in Lima underscores the influence of peripheral settlements on the form and structure of a major Latin American metro-city.

Barriadas in Lima: A Case Study

In Perú the word for an urban squatter settlement, barriada, is the equivalent of the Brazilian favela, the Venezuelan rancho or the Mexican colonia proletaria. Each country of the world has its own term for the region where the rate of urbanization has outstripped planning and building legislation and where cities are growing faster than those of the already urbanized and industrialized world.

The typical image which a barriada suggests—particularly to wealthier nations and even the wealthier classes of the poorer nations—is of the worst kind of slum; miserable shanty towns in which the poorest of the world's poor suffer miserable lives. Although this may indeed be the true picture in some areas, it is important to realize that in the Latin American context, this image does not adequately convey the real nature of the barriada phenomenon.

The barriada population in Lima has grown from an estimated 100,000 in 1958 (then about 10% of the total population) to an estimated 400,000 in 1964 which is over 20% of the total. This rapid growth, however, is merely another reflection of the high rate of urbanization experienced by Lima in the last two decades. The barriadas, in effect, represent the single most important physical

Belo Horizonte, Brazil. © *Manchete.*

expression of the present urbanization process in Latin America. As described earlier in this chapter, they constitute peripheral settlements of low-income groups. But today most barriada populations are not, by Peruvian and even by Lima standards, extremely poor. This fact is of course contradictory to the prevailing general opinion on economic conditions in squatter settlements and to the physical appearance of improvised shacks. Recent research has shown that generally the lives the people lead in their barriadas are a considerable improvement over their former condition, whether in the city slums from which they moved to the barriada or in the rural towns from which they moved into the city slums. A barriada family usually has its own plot of land and at least part of a fairly well-built dwelling which will be completed eventually, even though without such public utilities as water and sewers.[7]

[7] See Harris and Hosse, *Housing in Perú*, p. 588; and John C. Turner, "Dwelling Resources in South America," in *Architectural Design*, 33 (August 1963).

A scene in Cartagena, Colombia. Photo by author.

If the frequent and partially erroneous translation of barriada into English as slum has resulted in misconceptions outside of Latin America, the same misconception led the Peruvian upper and middle class into paranoic fear of a "cinturón de miseria"—a misery belt—surrounding the city and ready to cut it off and invade the residential areas to seize the homes of the wealthy. From the standpoint of the outside observer who lives in more sophisticated and economically developed countries these attitudes and conclusions are certainly comprehensible, for a barriada—especially in its earlier

Rio de Janeiro, Brazil © Manchete

stages of development—looks very much like a slum, and, by the usual definitions of slums as substandard dwellings, some barriada dwellings are slums. A distinction must, however, be made between the barriadas created before and after 1940. Most barriadas dating before 1940 have retained their slum characteristics and are few in number and located mainly in the eastern sector of the city. An example of this earlier type is shown in figure 7.1 where a chaotic agglomeration of shacks predominates. By contrast, the majority of barriadas dating from the early 1950s, mainly concentrated in the northern district of Carabayllo, have developed into highly formalized urban geometrical grid constructions (fig. 7.2). Fortunately, recent close contact with the people and a better understanding of them and their problems has changed official attitudes and policies in Perú; but only a few years ago barriadas were often regarded by technicians and administrators as a slum blight to be eradicated or a cancerous growth to be suppressed.[8]

[8] See Humberto Rodríguez-Camilloni, "The Barriada Problem in Lima Today" (unpublished paper, Yale University, New Haven, Conn., 1965).

FIG. 7.1 *A squatter settlement in Lima. Reprinted from Walter D. Harris and Hans A. Hossé,* Housing in Perú *(Washington, D. C.: Pan American Union, 1963). Reprinted by permission of the publisher.*

Fig. 7.2 *Pampas de Comas, an improved squatter settlement in Lima. Reprinted from Harris and Hossé*, Housing in Perú. *Reprinted by permission of the publisher.*

BARRIADA VERSUS CORRALÓN

It is also necessary to differentiate the barriada from the corralón, or center-city slum, which to the casual observer in Lima might appear to be indistinguishable from one another. The construction form of both the barriada and the corralón may appear to be a jumble of cane matting or adobe shacks. However, in spite of the superficial similarity, there are important differences. The barriada dwelling will almost certainly be improved either by self-help or government assistance, while the corralón will stagnate or decay. The great majority of corralónes are situated on small plots near the city center, market areas, or any other source of casual or unskilled labor. The barriadas are situated at some distance from the city center, along secondary roads; and they are much larger. Housing reports and personal interviews with the people reveal that the majority of the corralón inhabitants are appreciably poorer than the majority living in the barriadas; that the barriada inhabitant have lived in the

city a good deal longer; and that the corralónes constitute the principal reception site for rural immigrants. The general settlement
pattern of rural immigrants in barriadas and corralónes can be sum-
marized as follows: Inhabitants of the barriadas either come directly
to it or move first to the corralón. Thus, while the settlement in a
corralón is usually a one-stage movement, a barriada settlement
often occurs in two stages. A population will invade a corralón
directly after migrating from a rural town to Lima. A barriada, on
the other hand, will tend to be occupied by low-income populations
who have resided in Lima for some time. The corralón is often the
immigrant's or the destitute's best available solution for his housing
problem, since it represents the cheapest available accommodation
and is located near centers of casual employment. In the case of the
outlying barriada, immediate settlement by a rural immigrant is
restricted by the fact that barriada inhabitants have to pay for some
utilities and for transportation to their work centers.[9]

The barriada and the corralón have different origins and functions
as well as different destinies, despite the fact that they are both
types of clandestine settlement and superficially similar. The typical
corralón was previously, say twenty to forty years ago, a market
gardener's small holding. Then the owner or tenant found it more
profitable to sell or to rent tiny plots to immigrants or to families
evicted from other center-city slums. In the rare cases when the
population of these shanty settlements has become relatively stable,
all that the families have been able to do to improve their condition
is to turn their cane-matting shacks into adobe huts, as the tenancy
of their extremely small plots is too uncertain to justify the investment of any hard-earned savings that they may manage to accumu-
late. It is evident that sooner or later these isolated slum settlements,
often blocking the completion of city developments around them,
must be demolished and their inhabitants moved elsewhere.

The origin of the typical barriada is totally different. In the first
place, it is usually started by organized groups of families, some

[9] According to Harris and Hosse (*Housing in Perú*, p. 588) existing housing in
these squatter settlements is of a temporary and makeshift nature, and the community is largely made up of people who have organized with the specific objective
of eventual home ownership. "The fact that these families are residents in these areas
does not imply that they came, or presently are, without means or even savings. It is
not uncommon to encounter people in squatter settlements who have substantial
funds and can afford to make regular savings which they frequently want to invest
in housing."

threatened with eviction from center-city slums scheduled for demolition to make way for city improvements or new buildings, others unwilling to go on living in corralónes and determined to build themselves a better house in more open and healthier surroundings. In most cases, these families are led by a small group interested in the chances of profit through the control of the distribution of land. Hence, they select and invade a suitable area of marginal desert land belonging to the government. The de facto possession of the occupied land, together with the scale of such invasions and the political problems posed by attempting to frustrate them (without providing adequate alternatives), have often guaranteed their success.

The barriada, albeit slowly, as it will take the average family about twenty years to complete its house without the assistance of credit, will develop into a typical working- and lower-class suburb. In contrast, the corralón crystallizes into a typical labyrinth of slum courts which can only deteriorate and must eventually be eradicated.

Local geographical and cultural conditions are the bases of the differentiation of these two types of settlement in Lima. Yet in other cities and in quite a few areas of Lima itself, the barriada and the corralón are mixed. Real slums and quite respectable dwellings inevitably exist side by side in Lima as well as in the other major Latin American cities. But it is clear that if the two situations—that of the immigrant or destitute family seeking temporary shelter and that of the established family seeking better housing conditions— are confused the outcome will be a false formulation of the problem, which will in turn produce an unfortunate delay in the search for successful solutions.

LOCATION OF MAJOR BARRIADAS

The geographical location of the major barriadas in Lima is shown on map 7.1. Three distinct groups may be observed: a northern group in the Carabayllo district, often referred to as the Carabayllo complex; a central group between the districts of Lima and Callao or San Martín de Porres group; and a southern group scattered between the districts of Lima and Pachacamac. Most of the barriadas composing these three groups originated after 1940 and developed the characteristics of low-income suburban settlements briefly out-

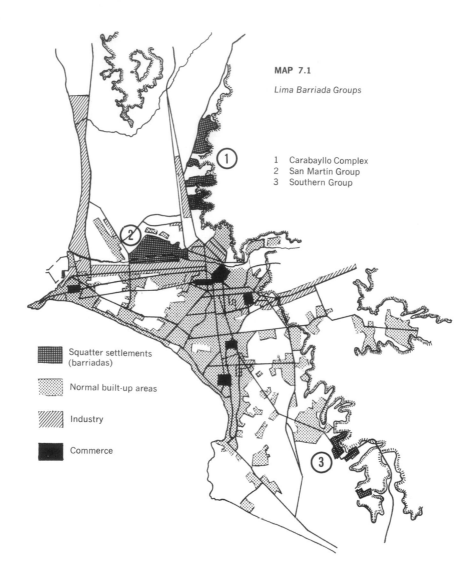

MAP 7.1

Lima Barriada Groups

1   Carabayllo Complex
2   San Martin Group
3   Southern Group

Squatter settlements
(barriadas)

Normal built-up areas

Industry

Commerce

lined above. All of them account for more than 80% of the physical growth experience by the metropolitan area of Lima from 1940 to 1960.

As pointed out in Chapter 6, Lima has been growing into a semi-circular form since 1950. The predominant tendency has been a linear growth in a northward and southward direction. It is evident from map 7.1 that this growth is but a direct expression of the expansion of the barriada groups, particularly of the northern and southern groups. In fact, these two groups alone account for the typical barriada settlement pattern, namely, the filling of the finger valleys forming a vertical chain running parallel to the Pan American Highway, the major access road to the center-city. The invasion of these valleys was most frequently carried out by organized groups and their success was guaranteed by the free appropriation of readily available desert land.

The Carabayllo complex consists of six major barriadas founded from 1958 to 1963, with populations varying from 970 to 5900 families. Nearest to the district of Lima in this group is Pampa El Ermitaño with 1800 families, dating from 1962. This barriada and Pampa de Cuevas immediately next to and above (invasion 1960, approximately 2000 families) present two cases of dynamic settlement and self-help improvement. The simple geometrical order given to both plans facilitated the fast allocation of plots with the necessary provision for the installment of basic urban utilities. It is interesting to compare the street layout of these two barriadas with that of the Tahuantinsuyo Project, a government-planned development for 4800 plots begun between 1961–62. Although the Tahuantinsuyo Project presents a looser plan, the basic layout is strikingly similar to those of the unaided self-help barriada settlements. It is located between Pampa de Cuevas and Pampa de Comas, the oldest and largest unaided self-help barriada in the Carabayllo complex (invasion 1958, approximately 5900 families). Barriadas Santa Rosa y Uchumayo (invasion 1959, approximately 970 families), Señor de los Milagros (invasion 1959, approximately 2000 families) and El Carmen (invasion 1961, approximately 2000 families) immediately adjacent to Comas complete the Carabayllo complex.

The San Martín de Porres or central barriada group differs fundamentally from the Carabayllo complex in origin and general characteristics. Chronologically, this group is much older. Invasions occurred between 1950 and 1952. It has an estimated population of 15,940 families. Fig. 7.3 shows a panoramic view of sections of Mirones and San Martín de Porres, separated by the Rimac River. But whereas the general plan presents a similar layout to that of Comas or most other barriadas in the northern group, San Martín has improved its conditions at a comparatively slow rate (until 1962 or twelve years after the invasion there were no public utilities) and many dwellings still retain typical slum characteristics. This would seem to suggest a substandard barriada, in general contrast to

Fig. 7.3 *Sections of Mirones and San Martín de Porras in Lima. Reprinted from Harris and Hossé,* Housing in Perú. *Reprinted by permission of the publisher.*

the Carabayllo complex. The proximity of San Martín to the center-city could probably explain, at least in part, the relatively lower standard of this barriada. The location of San Martín de Porres, in fact, is very close to the industrial corridor between Lima and Callao, offering easy, economical transportation to the working centers as well as the other benefits of direct attachment to the center-city. The urbanization of San Martín as a process of filling in of the empty areas between Lima and Callao could probably be compared to the filling in process between Lima and Chorrillos through the first decades of the present century. A basic difference, however, distinguishes the two processes: Lima and Chorillos became integrated through the urbanization of middle-income and high-income housing in the districts of San Isidro, Miraflores, and San Antonio; San Martín still represents the typical post-1940 low-income suburban development. By 1960 San Martín had reached its present size (approximately 15,940 families). Additional horizontal expansion was then prevented by two government-aided projects begun in 1961 located at the northern limits of barriada San Martín. These were the Conde Villa Señor and Valdivieso projects, to house approximately 2,750 families. Another factor which impeded the growth of San Martín was the new International Airport in Callao, which promoted a number of other government housing projects in the nearby areas.

FORMATION OF THE BARRIADAS: PAMPA DE COMAS

The development of urban squatter settlements in our time has not been confined to Latin American cities. In the wake of the physical devastation and economic dislocation brought about by the heavy bombings during World War II, the appearance of squatter settlements amidst the ruins of European cities was a not uncommon phenomenon. Similar agglomerations of makeshift housing are also to be found in developing countries in Africa and in the Middle and Far East. What distinguishes the postwar situation in Europe from the other cases is that in Europe this phenomenon was largely temporary. In Latin America, on the other hand, squatter settlements seem likely to become a permanent feature of the urban landscape.

In the case of Perú, one of the prime reasons for this is the continuing migration of people from rural areas to the urban centers. Indeed, there appears to be a direct correlation between the increasing percentage of rural migration to Lima and the growth of barriadas during recent decades.[10] In Lima, Arequipa and other major urban centers, the proportion of city-born dwellers in the barriadas is insignificant. The barriadas of Lima, for example, have few limeños. According to statistics, almost all the people in the barriadas originally came from the central and southern Andean

[10] The following is a chronological scale of the arrival to the barriadas in Lima: 1901–1910, 0.06%; 1911–1920, 0.42%; 1921–1930, 1.91%; 1931–1940, 7.11%; 1941–1950, 17.43%; 1951–1959, 73.07%. From Fondo de Salud y Bienestar Social, 1960, in Pablo Berkholtz-Salinas, *Barrios Marginales Aberración Social* (Lima, 1963), p. 36.

regions.[11] It may be pertinent to review at this point some of the primary motivations for these large rural migrations.

In April of 1961, a special symposium was held in Lima to study the causes of the continuous migration of the indigenous population to the coast.[12] The phenomenon was discussed as one of the most important sociological problems of the country. The participants eventually divided into two groups: Group 1 argued that the determinant factor of the migration was economic, while Group 2 stated that "social mobility" was the main factor. The former group maintained that a poor social and economic structure was the origin of poverty in the provinces, which in turn promoted the displacement of the rural dwellers to the large urban centers. The latter group, on the other hand, without ignoring the economic issues, gave prior importance to what they called factors of social mobility —emergency situations such as droughts or floods which caused sudden migrations of people who remained without any immediate economic prospects. The truth is, of course, that the factors cannot be limited to either group. The migration of such large numbers of people is no doubt the result of multiple factors, varying from family to family and person to person.

From the point of view of modern urban technology, barriadas still constitute inorganic portions of the city, for they lack the basic public utilities which in today's conception of urban life would be considered as requisite—namely, water supply, sewage, electricity, paved streets and sidewalks. To the sociologist this represents a problem of the transportation of people under the most precarious conditions: health in constant danger, a complete absence of education for children, an almost complete lack of economic capital, and no employment opportunities, though many willing hands seek work. In short, the basic problem appears to be one of a total disproportion between needs and resources. For a more specific view of the problem we turn to the results of a 1962 census of Pampa de Comas.

Pampa de Comas, with a population of about 30,000, forms part of the Carabyllo complex which has a total population of about 100,000. Dating from 1957, Comas is the oldest barriada in this

---

[11] See *Barriadas de Lima: Actitudes de los habitantes respecto a servicios públicos y privados* (Lima: Centro de Investigaciones Sociales por Muestreo, Ministerio de Trabajo y Comunidades, 1967), p. 42.

[12] Berckholtz-Salinas, *Aberración Social*, p. 38.

northern group. The initial invasion was begun by a group of families that had first settled in a slum in the center of Lima from which it had then been evicted. Two thousand families were interviewed along the 6 sq. km. extension of Comas. Results were recorded as percentages of the total of 2,000 families, and were as follows:[13]

1. Why did you come to Lima? Answers:
   51.33%—to work
   31.86%—to improve economic conditions (which is actually the same as "to work," hence adding to a total of 83.19%)
   10.50%—to join the family
   2.95%—to provide a better education for the children
   1.18%—obligatory military service
   1.18%—medical treatment

2. Why did you move from the city to the barriada? Answers:
   33.50%—lack of sufficient income to make life possible in the city
   57.0 %—to obtain a free lot of land and build a shelter
   3.0 %—impossible to afford costs of housing in Lima
   6.0 %—clearance of city shelter previously occupied (corralónes)
   0.5 %—to join other members of the family

3. Distribution of the population by sex and relationship to the head of the family:

Males 51.75%	Sons and daughters 75.53%
Females 48.25%	Wives 22.42%
	Other relatives 2.74%
	Friends, guests 1.30%

4. Distribution of the barriada population by age:

Age	%	Age	%
1—5	30.61	31—35	6.70
6—10	16.08	36—40	5.56
11—15	5.90	41—45	1.83
16—20	6.08	46—50	1.13
21—25	9.69	51—55	1.33
26—30	11.42	56—60	1.13

5. Do you have a permanent job? Answers:
   61.30% ...... permanent job
   38.13% ...... work only occasionally

[13] Ibid., pp. 43–47.

6. Monthly income of each family:

S/. (soles)[14]	%	S/. (soles)	%
150–300	8.62	900–1200	15.76
300–600	20.64	1200–1500	4.88
600–900	35.86	1500–1800	1.08

From these results, several important conclusions may be drawn:

(a) the percentage of children is high and accounts for more than one-half of the total population of the barriada of Comas;

(b) the percentage of the population above 35 years of age is relatively low;

(c) there are no people older than 60;

(d) only relatively few of the inhabitants suffer extreme poverty.

These statistics become all the more important when one realizes that the many improvements made in Pampa de Comas since the original invasion were entirely organized *and carried out by spontaneously formed associations of low-income groups*, there being no positive government intervention until 1961. Thus, Comas' present healthy physical aspect is an exemplary demonstration of the common people's initiative and the success of a self-help communal effort. Most houses in Comas are today either in their second or third stages of development.[15] Public utilities have already been installed and there are several schools.

Official government policies and agencies concerned with the barriada problem are many and varied. An important agency is the National Office of Urban and Regional Planning[16] which is an autonomous body whose main function is to act in an advisory capacity to the national and municipal governments. It is responsible for zoning and subdivision controls, the preparation of urban development plans, including aspects of long-range planning, and other related urban land-use matters. The actual implementation and execution of land-use plans and regulations prepared by this agency rests with the national and local governments.

Development controls for areas that present special problems to general urban growth were included in legislation passed in 1961 dealing with the rehabilitation and improvements of marginal squatter settlements. The National Housing Board is responsible for the enforcement of this legislation. The legislation provides for the

[14] Under the 1962 exchange rate, S/. 26.80 (soles) = 1 US $.
[15] Turner, *Dwelling Resources*, p. 375.
[16] Harris and Hossé, *Housing in Perú*, pp. 633–42.

control of future growth in areas surrounding the major urban centers. A special section deals with the legislation of property occupied by squatters and includes provisions for the establishment of appropriate community services in these problem areas. Provision is also made for some form of density control by limiting the gross density to 125 inhabitants per acre (300 per hectare). This regulation is intended to discourage the formation of new settlements without the consent of the Board. In particular, it declares all squatter settlements and other marginal developments in urban fringe areas illegal when undertaken outside the provisons of the legislation. As a means of enforcement, the Board has the right to withdraw financial aid to illegal settlements and to withhold aid to new developments.

Subdivision of new land and its incorporation into the urban complex play an important part in the expansion of cities. Regulations on subdivisions in Lima require a minimum lot size of 160 sq. m. with 8 m. frontage and 20 m. depth. Lots in most squatter settlements still fall below the minimum acceptable size, although the size of a lot there can vary from 120 sq. m. or less, to 45 sq. m. The type of housing built in the squatter areas usually does not allow for any front or side setbacks. Thus, even though a subdivision control code is in force, a substantial amount of Lima's recent urban development in squatter settlements has been outside the minimum standards.

In new housing projects sponsored by the state, minimum subdivision standards are applied. The satellite town of Ventanilla is an excellent example. Here, adequate provisions have been made for open space for recreation and other necessary neighborhood amenities such as schools, churches, and shopping facilities. It is fully recognized that congested major urban centers can be relieved of high densities and exorbitant population pressures by this type of satellite development; however, special attention must be paid to the provision of adequate transportation connections with the parent city and the provision of appropriate community services.

Under the application of Law 13517 for legislation and improvement of squatters settlements, 1964, 7,409 property titles were given to the people by the State and 11,691 lots were remodelled.[17] A sample distribution among the barriadas was as follows:

17 *El Perú Construye* (Lima, 1964), p. 299.

Squatter Settlements	*Property Titles*	*Lots*
El Carmen	40	
San Martín de Porres	2,202	
Mirones Bajo	526	
Santa Rosa-Comas	958	2,305
Señor de Los Milagros	1,581	900
Pampa de Comas	152	
Uchumayo		89
El Ermitaño		2,204

The barriada problem in Lima has often been approached solely in terms of the urban context. But obviously, in dealing with people who migrate from their rural homes in order to better satisfy their basic needs, the focus of action cannot be confined merely to the urban areas to which they come. Action must also be directed toward improving the rural conditions which pressed them to migrate in the first place.

The continuing migration of the indigenous population to the coast (and, hence, the continuing formation of barriadas), can certainly not be controlled unless living conditions in the highlands are improved. What is called for is a new approach both to rural and urban development. Such an approach requires coordinated effort by the government, the church, and all other significant political, social, and economic forces in the country, as well as the use of both private and public capital.

The improvement of living conditions in the highlands requires basic rural economic and social development, and to achieve this agrarian reform will have to be accelerated. But how does agrarian reform affect the barriadas? To begin with, Perú's economy is primarily based on agriculture and approximately 6 million people (the majority illiterate) work in agriculture. Yet the country has less than 0.5 acre of cultivated land per inhabitant. The low percentage of cultivated land, in turn, determines the low average income of the population. The situation is further complicated by the absence of capital and technological instruments to increase productivity of the cultivated lands.

An increase in the average income per inhabitant can be achieved in two ways: (a) through increase in productivity, and; (b) assuming a certain level of productivity, through an increase in income per man engaged in primary production, in relation to the income of the industrial countries which import part of the production. Productivity, in turn, is increased by: (a) adoption of modern techniques; and (b) a more efficient distribution of personnel so that optimum productivity can be obtained.

Through the agrarian reform the native farmer is given a piece of land to work with the necessary implements and ultimately becomes the owner of his property by gradually paying back the state with a percentage of his production. But technical training, systems of loans and credits, and cooperatives are just a few of the many facilities that are still urgently needed on a large scale. Further attention should also be given to improving the relations between the large land owners and the small farmers.

Nevertheless, even if measures for the overall improvement of rural life are vigorously pursued by all the relevant public and private agencies, it is still likely that squatter settlements will persist because there are a variety of complex factors that contribute to their existence. The continuing increase in population is one. The concentration of industry—a growing phenomenon—is another. By opening up new employment opportunities this process will inevitably attract increasing migration from rural areas even if conditions in these areas are improved. Legislation that simply prohibits the creation of new squatter settlements and uncontrolled developments in the marginal areas of urban centers cannot be effective. Instead the problem must be met by regional planning efforts directed at guiding migration into predetermined and well-prepared reception areas. This would benefit both the rural areas from which the migration stems and the urban areas to which it is directed. For whenever a serrano leaves the highlands he often disrupts the economic and social balance in his area, creating a problem there as well as in the urban center to which he moves. Thus every effort must be made to prevent premature abandonment of productive areas and so to delay the migratory movement. Such migration as does take place should be channeled to urban centers that have the facilities to absorb the new arrivals. Unless this can be done the squatter settlements will increasingly become sources of instability and decay in the urban centers of Perú.[18]

In the case of Lima there is one very special factor that must be taken into account, namely, its role as the seat of a highly centralized government. Perú, for many, is the metropolitan city called Lima.

---

[18] Harris and Hosse, *Housing in Perú*, pp. 641–42.

To stem the tide of migration to Lima it is essential that steps be taken toward political, economic, and social decentralization. Coupled with enlightened and dynamic rural development, such decentralization could go a long way toward decreasing the rate of migration to Lima, and this, in turn, would enable the city to provide better economic opportunities, better housing, and a generally improved standard of living for its inhabitants.

This chapter opened with a discussion of some of the major historical and geographical factors that have in the past influenced the form and structure of Latin American cities. We then focused on two factors which have in recent times assumed increasing importance in shaping Latin American urban areas: the rapid increase in urban population; and the related proliferation of squatter settlements on the periphery of urbanized areas. A case study of the barriadas in Lima, Perú, was presented as a concrete illustration of this increasingly widespread phenomenon. In the next chapter we examine the general pattern of the physical structure of Latin American cities.

8

Patterns of Urban Structure
in Latin America

Physical Structure of Cities

THE shape and size of a city may reflect quite accurately its complexity and stages of development. In general, small cities conform to a linear or circular shape with little or no functional differentiation between adjacent areas. Large metropolises acquire rather more complicated forms, usually fan-shaped, with more or less distinct functions between one area and another, particularly in terms of land use. Quite naturally, the shapes of cities evolve by growth or transformation from an original circular, semicircular or linear pattern (see Chapter 7, pp. 206–08).

In many cases the phenomenon of growth is explained by the sudden development of areas that were previously considered unsuitable for settlement. The specific reasons, however, may vary from place to place. Thus, in Bogotá large estates were converted for development. In the southern region of São Paulo, artificial lakes were created. Empty desert land around Lima facilitated barriada development. New road construction promoted settlement in peripheral areas of Buenos Aires and Santiago.

DETERMINANTS OF SIZE

As can be seen from the following examples, the historical development of Latin American cities reveals a slow progression from very simple to more complex shapes.

Buenos Aires has had at least three main stages in the develop-

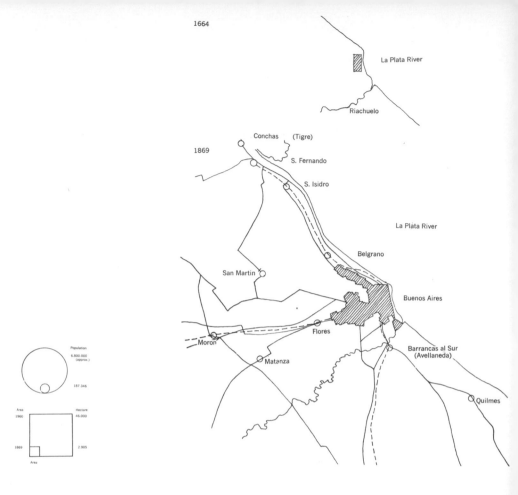

FIG. 8.1 *Buenos Aires: Historical Stages in the Development of Urban Shape: 1664, 1869, 1960.*

ment of its urban shape (see fig. 8.1).[1] The first was from its foundation in 1580, until 1870. During this period the city was compact in form, and oriented to the port. The nearby satellite towns were only small agricultural settlements, and not integrated into the core shape of Buenos Aires. From 1870 to 1940, however, these small towns experienced a rapid growth in population, and Buenos Aires began to acquire a fragmentary shape. Several factors accounted for this development. The establishment of Buenos Aires as the Federal Capital of the Argentine Republic in 1880, for instance, reinforced

---

[1] 1664 and 1849 maps of Buenos Aires from Francisco de Aparicio and Horacio di Frieri, *La Argentina Suma de Geografía*, 9 (Buenos Aires: Ediciones Pueser, 1963), pp. 37, 148. Population figures from vol. 9, p. 138. The area and population scales are based on these figures.

Buenos Aires Metropolitan Area
1960
SCALE 1:250,000

the importance of the city and attracted heavy foreign immigration. Another factor was the commercial exploitation of the agricultural products of the humid Pampa, which brought a network of railroads directed to the port of Buenos Aires. Along the railroad lines new small towns were established while the existing ones began to grow rapidly. The third stage in the evolution of the city's shape began about 1940 and continues to the present day. During this time the towns have merged and formed a single fan-shaped metropolis. The present tendency of growth is through the periphery of the fingers, although another important element has recently intruded to change the urban shape, namely, highways that do not follow the traditional urban areas but rather traverse the vacant land between the developed fingers of the city.

Caracas has had a linear shape due to its position in a deep valley

Caribbean Sea

La Guaira

1830

Caracas

Dos Caminos

Sabana Grande

Petare

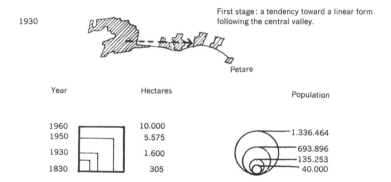

1930

First stage: a tendency toward a linear form
following the central valley.

Petare

Year		Hectares	Population
1960		10.000	1.336.464
1950		5.575	693.896
1930		1.600	135.253
1830		305	40.000

of the Caribbean coastal range (see fig. 8.2).[2] Its present shape is still linear, but more complex since growth of the city has also followed the secondary valleys that open into the central valley. Two main stages in the development of the form may be observed. The first stage, until 1930, was characterized by a linear growth structured about the spine of the central valley. The main valley was then almost completely settled and the city began to overflow. After 1930, as a result of the oil boom, Caracas witnessed a rapid increase in population. In the second stage, urban development

[2] Figure for 1830 from Pedro J. Gonzaléz, "Problemes d'Habitation a Caracas," *La Vie Urbaine* 2 (April-June, 1961): 118–21. Figures for 1930 and 1950 from Janine Brisseau, "Les barrios de Petaré," *Les Cahiers d'Outre-Mer* 61 (1963:) 8. Population figures from "Area Metropolitana de Caracas," *Noveno Censo General de Población 1961* 6 (Caracas: Ministerio de Fomento, Dirección General de Estadística y Censos Nacionales, 1964). Population and area scales based on the above.

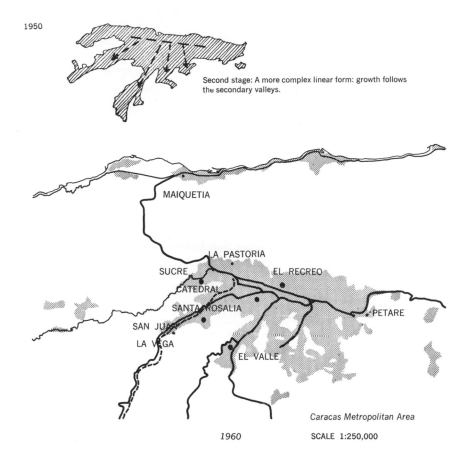

1950

Second stage: A more complex linear form: growth follows the secondary valleys.

MAIQUETIA

LA PASTORIA

SUCRE   EL RECREO

CATEDRAL

SANTA ROSALIA

SAN JUAN   PETARE

LA VEGA

EL VALLE

Caracas Metropolitan Area

1960   SCALE 1:250,000

Fig. 8.2 *Caracas: Historical Stages in the Development of Urban Shape: 1830, 1930, 1950, 1960.*

occurred not only in the valleys that open into the southern section, but also on the southern valley slopes.

São Paulo was founded in 1554 as a mission place on a small hill near the confluence of the Tietê and Tamanduatei rivers. The choice of this location was determined by the facilities for military defense and river communication. The shape of the city did not change from that time until the second half of the nineteenth century (fig. 8.3).[3]

[3] Historical maps, 1881, 1905 and 1920 from Aroldo de Azevedo, *A Cidade de São Paulo* (São Paulo: Companhia Editors Nacional, 1958). Population figures from Internation Urban Research Institute Studies, *The World's Metropolitan Areas* (Berkeley: University of California Press, 1959). Population and area scales based on the above.

São Paulo was then confined to the hill on which it was founded
with only very small settlements in its vicinity. The lowlands along
the rivers were the main physical barrier to development. A second
period in the development of urban shape occurred from 1870–80
to 1920–30. During this time the city began to expand, due to an
increase in the production of coffee and cotton and to the establishment of industries within the metropolitan area. The railroad lines
were a major influence on the physical shape of the city which, in
order to avoid the hilly areas, were laid along the valley of the Tieté
River (toward Rio de Janeiro and the interior of the state) and the
Tamanduatei River (toward Santos). The urban area in this period
was composed of fragmentary units divided mainly by the rivers.
A third period in the formation of São Paulo started in the 1920s. By

1881   Tieté River

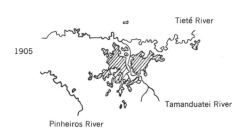

1905   Tieté River

Tamanduatei River

Pinheiros River

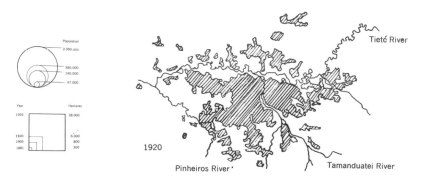

1920   Tietó River

Pinheiros River   Tamanduatei River

that time the work to channel the rivers had begun. The dams and lakes in the southern section of the city were created, and a new layout of radial avenues starting from the city was established. Today the city has continued to grow along the main avenues while industry has taken advantage of new flat land along the rivers for its location.

Lima was founded in 1535 in the Rimac Valley, approximately five miles from the sea. The original layout of the city was the typical Spanish colonial gridiron plan—a square seven blocks to a side, with each block 400 square feet. The port of Callao was established on the coast, as Lima had to perform the major role of capital of the Viceroyalty of Perú. The road connecting the port and the city re-

1955

FIG. 8.3 *São Paulo: Historical Stages in the Development of Urban Shape: 1881, 1905, 1920, 1955.*

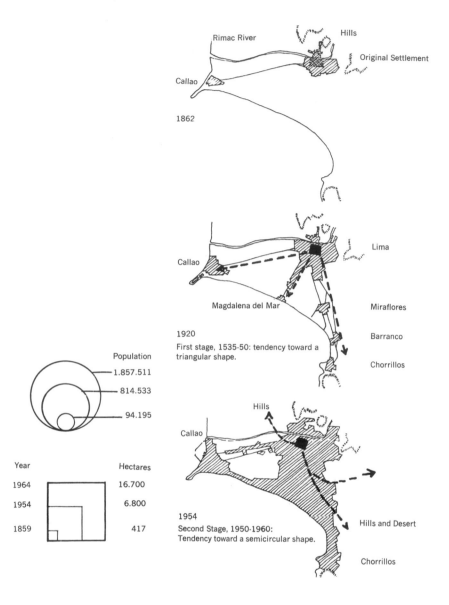

Rimac River

Hills

Original Settlement

Callao

1862

Callao

Lima

Magdalena del Mar

Miraflores

1920
First stage, 1535-50: tendency toward a
triangular shape.

Barranco

Chorrillos

Population

1.857.511

814.533

94.195

Hills

Callao

Year

Hectares

1964

16.700

1954

6.800

1859

417

1954
Second Stage, 1950-1960:
Tendency toward a semicircular shape.

Hills and Desert

Chorrillos

mained the main transportation link between the sea and the hinterland throughout the nineteenth century (see fig. 8.4).[4]

During the seventeenth century the city was fortified with walls,
as a protection against frequent pirate attacks. This contributed to a

[4] Historical maps 1862, 1920 and 1954 from *Guía de Ciudades del Perú* (Lima:
Oficina Nacional de Planeamiento y Urbanismo, 1955). Population and area scales
and population figures from J. Bromley and J. Barbagelata, *Evolución Urbana de la
Ciudad de Lima* (Lima: Publicación del Concejo Provincial de Lima, 1945), and
Guía de Ciudades del Perú.

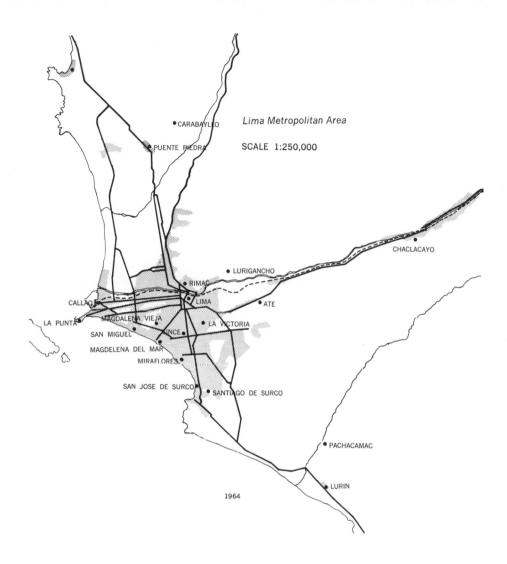

FIG. 8.4 *Lima: Historical Stages in the Development of Urban Shape:*
1862, 1920, 1954, 1964.

growth within restricted boundaries, resulting in a very compact
pattern. It was only in the second half of the nineteenth century
that these walls were demolished and the city began to expand toward the agricultural lands of the southern section of the Rimac
Valley. This expansion was facilitated by the establishment of three
main electric car lines at the beginning of the present century:
Lima-Callao, Lima-Magdallena del Mar, and Lima-Chorrillos.
Metropolitan growth, then, was clearly channeled in a southward

direction with a consequent change in the overall form of the urbanized area. Later, when the automobile arrived in Lima, avenues were laid following the pattern already established by the electric car and a large migration from the central city occurred. First, the high-income groups settled in the vicinity of Miraflores and San Isidro, taking advantage of the proximity of resorts and the availability of cheap land. Thus the area between the southern districts of Chorrillos, Barranco, Miraflores and Lima built up, and Lima acquired a triangular form with the main vertex in the center-city.

After 1950 Lima began to expand toward the folds of the hills, toward the banks of the Rimac River and toward the sections of desert land—all places that had been rejected by the city for more than four hundred years. The main reason for this new pattern of growth was the rapid increase of the urban population, a large portion of which has a very low income. The attraction of these places (the hills and desert) was that they were vacant, useless for agricultural purposes and publicly owned. The new trend of growth again changed the physical configuration of the city, and also changed former physical barriers into elements which stimulated growth.

DETERMINANTS OF SHAPE

Generally speaking, the shape of a city is conditioned by: (1) the physiographic characteristics of the site, i.e. mountains (Quito, Bogotá), rivers (Buenos Aires), desert lands (Lima), flat valleys (Caracas, La Paz); (2) the location of external nodes of economic activity in the surrounding regions, i.e. natural resources, commercial centers and tourist attractions which define the orientation of major roads, channeling and promoting development; (3) the relative magnitude of the different activities that take place in the city. The location of industry, for instance, may largely influence a general shape, since it is a real barrier which segregates surrounding residential development. A railroad line that crosses a city from one end to the other produces a similar effect. High densities may find physical expression in old residential complexes of row houses, quite different in general shape from loose, low density patterns; (4) the technology of transportation used. In Buenos Aires, a mass transit system (especially railroads) defined a finger-like form along its routes. The extensive and expanding use of the automobile in Caracas today—as in almost all first- and second-rank cities—justified the proliferation of expanded development in the fringes.

Figure 8.5 shows the shape and size of all the first-rank Latin American cities. To facilitate comparisons, all the maps were drawn

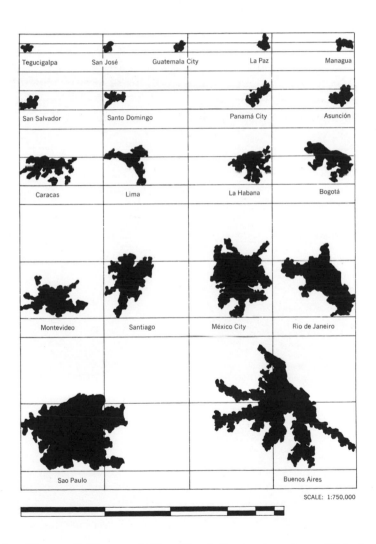

SCALE: 1:750,000

Fig. 8.5 *Size and Shape of First-Rank Latin American Cities.*

according to the same scale (1: 750,000 cm.). The cities are arranged by rank-size, from the smallest city, Tegucigalpa, to the largest city, Buenos Aires. The shape seems to be generally dependent on the size of the cities. Thus smaller cities like Managua tend to become semi-circular. As other larger semicircular cities grow in size, "fingers" begin to appear—Buenos Aires, La Habana, Montevideo. However, it is interesting to observe that the ratio between the shortest and the longest distances of developed areas measured from the center of the cities seem to be independent of the size. For example, the shortest and longest distances measured in kilometers for Managua and Montevideo are, respectively, 1.7, 4.2 and 6.0, 13.2. But the ratio between the two distances is the same in both cases, 0.4.

The recent urban population explosion, of course, has changed the shapes of most Latin American cities. But the population increase has not affected all the districts of the cities in the same way.

TABLE 8.1

CHANGE IN POPULATION DENSITY BY DISTRICT IN BUENOS AIRES
(persons per km.^{2})

	DENSITY		PERCENT
DISTRICT	1947	1957	OF CHANGE
Tigre	1.7	2.2	33.3
San Fernando	19.4	33.1	70.5
San Isidro	16.7	29.1	74.4
Vicente López	44.1	66.9	51.6
G. Sarmiento	2.4	4.3	78.9
M. Moreno	.8	1.9	125.6
Merlo	1.2	3.5	200.0
Morón	8.6	17.5	104.2
G. San Martín	27.5	47.1	71.2
Capital Federal	149.8	187.7	25.2
Avellaneda	52.6	67.9	29.1
Matanza	2.9	7.7	165.2
Echeverría	.5	1.1	118.7
A. Brown	3.6	7.8	114.8
Lomas de Zamora	12.9	20.9	62.5
Lanus	58.2	89.2	53.3
Quilmes	3.8	7.2	89.0
F. Varela	.5	1.2	129.4
Total			43.0

SOURCE: Elaborated using data from Francisco de Aparicio and Horacio di Frieri, *La Argentina, Suma de Geografía*, vol. 10 (Buenos Aires: Ediciones Peuser, 1963), p. 158.

Generally, the main increase of population density has occurred in the peripheral areas, while the central areas of the cities have lost population or have grown at a smaller rate than the whole city.[5]

The population density of Buenos Aires between 1947 and 1957 showed three kinds of changes (see table 8.1). In the central area of the metropolitan city (Federal Capital, Avellaneda), the rate of

TABLE 8.2

CHANGE IN POPULATION DENSITY BY DISTRICT IN CARACAS
(persons per km.²)

		DENSITY		PERCENT OF CHANGE	
DISTRICT	1941 [a]	1950 [b]	1961 [b]	41–50	50–61
Altagracia	61.5	85.5	105.7	38.9	23.6
Candelaria	54.6	74.0	109.8	35.3	48.3
Catedral	106.6	150.5	284.5	41.1	89.0
La Pastora	29.4	50.3	68.9	70.7	37.1
San Agustín	145.6	216.5	236.2	48.6	9.0
San José	30.4	46.0	88.3	51.1	91.9
San Juan	73.4	128.2	166.6	74.7	29.8
Santa Rosalia	34.8	78.1	147.0	127.2	88.1
Santa Teresa	78.5	84.8	146.8	8.0	72.9
Sucre	10.6	35.6	64.4	234.1	80.9
Antimano	1.5	2.7	8.4	77.7	209.9
El Recreo	14.5	30.9	56.4	111.9	82.4
El Valle	2.7	7.3	21.1	163.8	188.7
La Vega	3.8	9.7	32.1	153.9	231.0
La Baruta	.7	1.1	7.3	41.7	558.0
Chacao	34.9	12.2	30.3	250.1	148.1
El Hatillo	.2	1.4	2.0	386.2	43.9
Leoncio Martínez		7.7	20.3		162.2
Petaré		7.7	28.3		266.0
Total	9.9	19.2	37.0	93.1	92.5

SOURCES:
 a. Elaborated with data from *Plano Regulador de Caracas, Estudio Preliminar* (Caracas: Ministerio de Obras Públicas, 1951).
 b. Noveno Censo General de Población, 1961 (Caracas: Dirección Nacional de Estadística y Censo, 1964).

[5] A pilot study of this process for cities where data was readily available (Caracas, Lima, Managua and La Habana) revealed that densities consistently increase along with population until some point, which may be called the point of maturity of the city, where they start decreasing sharply. Although more similar data would be needed to sustain this theory, the pattern seems to prevail throughout Latin America, with local variations. The turning point varies in time from city to city depending upon the degree of maturity of the city.

TABLE 8.3

CHANGE IN POPULATION DENSITY BY DISTRICT IN LIMA

(persons per km.²)

	DENSITY		PERCENT
DISTRICT	1940	1961	OF CHANGE
Barranco	72.2	164.6	127.8
Bellavista	11.1	58.7	427.3
Breña	155.6	303.6	95.4
Callao	14.1	33.7	135.7
Chorrillos	1.7	7.9	364.7
Lima	75.1	112.5	49.3
Lince	106.8	276.8	160.3
La Victoria	41.6	155.0	278.0
La Punta	74.8	123.8	66.2
La Molina-Ate		4.8	
Miraflores	48.9	97.2	102.1
Magdalena del Mar	44.8	153.2	247.7
Pueblo Libre	35.7	110.6	214.3
Puente de Piedra		.5	
Rimac	22.8	57.6	159.0
Surco		14.6	
San Miguel	4.1	22.0	450.0
Surquillo		76.3	
San Isidro	9.4	39.1	333.3
Santa Rosa			
S. Martín de Porres		16.8	
Villa Maria del triunfo			
Comas			
Jesus Maria	40.8	151.4	277.5
Total	2.3	7.1	202.9

SOURCE: Elaborated with data from, Oficina National de Planeamiento y Urbanisma, Perú, density map, 1960, and Dirección Nacional de Estadística y Censo, Perú, Censo 1940.

increase was lower than that for the whole city. The second area, a peripheral one, showed the highest values; and the third area, a transition one, showed medium values. In Caracas one may observe the same pattern of increase of density; the central areas has increased its population density at a rate lower than that of the whole city, while the peripheral areas have the highest rate. The districts that have the highest rates within the peripheral areas are located outside the traditional limits of the city, that is, outside the central valley (table 8.2). In Lima there is a process of filling the areas between the major centers of the city—Lima, Callao, Miraflores—and a process of growth in the periphery of the metropolitan area. Also, the rate of population density increase presents the same pattern as

Buenos Aires and Caracas—a lower rate of increase in the old centers and a higher rate of increase in the periphery (table 8.3). The density pattern in São Paulo presents three concentric rings: the first one—the center of the city—shows a decrease in population density between 1940 and 1950. The ring is surrounded by a second ring which presents an increase that is lower than the rate of increase for the whole city. The third ring, on the other hand, shows a rate of increase higher than that for the whole city.

Generalized Residential Patterns by Income Groups

The highest population densities in Latin American cities are found in the central areas and in the peripheral areas corresponding to the squatter settlements. The central residential areas of high density generally are central slums. The high percentages of squatter settlements in cities like Caracas (38%) and Lima (21%) have practically divided these cities into two sections, each one corresponding to one income group (see map 8.1). In Caracas both the high- and the low-income groups have migrated away from the central area of the city. The high-income groups are now located in the central valley toward the east, mainly in the Chacao district, in the vicinity of the Caracas Country Club. The low-income groups have moved to the western end of the valley and are tending to expand out of the central valley. The city is thus divided into two main sectors, with low-income groups to the west, and high-income groups to the east.

In Lima the high-income groups have migrated away from the central area of the city toward the south. This migration began about 1940 and has since established a sector of high- and middle-income groups between Lima and Miraflores. The low-income groups reside in central slums, corralónes, or in peripheral squatter settlements, the barriadas.

In Buenos Aires the residential areas have grown up following the major lines of mass transit and have formed a radial pattern starting from the center of the city. The high-income groups are located in a sector that extends from the center of the city in a northward direction along the river. The low-income groups are located in the lowlands of the Matanzas River or in small nuclei

MAP 8.1

Caracas and Lima: Residential and Industrial Patterns.

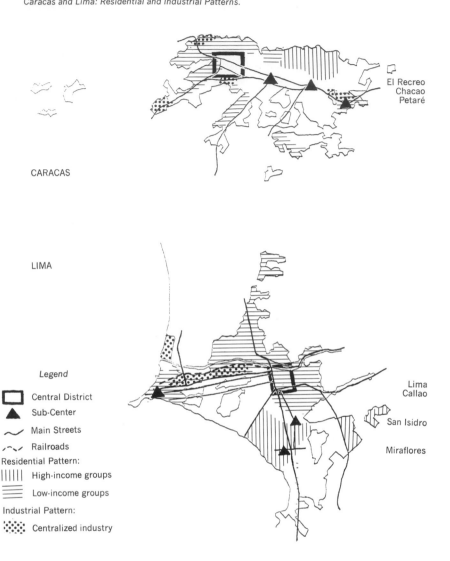

CARACAS

El Recreo
Chacao
Petaré

LIMA

Legend

☐ Central District
▲ Sub-Center
∿ Main Streets
⌁ Railroads

Residential Pattern:
|||||| High-income groups
≡ Low-income groups

Industrial Pattern:
⠿ Centralized industry

Lima
Callao

San Isidro

Miraflores

surrounding the industrial areas (Avellaneda or General San Martín). Some low-income groups take advantage of public land along the railroad lines (see map 8.2).

In São Paulo (map 8.3) the high-income groups have maintained a relatively central location—Jardim Paulista, Jardim America, Perdizes—due to the existence of developments in which industrial and commercial activities were not allowed. The low-income groups are located in the vicinity of the industries and in the lowlands near the rivers.

In the peripheral areas of most of the first-rank Latin American cities, one may find three major types of residential developments: the squatter settlements, the public housing developments and the high-income suburban developments. Each of these areas is characterized by a different density. The suburban one has a low density of approximately 50 persons per hectare, while the squatter area has an extremely high density of approximately 400 persons per hectare. By contrast, some public housing developments have even higher

MAP 8.2

Buenos Aires: Residental and Industrial Patterns

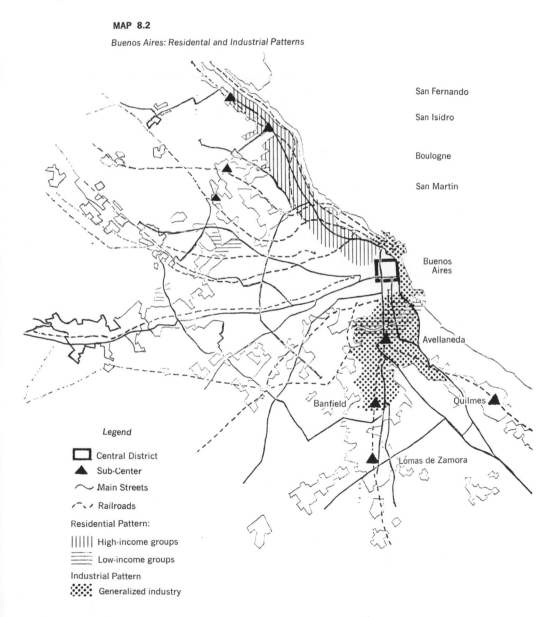

San Fernando

San Isidro

Boulogne

San Martín

Buenos Aires

Avellaneda

Banfield

Quilmes

Lómas de Zamora

Legend

☐ Central District

▲ Sub-Center

∿ Main Streets

⌒⌒ Railroads

Residential Pattern:

||||| High-income groups

≡ Low-income groups

Industrial Pattern

▦ Generalized industry

MAP 8.3

Sao Paulo: Residential and Industrial Patterns.

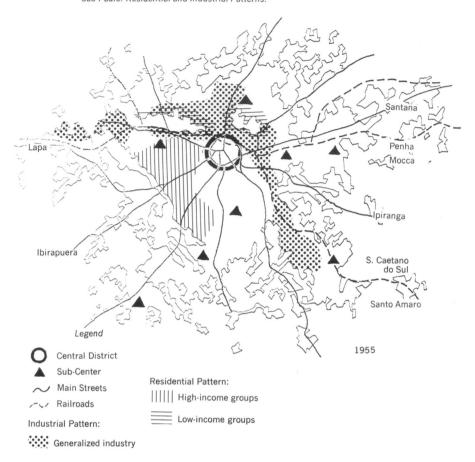

Lapa

Santana

Penha
Mocca

Ipiranga

Ibirapuera

S. Caetano
do Sul

Santo Amaro

1955

Legend

◯ Central District

▲ Sub-Center

〰 Main Streets

〰 Railroads

Industrial Pattern:

⣿ Generalized industry

Residential Pattern:

||||| High-income groups

≡ Low-income groups

densities, as in the case of the Banco Obrero development in Caracas which has 615 persons per hectare.

The traditional location of the low-income groups had been the central slums, but the present urban growth has been so rapid and of such magnitude that the residential sector in the center of the cities could not support it. The growth of the cities has also increased the commercial and government activities in the center of the cities, leading to the removal of central slums and the reduction of the residential sector in the central districts.

The residential pattern in the peripheral areas presents a different layout and grain according to the type of development. As suggested in the case study of barriadas in Lima in the preceding chapter, squatter settlements may be differentiated according to their age. The older ones located on hills do not present a regular street pattern. They lack roads, and the housing units tending to follow the natural contour of the terrain in their orientation. This type of residential organization contrasts sharply with the layout of suburban middle-income developments which present an ordered street subdivision pattern. Some squatter settlements improve with time, their streets becoming more defined, thus making them resemble middle-income developments. The Banco Obrero development in Caracas is an example of a peripheral public housing project. The layout of large blocks in this case necessitated the movement of large portions of land, thus completely changing the landscape of the city. Contemporary high-income residential areas tend to follow a loose pattern related to the topography of the area on the one hand and to access to roads suitable for automobile traffic on the other. This type of layout presents smooth curves which contrast with the traditional gridiron street patterns.

Generalized Industrial Patterns

The internal structure of a city is, to a degree, a result of its population size and degree of industrialization. In small or preindustrial cities there is relatively little complexity of functions and the main economic and social activities of the city tend to be carried out within one or more localized focal points. But as the city grows and becomes more industrialized the activities become more sharply differentiated among themselves so that they tend to locate at different points within the city and particular functional foci begin to appear. This may be illustrated at once by reference to three first-rank Latin American cities: La Paz, a small capital city, with a population of between 300 and 400 thousand and with a relatively low degree of industrialization; Lima, with a population of around 2 million and now in the process of industrialization; and Buenos Aires, the largest city in Latin America and already highly industrialized.

In La Paz one finds that, following the traditional pattern, the main activities of the city are undispersed and are carried on around the Plaza de Armas. In Lima the general pattern of the internal structure remained very similar to that of La Paz until 1940. Since that time, which marked the beginning of the industrialization of the whole city, there has been a general movement of the upper class away from the center-city toward the periphery. As a result of this, commercial centers such as Miraflores and Callao are now appearing in the suburbs and industrial areas are becoming clearly defined. In contrast to La Paz and Lima, Buenos Aires offers an example of a mature city. It presents a hierarchy of already established centers and a spatial differentiation of activities.

In Buenos Aires the location of industry has strongly depended on access to the seaport and the railroads. If one recalls that the port areas are localized in the lower part of the Barranca and at the mouth of the Riachuelo, one may notice that there has been a physical separation between the center of the city and the industrial areas. At present industry is more heavily concentrated on both banks of the Riachuelo and in Avellaneda, with some nuclei also in San Martín, Tres de Febrero and Boulogne. Aside from these nuclei, industry is characterized by its sprawl over the entire urban area. In the last ten years, in each of the peripheral districts of the city the number of industrial establishments has more than doubled. This fact suggests that population and industry are undergoing a parallel centrifugal process of dispersion.

In São Paulo the industrial process started at the beginning of the century, between 1907 and 1920. At first, industry took advantage of the railroad system established for the exploitation of coffee, and on this account was localized in the low areas of the city, following the railroad lines. But when the rivers were channeled, industry moved into the central areas of the city that had not been developed before because of the possibility of flooding. In a second stage, industry spread all over the urban area until finally a complex of satellite industrial towns sprang up around the central core of São Paulo.

In Lima, the process of industrialization began at a later time than in Buenos Aires or São Paulo and has proceeded on a smaller scale than in these two cities. Another important difference is that industry in Lima is located in a linear pattern, mainly along two corridors: one between Lima and Callao and the other along the northern coast of Callao—the latter one being chiefly occupied by fish product industries. This linear shape expresses the influence of the railroad and of the major transportation roads connecting Callao and Lima. The natural distribution of industry along the main avenues that join the center of Lima with Callao—Avenida Argentina, Avenida Colonial and Avenida Venezuela—is, in fact, a notable

São Paulo, center-city: In the area of Nucleo Antiguo are the banks and the major commercial and business enterprises.

characteristic of the general plan of the city. Its linear arrangement facilitates access to transportation and creates a favorable interrelationship between residential and working areas. These characteristics were a basic consideration in the elaboration of the Master Plan for the metropolis (published in *Lima Metropolitana*) by the Oficina Nacional de Planeamiento Urbano (ONPU) in 1954.

Some of the industrial areas are very near the center of the city. This, however, did not come out of an early industrial development, but rather was due to a sudden growth of the city which transformed previously peripheral areas into central ones. Urbanization along the main roads has led to the surrounding of large agricultural areas by residential areas. But as the price of the agricultural land was considerably raised, it remained beyond the financial reach of the average middle-income family. Finding the means to allow the organic growth of the city in places as yet untouched by speculation presents one of the current problems in new planning policies.

Caracas' industrial growth and location pattern is similar to that of Lima. The most significant tendency has been the expansion of industry from the central valley in the direction of Valencia. This has been reinforced by the construction of a rapid expressway linking the two cities. The fact that the central valley is now almost completely developed suggests that in the future a conurbation between Caracas and Valencia may result from this decentralization of industry.

Structure of the Center-City

Because the population of Latin America has a relatively low purchasing power[6] and because the retail trade is mainly oriented to the pedestrian, the center-city has always been the major retail center. The center-city has the largest threshold and is the point in the city most easily accessible from all other points by means of mass transit. Thus Buenos Aires and São Paulo have a large movement of daily railroad commuters,[7] while most of the other first-rank Latin American cities depend on bus or taxi systems of mass transit. The major railroad or bus terminals have a similar location pattern in these cities: they are to be found in the transition area of the core, so that they clearly define the central area of the city. The local

[6] Per Capita Consumption Expenditures in Selected Countries, 1958

Country	US $
Argentina	311.5
Brazil	107.3
Perú	103.4
Venezuela	357.5
United States	1,510.6

SOURCE: *Yearbook of National Accounts Statistics, 1963* (New York: United Nations, 1964).

[7] Evolution of Suburban Transit in Argentina and Brazil

	1950		1960	
	No.	Index	No.	Index
Argentina				
Passengers (millions)	435	100	536	123
Passengers/Km. (Mil.)	6,269	100	8,747	140
Average distance (Km.)	14.4		16.3	
Brazil				
Passengers (millions)	250	100	332	133
Passengers/Km. (Mil.)	4,240	100	8,215	194
Average distance (Km.)	17.0		24.7	

SOURCE: CEPAL, *El Transporte en América Latina* (New York, 1965), p. 44.

passenger services have their terminals within the central areas such as Lima (see fig. 8.6). The first city in Latin America to have a subway system is Buenos Aires (Mexico City's system has just been completed) but this system is mainly a connection between the major railroad stations that carry out the heavy commuter traffic. Several points of retail concentration are to be found along major arteries from the central district to the residential areas, or at the centers of smaller towns that have been absorbed by the city. In Buenos Aires, the main suburban commercial centers are located near the railroad stations—at the original centers of formerly independent towns (see fig. 8.7).

In most Latin American cities the major commercial and financial enterprises are still located in the center of the city. The suburbanization of these activities has not taken place, for instance, as it has in the United States. More akin to European and Asiatic cities, the chief retail outlets in Latin American cities are thousands of small shops located in the core of the city. Planned regional centers are rare; and when retail stores move out from the central district, they go to the center of the suburbs rather than to the peripheral areas.[8] As the first- and second-rank cities grow, however, one can expect the location of industry, shopping centers and other activities to occur simultaneously with the development of new housing systems. In fact new suburban areas in Bogotá and Miraflores in Lima already give evidence of this trend. Here, suburban satellite shopping centers, office buildings and theaters are the focus of planned residential areas.

Most urban retail stores are localized in particular areas of the center-cities and often concentrated on main shopping streets such as Jirón de la Unión in Lima, Santa Fé and Florida in Buenos Aires, Avenida São Joao in São Paulo and Carrera 7 in Bogotá. Financial activities in effect define a special district in São Paulo and Buenos Aires. The center-city of São Paulo contains two foci, Nucleo Antiguo and Nucleo Novo (fig. 8.8). In the area of Nucleo Antiguo are located the banks and the major commercial and business enter-

[8] In Santiago, Bogotá and Lima, Sears Roebuck stores are located in outlying residential areas with a few other stores; but in Rio de Janeiro, Caracas and México City, the Sears stores are located in midtown areas. In Lima, Sears actually has two locations: one in the center-city and the other in a residential section between the city and Miraflores. However, in 1965 Sears was forced to double the total floor space of the central-district building, instead of expanding the outlying store.

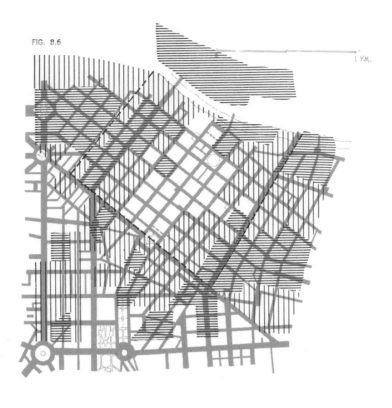

FIG. 8.6

1 KM.

Population density
persons per hectare:

more than 400

more than 200

FIG. 8.6 *Lima: Districts of Activity and Density of Population in the Center-City.*

prises. This same area corresponds roughly to the general location of the original settlements from which the modern city grew. However, few of the government activities are carried on in this section of the center—as opposed to Buenos Aires, where the financial district and the government district are located quite close to each other.

The galería is perhaps the most interesting shopping development in the central areas of a number of Latin American cities such as Lima, Santiago, São Paulo, Buenos Aires and Rio de Janeiro. As an

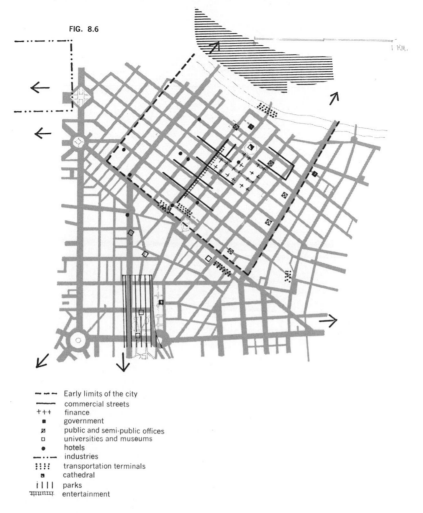

FIG. 8.6

1 KM.

- - - Early limits of the city
——— commercial streets
+ + + finance
▪ government
▨ public and semi-public offices
▢ universities and museums
● hotels
— ·· — industries
⋮⋮⋮⋮ transportation terminals
▣ cathedral
ᵢ l l l parks
ⅉⅉⅉⅉⅉ entertainment

example of retail architecture, it is comparable to the arcades found in the United States. A galería usually joins two streets by means of a roofed arcade, broken at several levels and with access from four streets. Small adjacent shops about 12 to 25 feet wide, are arranged at either side of the covered arcade. In São Paulo, for example, a new galería with five levels has been built in the center of the downtown area on the Avenida São Joao. In Lima, Galería Boza, a smaller scale example, may be found just off Jirón de la Unión, the main shopping street.

Hotels constitute the primary residential buildings in the center of most of the Latin American cities. Their location defines a specific area that is generally near the financial and government centers.

- - - Early limits of the city
———— commercial streets
+ + + finance
■ government
⊠ public and semi-public offices
□ universities and museums
• hotels
— ‥ — industry
⫶⫶⫶ transportation terminals
◧ cathedral
| | | | | parks
▥▥▥▥ entertainment street

FIG. 8.7 *Buenos Aires: Districts of Activity and Population Density in the Center-City.*

Population density
persons per hectare

more than 400

more than 200

FIG. 8.8 *São Paulo: Districts of Activity in the Center-City*

Many hotels are located next to the main shopping street which has a close relationship to the major national transport terminals. New hotels are currently being planned for a site in downtown Lima reinforcing the traditional center-city location. However, in Guatemala City a new hotel is located some distance from the central plaza on a main avenue connecting with the airport.

Government activities in Latin American cities have traditionally been located in the immediate vicinity of the plaza de armas, since

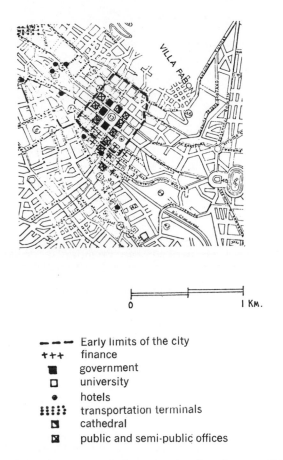

VILLA PABON

0	I KM.

- - - Early limits of the city
+++ finance
■ government
□ university
● hotels
⁞⁞⁞⁞⁞ transportation terminals
◣ cathedral
◪ public and semi-public offices

FIG. 8.9 *La Paz: Districts of Activity in the Center-City.*

the Spanish colonial governments built the viceroyal palace, the city hall and the cathedral around the main square. In most capital cities the presidential palace has remained adjacent to the central plaza; but with the division of power into the executive, legislative and judicial branches, government activities are no longer restricted to the area immediately surrounding the main square and have begun to spread out over the central area of the city.

In La Paz government activities are concentrated around the Plaza Murillo, where the Presidential Palace and the Congress are located (see fig. 8.9). In Caracas the government offices are divided between Plaza Bolívar and the new Centro Simón Bolívar to which the Presidential Palace and the ministries have now been moved. This famous modern center includes two thirty-story office towers. The government offices occupy the upper floors while the street and lower levels are taken up by shopping areas, restaurants, and parking areas, with the super highway, Avenida Bolívar, passing under the lower shopping level. In Lima, government activities are more dispersed, the Congress Building being located at some distance from the Plaza de Armas.

In Buenos Aires the activities of public and semipublic institutions occupy a major part of the center of the city and the immediately surrounding area. A line drawn on a map to include all of the government buildings bounds an area which also embraces the other most important activities of the city. The trio of buildings housing the three branches of the Argentine government in Buenos Aires stand at the vertices of a triangle, one side of which is formed by Avenida de Mayo, connecting the Presidential Palace and the Congress and another side by Avenida Presidente Saenz Peña, running between the Presidential Palace and the Palace of Justice.

São Paulo is a peculiar case because it is not a national capital but the capital of the state of São Paulo. The importance of the city lies not in its government functions but rather in its particularly highly developed industrial capacity and financial power. An indication of the increasing importance of São Paulo as an industrial city is the fact that the government buildings, formerly located in the immediate center of the city, have been moved to locations more removed from the center.

Latin American cities have relatively few open spaces in relation to the sizes of their population. In 1954, for instance, Lima had only approximately 33 square feet of open space per person. (Although the suggested ideal figure varies from city to city, some standards have placed it at 250 square feet per person.)[9] This shortage of open space is partly due to the continuous housing that makes the center-cities very compact, and partly to the Spanish tradition which made the plaza de armas virtually the only open space in the city. Thus today the major open spaces in Latin America are found away from the center of the city, usually in the direction of the best residential areas, the private areas of recreation such as country clubs or golf courses, and resort places along rivers or the sea. Of these open spaces, the private areas of recreation are generally located in the peripheral areas of the city, but only in those sectors where the

[9] Oficina Nacional de Planeamiento y Urbanismo, *Lima Metropolitana* (Lima, 1954), p. 11.

high-income groups reside. In Caracas one may find the districts of Altamira, La Castellana and El Pedregal, near the Caracas Country Club; in Lima, the Country Club is in San Isidro; in Buenos Aires almost all the private areas of recreation are in the northern part of the city, mainly in Palermo, Vicente López, San Isidro and Tigre.

The main recreational facilities in the central districts of Latin American cities are the movie houses, theaters and public parks. In large cities like Buenos Aires or São Paulo, theaters form a special section within the central area; in smaller cities like Lima, they are part of the main shopping street. Public parks are located toward the outskirts of the central area, in the direction of the high-income residential areas. This is the case for the main public parks in Buenos Aires, the Reserva Park in Lima, the Japonés Park in Santiago and Los Caobos Park in Caracas.

Common Elements in the Structure of Latin American Cities

The preceding observations are confined to the large cities and, in the majority of cases, the capitals of Latin American countries, because most of the available reliable data is limited to these first-rank cities. Thus they do not claim to characterize the typical Latin American city. The population and characteristics—economic conditions, social patterns—of the capital city are generally quite different from those of other cities of a given country. The range of variation among the capitals of the different countries, however, diminishes the significance of this distortion. For example, we can compare Managua, having 234,600 inhabitants, with Buenos Aires, encompassing a population almost twenty-five times greater, 6.7 million, and with differences of complexity to match.

The spatial arrangement of functions within the Latin American cities is undergoing radical changes, mainly as an effect of the rapid growth of population and the consequent occupation of available land. The resulting network of streets and the patterns of land use are far from an orderly development; indeed, the juxtaposition of dissimilar elements is the rule.

The case of México City is very representative in this respect. Acres that were peripheral ten or twenty years ago, when industries were occupying large tracts of land, have now been engulfed by residential development and peripheral squatter settlements located side by side with good residential areas.

The case of Caracas, with a different general shape conditioned by the topography, is structurally similar. Since industrialization started at a later stage in Caracas, industry still occupies peripheral areas, but is dispersed in at least five or six major locations around the city. Peripheral squatter settlements or ranchos concentrate more heavily in the areas surrounding the central core, but are also dispersed along the valleys at regular spacing within the good residential neighborhoods.[10]

In very general form, the common elements of the structure of Latin American cities can be grouped as follows:

(1) *Peripheral Settlements of Low-Income Groups:* These exist in almost all first- and second-rank cities in Latin America, and are proliferating at a fantastic rate. Their most dramatic growth occurred during the 1940s and 1950s and they continued to grow in the 1960s. Peripheral dwellings are generally first constructed of scrap materials, but are in some cases improved over time and become permanent elements of the urban structure. Lima, as we have seen, provides a striking example of this.

Density in peripheral settlements is usually very high, due to the large-sized families of their inhabitants and the compact number of individual housing units. The people are generally rural migrants, who have either come directly from the country or have moved to the peripheral dwellings after a period of residence in the center-city slums. As shown in this study, peripheral settlements are not degraded areas; on the contrary, their dwellers are frequently quite energetic and have shown a capacity for a high degree of organization and a desire for self-improvement. Physically, even when sanitary and other environmental conditions are poor, the settlements have several valuable characteristics, such as cohesiveness and interesting clustering forms.

(2) A *Mature, Compact Central Area of Representative Character:* The form and structure of the central area stem from the original function of the city in Latin America. With only a few exceptions[11] it is possible to define a central core not disrupted by industry which

[10] Emrys Jones, "Aspects of Urbanization in Venezuela," *Ekistics* 18 (1964).

[11] Namely, São Paulo and Buenos Aires, the most industrialized cities in Latin America.

developed about the main open space of the cities—the plaza de armas or plaza mayor. This central area was designed in every case to house the seat of the government and major civic buildings. Traditionally, it became a good residential area with high population densities. Within the central area, there are clearly recognizable sectors such as the main business district, the hotel and theater district, the bank district, and the area of the government palace, town hall and ministries.

(3) *High-Income Residential Areas:* These are located in one sector, toward the outlying areas (Lomas de Chapultepec in México City, Chapinero-Chico in Bogotá, Miraflores-San Antonio in Lima, San Isidro in Buenos Aires, Providencia-El Golf-Los Condes in Santiago). High-income groups have generally moved in the direction of the better lands of the city as far as natural conditions, vegetation, and scenery are concerned. They have generated new forms of recreation such as golf, boating, and country clubs. The physical layout in these residential areas is remarkably less dense and more homogeneous than in any other sector of the city. Characteristic dwellings in such sectors are one-story houses with front yards, only occasionally interspersed with isolated multi-family buildings. Broad avenues connect this sector with the central area, since the number of automobiles per family here is the highest in the city. In Santiago de Chile, for instance, 50 percent of all the automobiles in the city are concentrated in the high-income sector of Providencia-Los Condes.

(4) *Peripheral Industry:* In most of the cities in Latin America, industry has been a late-comer. For this reason, it has generally located in peripheral areas, in discontinuous zones, and spread all around the developed land along railroad tracks and major routes.

(5) *Dependence on Mass Transit, with Increasing Importance of the Automobile:* This dependence makes cities in Latin America generally more dense and compact along main routes of mass transit than is the case for cities in North America. It also determines the location of service functions along these lines. But, as mentioned previously, the high-income residential areas have a much lower density and reflect the increasing importance of the automobile in Latin America. For example, from 1960 to 1965, there was an increase from one to two million automobiles in Brazil. The impact of the automobile on the cities is aggravated by the inadequacy of the

road network to handle traffic; traditional streets are narrow, inter-
sections are inappropriate, and parking space is scarce. In short,
Latin American cities today face the same traffic problems as the
rest of the world.

(6) *Commercial Pattern Composed of Scattered Small Shops and
Main Shops Centralized in One or Two Centers:* There are very few
planned regional shopping centers, and the department stores generally occupy a subordinate position. There seems to be a much
larger number of stores than needed in proportion to the volume of
sales or the purchasing power of the population. A reason for this
may be found in the fact that the small shop is a type of disguised
unemployment. In cities like Lima and Bogotá the new secondary
centers are more important and varied and of better quality than
the traditional shopping centers (San Isidro in Lima, Chapinero in
Bogotá). The old traditional shopping center is characterized by
the dominance of a main shopping street (four or seven blocks).
Many main streets are enclosed by commercial galleries, a superb
example of retail architecture if properly done. As a retailing device,
it works very well, since it is a sheltered space which permits access
from several streets.

(7) *Presence on the Urban Landscape of a Natural Element:*
For one reason or another, cities in Latin America seem to have a
more direct relation with the natural landscape than those in other
parts of the world. The extreme example is Rio de Janeiro, whose
form is completely conditioned by the hills, mountains, and the bay.
There is almost no city which does not have a very strong element of
the landscape—the Andes in Santiago, La Paz, Quito, Bogotá,
Caracas, the river in Buenos Aires and Montevideo, and the desert,
the sea and the Andes in Lima. In almost all of these cases, the
natural elements have been crucial factors in shaping the general
form of the city and in giving particular interest to different sub-
sections.

This general review emphasizes two main characteristics of the
Latin American city today: first, that it is undergoing rapid structural changes, influenced by some *native* factors, the most dramatic
being the proliferation of squatter settlements, and some *induced*
factors, either from abroad, as an imitation, or as the natural response to the attainment of higher standards of living and technological levels such as industrialization of cities, changing commercial
patterns, increasing popularity of private automobiles and improve-

ments in highway construction. Secondly, in view of these changes, it is extremely difficult to specify historical patterns, and from these define what the Latin American city is today. It would perhaps be more appropriate to approach the problem by looking at what the Latin American city is becoming today and to consider the integral relationship of rural-urban development policies to national, social, and economic development goals. The external influence on the internal structure of Latin American cities is increasingly important, and must be taken into account in any attempt to deal with the problems created by rapid growth change.

Appendix

TABLE 1

PERÚ: RANKING ORDER OF CITIES OVER 5,000 INHABITANTS, 1961

RANK	CITY	POPULATION	RANK	CITY	POPULATION
1.	Lima [a]	1,845,910	33.	Pativilca	15,325
2.	Arequipa [b]	222,377	34.	La Brea (Negritos)	14,810
3.	Trujillo	100,130	35.	Tarapoto	13,907
4.	Chiclayo	95,667	36.	Nazca	13,587
5.	Cuzco [c]	79,857	37.	Jauja	12,751
6.	Piura	72,096	38.	Mollendo	12,483
7.	Huancayo [c]	64,153	39.	Catacaos	12,135
8.	Chimbote	59,990	40.	Ferreñafe	12,112
9.	Iquitos	57,777	41.	Pacasmayo	11,956
10.	Sullana	50,171	42.	Yurimaguas	11,655
11.	Ica	49,097	43.	Huaral	11,481
12.	Talara	27,957	44.	Barranca Lima	11,320
13.	Tacna	27,499	45.	Monscfú	11,141
14.	Pucallpa	26,391	46.	Huancavelica	11,039
15.	Chosica	25,248	47.	Sicuani	10,664
16.	La Oroya	24,724	48.	Lambayeque	10,269
17.	Huánuco	24,646	49.	Ilo	9,986
18.	Puno	24,459	50.	Paita	9,615
19.	Ayacucho	23,768	51.	Abancay	9,053
20.	Huacho	22,806	52.	Chaclacayo	8,698
21.	Cajamarca	22,705	53.	Quillabamba	8,644
22.	Pisco	22,112	54.	Yanahuara	8,535
23.	Cerro de Pasco	21,363	55.	El Alto	8,496
24.	Tumbes	20,885	56.	Pachacamac	8,475
25.	Chincha	20,817	57.	Chupaca	8,383
26.	Juliaca	20,351	58.	Moyobamba	8,373
27.	Huarás	20,345	59.	Puquio	8,144
28.	Chulucanas	19,714	60.	Máncora	7,943
29.	Chocope	19,049	61.	Moquegua	7,765
30.	Saña	18,421	62.	Ayaviri	7,553
31.	Chepén	16,119	63.	San Pedro de Lloc	7,497
32.	Tarma	15,452	64.	San Vicente de Cañete	7,184

SOURCE: Dirección Nacional de Estadística y Censos, Perú, *Boletín de Estadística Peruana, Year VI,* no. 6 (Lima: Ministerio de Hacienda y Comercio, 1963).

NOTES:

    a. Lima's population includes the metropolitan area, as well as Callao.

    b. Metropolitan area of Arequipa.

    c. Urban areas, as defined by the census.

RANK	CITY	POPULATION	RANK	CITY	POPULATION
65.	Llama	7,139	82.	Huamachuco	5,730
66.	Eten	6,999	83.	Huanta	5,728
67.	Guadalupe	6,882	84.	Celendín	5,646
68.	Chachapoyas	6,860	85.	Tabalosos	5,344
69.	Paucarpata	6,792	86.	Cajabamba	5,253
70.	Marcona	6,744	87.	Huarmey	5,232
71.	Colan	6,646	88.	Tingo María	5,208
72.	Ilabaya	6,563	89.	Puente Piedra	5,182
73.	Morococha	6,519	90.	Sechura	5,157
74.	Imperial	6,345	91.	Camaná	5,120
75.	Pimentel	6,252	92.	Juanjuí	5,105
76.	Querecotillo	6,205	93.	Santiago de Chuco	5,060
77.	Chancay	6,145	94.	Junín	5,004
78.	La Unión	6,047	95.	Casma	4,975
79.	Cerro Colorado	6,002	96.	Chota	4,961
80.	Motupe	5,864	97.	Puerto Maldonado [d]	3,518
81.	Paiján	5,815			

d. Although Puerto Maldonado does not have 5,000 inhabitants, it is considered because it is the capital of the Departamento of Madre de Dios.

TABLE 2

CHILE: RANKING ORDER OF CITIES OVER 5,000 INHABITANTS, 1960

RANK	CITY	POPULATION	RANK	CITY	POPULATION
over 100,000			over 20,000		
1.	Santiago	1,983,945	13.	Lota	48,693
2.	Valparaíso [a]	384,324	14.	Arica	43,334
3.	Concepción-Talcahuano	314,412	15.	Puente Alto	43,238
over 50,000			16.	Pto. Montt	41,681
4.	Antofagasta	87,860	17.	La Serena	40,854
5.	Temuco	72,132	18.	San Antonio	39,619
6.	Talca	67,463	19.	Los Angeles	35,511
7.	Chillán	66,771	20.	Coronel	33,870
8.	Valdivia	61,334	21.	Coquimbo	33,794
9.	Osorno	54,693	22.	Curicó	32,562
10.	Rancagua	53,318	23.	Copiapó	30,123
11.	Punta Arenas	51,200	24.	Quillota	29,447
12.	Iquique	50,665	25.	Linares	27,562

SOURCE: Dirección de Estadística y Censos, Republica de Chile, *Entidades de Población 1960* (Santiago, 1962).
NOTE: *a.* Includes Viña del Mar.
  b. Total Population in Cities over 5,000: 4,496,268.

RANK	CITY	POPULATION	RANK	CITY	POPULATION
26.	Tomé	26,942	59.	Llolleo	9,846
27.	Quilpué	26,558	60.	Curacautín	9,601
28.	Calama	26,116	61.	Constitución	9,536
29.	Ovalle	25,282	62.	Puerto Natales	9,399
30.	Chuquicamata	24,798	63.	Villarrica	9,122
31.	San Fernando	21,779	64.	Coihaique	8,782
32.	Tocopilla	21,580	65.	San Javier	8,541
33.	Los Andes	20,448	66.	Molina	7,615
over 10,000			67.	Rio Bueno	7,544
34.	San Felipe	19,040	68.	Ancud	7,390
35.	Angol	18,637	69.	Llay-Llay	7,049
36.	La Calera	18,134	70.	Castro	7,001
37.	Cauquenes	17,836	71.	Loncoche	6,497
38.	Chiguayante	17,568	72.	Quintero	6,486
39.	Maipú	16,740	73.	Pitrufquén	6,483
40.	Vallenar	15,693	74.	Lebu	6,461
41.	Villa Alemana	15,650	75.	Nueva La Imperial	6,442
42.	Penco	15,483	76.	Potrerillos	6,168
43.	Melipilla	15,467	77.	El Bellotto	6,086
44.	Limache	14,448	78.	Santa Cruz	5,906
45.	Victoria	14,215	79.	Carahue	5,891
46.	Barrancas	13,743	80.	Bulnes	5,831
47.	San Carlos	13,598	81.	Graneros	5,644
48.	Parral	12,973	82.	Collipulli	5,572
49.	La Unión	11,558	83.	Puerto Aysen	5,488
50.	Talagante	11,500	84.	Cañete	5,487
51.	Pedro de Valdivia	11,028	85.	Peñablanca	5,386
52.	Rengo	10,989	86.	Andacollo	5,381
53.	Mulchen	10,729	87.	Concón	5,381
54.	Peñaflor	10,470	88.	Taltal	5,291
55.	Lautaro	10,448	89.	Chanaral	5,216
56.	Illapel	10,395	90.	La Ligua	5,095
57.	Puerto Varas	10,305	91.	El Monte	5,083
over 5,000 [b]			92.	Cartagena	5,022
58.	Traiguén	9,990			

TABLE 3

HONDURAS, EL SALVADOR AND GUATEMALA: INDICES OF ECONOMIC AND SOCIAL DEVELOPMENT

INDEX	HONDURAS	EL SALVADOR	GUATEMALA
Area sq. mi.[a]	43,277	7,722	42,040
Pop.[c] 1961	1,884,765	2,576,366	4,284,473(1964)
GDP per capita 1964 [a]	US$201	US$314	US$307
Life expectancy[b]	38	51	37
% labor force in agric. [b]	66	60	65
Illiteracy rate, %, 1964 [b]	55–50	55–50	65–60
% pop. in cities over 100,000 [c]	8.2	12.7	13.4
% pop. in cities 20,000–100,000 [c]	4.4	6.6	2.1

SOURCES:

a. Social Progress Trust Fund, 1965, Fifth Annual Report (Washington, D.C.: Inter-American Development Bank), pp. 326, 347, 386.

b. Economic Development of Central America (New York: Committee for Economic Development, 1964), p. 10; p. 34.

c. See Appendix, tables 4–7.

TABLE 4

HONDURAS: POPULATION CHANGE BY DEPARTMENTS, 1901–1961

	CUMULATIVE PERCENTAGE CHANGE					
DEPARTMENT	CENSUS 1901 [a]	CENSUS 1916 [a]	CENSUS 1930 [a]	CENSUS 1940 [a]	CENSUS 1961 [b]	POPULATION 1961 [b]
Atlántida	100	138	370	497	1100	92,914
Colón	100	94	230	223	306	41,904
Comayagua	100	108	144	186	344	96,442
Copác	100	76	106	132	208	126,183
Cortés	100	139	267	400	955	200,099
Choluteca	100	105	152	195	341	149,175
El Paraíso	100	102	141	170	276	106,823
Francisco Morazán	100	105	172	196	361	284,428
Intibuca	100	148	147	200	284	73,138
Islas de la Bahía	100	118	116	147	195	8,961
La Paz	100	112	143	178	226	60,600
Lempira	100	107	135	163	237	111,546
Ocotepeque [c]		100	159	198	234	52,540
Olancho	100	103	120	145	257	110,744
Santa Bárbara	100	119	170	222	423	146,909

	CUMULATIVE PERCENTAGE CHANGE					
DEPARTMENT	CENSUS 1901 [a]	CENSUS 1916 [a]	CENSUS 1930 [a]	CENSUS 1940 [a]	CENSUS 1961 [b]	POPULATION 1961 [b]
Valle	100	86	121	160	248	80,907
Yoro	100	108	213	318	678	130,547
Total Republic	100	113	157	203	375	1,873,860

SOURCES:

  a. *Honduras: Summary of Biostatistics* (Washington, D.C.: U.S. Dept. of Commerce, Bureau of Census, 1944).

  b. *Cifras Definitivas de Población y Viviendas en Cabeceras Municipales y en Aldeas y Caserios, Abril, 1961*(Tegucigalpa: Dirección General de Estadística y Censos, 1963).

NOTE:

  c. Territorial change.

TABLE 5

EL SALVADOR: POPULATION CHANGE BY DEPARTMENTS, 1900–1961

	CUMULATIVE PERCENTAGE CHANGE					
DEPARTMENT	CENSUS 1900 [a, c]	ESTIM. 1915 [a]	CENSUS 1930 [a]	ESTIM. 1940 [a]	CENSUS 1961 [b]	POPULATION 1961 [b]
Santa Ana	100	132	152	194	275	265,918
Ahuachapán	100	142	187	230	309	133,389
Sonsonate	100	130	165	192	275	170,962
La Libertad	100	128	159	185	274	208,269
San Salvador	100	129	140	161	344	475,266
Chalatenango	100	169	243	312	385	132,826
Cuscatlán	100	147	194	233	264	115,501
La Paz	100	146	198	241	296	134,065
San Vicente	100	151	206	254	301	115,390
Cabanas	100	161	208	312	389	97,075
San Miguel	100	142	196	249	357	237,416
Usulután	100	146	206	257	344	212,114
Morazán	100	193	300	395	479	122,182
La Unión	100	169	278	373	565	152,507
Total Republic	100	140	186	228	329	2,572,880

SOURCES:

  a. *El Salvador: Summary of Biostatistics* (Washington, D.C.: U.S. Dept. of Commerce, Bureau of Census, 1944).

  b. *Anuario Estadístico* (San Salvador: Dirección General de Estadística y Censos, 1963).

NOTE:

  c. According to 1901 census.

TABLE 6

GUATEMALA: POPULATION CHANGE BY DEPARTMENTS, 1893–1964

DEPARTMENT	CENSUS 1893 [a]	CUMULATIVE PERCENTAGE CHANGE ENUM. 1921 [b]	ESTIM. 1934 [b]	ENUM. 1940 [b, d]	CENSUS 1950 [c]	CENSUS 1964 [c]	POPULATION 1964 [c]
Guatemala	100	157	187	216	297	550	813,696
El Progreso [e]				100	125	141	66,734
Sacatepequez	100	85	125	194	141	188	80,479
Chimaltenango	100	81	225	167	208	301	163,753
Escuintla [e]	100	210	234	551	387	843	269,813
Santa Rosa [e]	100	155	219	359	232	329	155,488
Sololá [e]	100	101	105	124	118	155	108,815
Totonicapán	100	105	104	103	111	156	139,636
Quetzaltenango	100	141	170	210	166	242	268,962
Suchitepequez [e]	100	261	299	482	329	493	186,299
Retalhuleu [e]	100	177	137	252	241	442	122,829
San Marcos	100	197	208	229	260	372	332,303
Huehuetenango	100	117	132	151	171	245	286,965
El Quiche	100	149	161	171	189	267	247,775
Baja Verapaz	100	115	113	175	121	175	95,663
Alta Verapaz	100	163	192	280	188	258	259,873
Petén	100	116	145	170	235	396	26,720
Izabal [e]	100	233	352	1124	744	1546	114,404
Zacapa [e]	100	125	120	308	147	203	95,976
Chiquimula	100	138	175	226	177	237	151,241
Jalapa [e]	100	143	165	375	226	294	97,996
Jutiapa	100	178	199	379	263	377	199,053
Total Republic	100	147	166	241	205	314	4,284,473

SOURCES:

a. *Censos General de la Republica* (Guatemala City: Dirección General de Estadística, 1894).

b. *Guatemala: Summary of Biostatistics* (Washington, D.C.: U.S. Dept. of Commerce, Bureau of Census, 1944).

c. *Trimestre Estadístico* (Guatemala City: Dirección General de Estadística, 1964).

NOTES:

d. The results of the 1940 census were later recognized as being inexact by official sources.

e. Territorial change.

TABLE 7

GUATEMALA, EL SALVADOR AND HONDURAS:
FIRST 12 CITIES IN ORDER OF POPULATION

RANK	HONDURAS 1961 CENSUS [a]		EL SALVADOR 1961 CENSUS [b]		GUATEMALA 1964 CENSUS [c]	
1	Tegucigalpa [d]	154,429	San Salvador [d]	319,110	Guatemala [d]	572,937
2	San Pedro Sula	58,635	Santa Ana	73,429	Quetzaltenango	45,195
3	La Ceiba	24,863	San Miguel	40,166	Escuintla	24,832
4	Puerto Cortés	17,048	Nueva San Salvador	27,176	Puerto Barrios	22,242
5	El Progreso	13,797	Sonsonate	23,798	Mazatenango	19,506
6	Tela	13,619	San Vicente	15,500	Chiquimula	14,760
7	Choluteca	11,483	Chalchuapa	13,440	Retalhuleu	14,366
8	Comayagua	8,474	Ahuachapán	13,307	Coatepeque	13,657
9	Santa Rosa	7,964	Usulután	12,532	Antigua	13,576
10	Juticalpa	7,210	Zacatecoluca	12,298	Amatitlán	12,225
11	Danlí	6,325	La Unión	11,544	Zacapa	11,173
12	Siguatepeque	5,993	Cojutepeque	11,494	Tiquisate	10,348

SOURCES:
a. *Cifras Definitivas de Población y Viviendas en Cabeceras Municipales y en Aldeas y Caserios, Abril, 1961* (Tegucigalpa: Dirección General de Estadística y Censos, Honduras, 1963).
b. *Anuario Estadístico* (San Salvador: Dirección General de Estadística y Censos, El Salvador, 1965).
c. *Trimestre Estadístico* (Guatemala: Dirección General de Estadística, Guatemala, 1964).
d. Includes rural municipal population, according to metropolitan definition, (Tendencias de Localización y Crecimiento de la Población Urbana Latinoamericana) Unpublished mimeograph (Washington, D.C.: Pan American Union, 1964).

[277]

TABLE 8

TRADE AMONG CENTRAL AMERICA COUNTRIES
(Thousands of Dollars)

YEAR	IMPORTING COUNTRY	GUATEMALA	EL SALVADOR	HONDURAS	NICARAGUA	COSTA RICA	TOTAL
1950	Guatemala	—	1,577	164	50	2	1,795
	El Salvador	272	—	2,125	470	23	2,890
	Honduras	158	1,795	—	243	43	2,239
	Nicaragua	25	198	68	—	96	388
	Costa Rica	44	155	464	311	—	975
	TOTAL	499	3,725	2,821	1,074	164	8,287
1956	Guatemala	—	745	637	a	203	1,586
	El Salvador	1,878	—	5,377	500	307	8,063
	Honduras	30	1,290	—	82	33	1,436
	Nicaragua	41	950	63	—	410	1,466
	Costa Rica	71	557	66	234	—	929
	TOTAL	2,020	3,542	6,143	816	953	13,480
1963	Guatemala	—	12,658	4,603	2,909	568	20,738
	El Salvador	11,538	—	7,850	2,205	2,322	23,915
	Honduras	2,047	10,771	—	230	159	13,207
	Nicaragua	196	2,444	458	—	926	4,024
	Costa Rica	395	2,071	345	1,538	—	4,349
	TOTAL	14,176	27,944	13,256	6,882	3,975	66,233

SOURCE: J. Abraham Bennaton Ramos, "El Mercado Común Centroamericano: Su Evolución y Perspectiva" unpublished (Tegucigalpa: Universidad Nacional Autónoma de Honduras, 1964).
NOTE: *a.* Less than a thousand dollars.

TABLE 9

POPULATION GROWTH OF SELECTED MAJOR LATIN AMERICAN CITIES

CITY	INTEGRANTS	TOTAL	TOTAL
Asunción	Municipio:	*1953*	*1962*
	Asunción	206,634	305,160
Bogotá	Integrant:	*1951*	*1960*
	Bogotá	648,624 (1) [a]	1,048,870
	Bosa	16,613 (2)	41,970
	Fontibón	16,468 (3)	30,070
	Usaquen	11,207 (4)	21,100
	Usme	10,794 (5)	20,160
	Engativa	5,782 (7)	16,240
	Suba	6,062 (6)	9,770
		715,550	1,188,180
Guatemala City	Municipality:	*1950*	*1964*
	Guatemala	294,344	572,937
Cuayaquil	Parroquia urbana:	*1950*	*1962*
	Guayaquil	266,637	567,895
La Habana	Municipalities:	*1953*	*1960*
	Habana	787,765	
	Marianao	229,576	
	Guanabacoa	112,333	
	Santiago de las Vegas	32,891	
	Bauta	29,499	
	Regla	26,755	
	Santa María del Rosario	21,600	
		1,240,419	1,594,000
La Paz	City:	*1950*	*1960*
	La Paz	321,073	347,394
	Province:		
	Murillo	25,057	30,925
		346,130	378,319
Managua	Municipality :	*1950*	*1963*
	Managua	140,334	234,600
Montevideo	Departamento:	*1950*	*1963*
	Montevideo	768,413	1,202,890
Port-au-Prince	Communes:	*1950*	*1960*
	Port-au-Prince		
	Petionville		
		216,170	240,000

CITY	INTEGRANTS	TOTAL	TOTAL
Quito	Parroquia urbana: Quito	*1950* 212,135	*1962* 510,286
Rio de Janeiro	1. Federal District State: Rio de Janeiro Municipalities & Districts:	*1950* 2,377,451 (1)	*1960* 3,307,163
	2. Nova Iquacu Nova Iquacu Bedford Roxo Cava Queimados	145,649 (3) 90,749 23,750 12,376 18,774	359,364
	3. São Goncalo Neves Sete Pontes São Goncalo Ipiiba Monjolo	127,276 (4) 52,424 30,706 28,003 10,456 5,687	247,754
	4. Niteroi Niteroi Itaipu	186,309 (2) 182,039 4,270	245,467
	5. Duque de Caxias Duque de Caxias Imbarie	92,459 (5) 73,527 18,932	243,619
	6. São Joas de Meriti São Joas de Meriti Coelho da Rocha São Mateus	76,462 (6) 43,790 21,394 11,278	191,734
	7. Nilopolis Nilopolis Olinda	46,406 (7) 30,711 15,695	96,553
		3,052,012	4,691,654
San José	Cantones: Cantón Central Goicoechea Tibas Montes de Oca Desamparados Escazú Moravia Alajuelita	*1950* 111,820 (1) 21,093 (2) 10,594 (3) 9,916 (4) 5,727 (5)	*1963* 172,193 44,707 24,575 24,536 22,199 14,601 11,898 5,769
		159,150	320,478

CITY	INTEGRANTS	TOTAL	TOTAL
San Salvador	Districts and Municipalities:	*1950*	*1961*
	San Salvador	171,270 (1)	255,744
	Villa Delgado	19,333 (2)	32,631
	Mejicanos	14,406 (3)	28,491
	Soyapango	9,530 (4)	20,440
	Cuscatancingo	4,160 (5)	11,234
	Ayutuxtepeque	2,230 (6)	2,736
		220,929	351,276
Santo Domingo	District:	*1950*	*1961*
	Santo Domingo	239,464	477,000 (est.)
Tegucigalpa	Central District:	*1950*	*1961*
	Tegucigalpa	99,948	164,941

SOURCES: Statistics from Country Census (see Bibliography). Estimates for Port-au-Prince and La Habana, 1960 from *Demographic Yearbook*, 1965.
NOTE: *a.* Numbers in parentheses indicate rank.

Adams, R. N. *Cultural Surveys of Panamá, Nicaragua, Guatemala, El Salvador, Honduras.* Washington, D. C.: Pan American Sanitary Bureau, 1957.

Agarwala, A. N., and Psinch, S. *The Economics of Underdevelopment.* New York: Oxford University Press, 1963.

Alexander, J. W. "The Basic-Nonbasic Concept of Urban Economic Function." In *Readings in Urban Geography,* edited by Mayer and Kohn. Chicago: University of Chicago Press, 1959.

Alonso, William. "The Form of the Cities in Developing Countries." *Papers and Proceedings of the Regional Science Association,* 11 (1963).

Altamira Y Crevea, Rafael. *Ensayo Sobre Felipe II.* Mexico: Gráficas Reunidas, 1959.

Anderson, Nels. *The Urban Community: A World Perspective.* New York. Henry Holt, 1959.

Andrew, Frank. "La Inestabilidad Urbana en America Latina." *Cuadernos Americanos* 25/144 (January-February, 1966).

Aparicio, Francisco de, and Di Freieri, Horacio. *La Argentina, Suma de Geografía,* vols. 6, 7, 9, 10. Buenos Aires: Ediciones Peuser, 1963.

Arca Parró, Alberto. *El Medio Geográfico y la Población del Perú.* Lima: Imprenta Torres Aguirre, 1945.

Azevedo, Aroldo de. *A Cidade de São Paulo,* vols. 1–4. São Paulo Companhia Editora Nacional, 1958.

Banco Central de Honduras. *Memoria.* Tegucigalpa, 1964.

Banco Central de Reserva Del Perú. *Actividades Productivas del Perú.* Lima, 1961.

———. *Plan Nacional de Desarrollo Económico y Social del Perú 1961–1971,* vol. 1. Lima, 1962.

———. *Renta Nacional del Perú 1942–1955.* Lima, 1957.

Banco De La Republica, Departamento de Investigaciones Economicas, Colombia. *Atlas de la Economía Colombiana.* Bogotá: Imprenta del Banco de la República, 1959.

Banco Nacional De Comercio Exterior, México. *México 1960.* México, 1960.

Banco Obrero De Caracas. *Proyecto de Evaluación de los Superbloques.* Caracas: Centro Interamericano de Vivienda y Planeamiento (CINVA).

Baron-Castro, R. *La Población de El Salvador.* Madrid: Instituto Gonzalo Fernández de Oviedo, 1942.

Barrera, Isaac J. *Quito Colonial.* Quito: Imprenta Nacional, 1922.

Baudin, Louis. *A Socialist Empire—The Incas of Perú.* Princeton; Van Nostrand, 1961.

Bayitch, S. A. *Latin America, A Bibliographical Guide to Economy, History, Law, Politics and Society.* Coral Gables, Florida; University of Miami Press, 1961.

Bazzanella, W. *Problemas de Urbanizacao na America Latina, Fontes Bibliograficas.* Rio de Janeiro: Centro Latino Americano de Investigaciones en Ciencias Sociales, 1960.

Beals, Ralph. "Urbanism, Urbanization and Acculturation." In *Readings in Latin American Social Organization.* East Lansing, Michigan: Michigan State College, 1953.

Belaúnde, Victor Andrés. *Meditaciones Peruanas.* 2d ed. Lima: Talleres Gráficos Villanueva, 1963.

Belaúnde-Terry, Fernando. *La Conquista del Perú por los Peruanos.* Lima: Ediciones Tawantinsuyu, 1959.

———. "Iquitos," "Belén," "Vilcashuamán," "Machu Picchu." *El Arquitecto Peruano* 26 (May-June, 1962).

———. *El Perú Construye.* Lima: Minerva, 1965.

———, and Tedeschi, Enrico. "La Plaza de Armas del Cuzco." *El Arquitecto Peruano* 24 (July-August, 1960).

Bennaton-Ramos, J. A. "El Mercado Común Centroamericano: su Evolución y Perspectiva." Unpublished thesis for degree of Lic. en Ciencas Económicas, Universidad Nacional Autónoma de Honduras, 1964.

Bennett, Wendell C. *The Andean Highlands—An Introduction.* Handbook of South American Indians. Washington, D. C.: The Smithsonian Institution, 1946.

———, and Bird, Junius. *Andean Culture History.* Handbook Series, no. 15. New York: American Museum of Natural History, 1949.

Berckholtz-Salinas, Pablo. *Barrios Marginales, Aberración Social.* Lima, 1963.

Berry, B. J. L. "City Size Distributions and Economic Development." In *Regional Development and Planning.* Edited by Friedmann and Alonso. Cambridge, Mass.: The MIT Press, 1964.

———. "Urbanization and Basic Patterns of Development." In *Urban Systems and Economic Development.* Edited by Pitts. Eugene, Oregon: School of Business Administration, University of Oregon, 1962.

———, and Garrison, W. L. "Alternate Explanations of Urban Rank-Size Relationship." In *Readings in Urban Geography.* Edited by Mayer and Kohn. Chicago: University of Chicago Press, 1959.

Beyer, Glenn H., ed. *The Urban Explosion in Latin America.* Ithaca, N.Y.: Cornell University Press, 1967.

Bingham, Hiram. *Lost City of the Incas.* New York: Duell, Sloan and Pearce, 1948.

Bobadilla, J. A. "Importancia de las Obras de Infraestructura en el Desarrollo Economico de Centroamerica." Lecture, Tegucigalpa, June 16, 1962.

Bogree, Donald J. "Migration and Distance." *American Sociological Review* 14 (1949).

Bohan, M. L. and Pomeranz, M. *Investment in Chile.* Washington, D. C.: U. S. Department of Commerce, 1960.

Bollaert, William. *Antiquarian, Ethnological and other Researches in New Granada, Ecuador, Peru, and Chile, with Observation on the Pre-Incarial, Incarial, and other Monuments of Peruvian Nations.* London: Trübner & Co., 1860.

Bonet, Antonio. "Remodelamiento de la zona sur de Buenos Aires." *Cuaderno de Arquitectura* 37 (1959).

Borkoff, Alvin. *The Sociology of Urban Regions.* New York: Appleton-Century-Crofts, 1962.

Bourricaud, Francois. *Changements a Puno: Etude de Sociologie Andine.* Paris: Universite de Paris: De Hautes Etudes de l'Amerique Latine, 1962.

Breese, Gerald Williams, ed. *The City in Newly Developing Countries: Readings on Urbanism and Urbanization.* Englewood Cliffs, N.J.: Prentice-Hall, 1969.

———. *Urbanization in Newly Developing Countries.* Edited by Wilbert E. Moore and Neil J. Smelser. Englewood Cliffs, N.J.: Prentice-Hall, 1966.

Breuer, Marcel. "Nouveau Centre Urbain, Caracas." *L'Architecture D'Aujourd 'hui* 88 (January-March, 1960).

Brisseau, Janine. "Les 'barrios' de Petaré." *Les Cahiers d'Outre-Mer*, 61 (1963).

Bromley, J. and Barbagelata, J. *Evolución Urbana de la Ciudad de Lima.* Lima: Publicación del Consejo Provincial de Lima, 1945.

Browning, Harley L. "Recent Trends in Latin American Urbanization." *The Annals of the American Academy of Political and Social Science* 316 (March, 1958).

Brush, J. E. and Bracey, H. E. "Rural Service Centers in Southwestern Wisconsin and Southern England." in *Readings in Urban Geography.* Edited by Mayer and Kohn. Chicago: University of Chicago Press, 1959.

Burgess, Ernest W. "The Growth of the City; An Introduction to a Research Project." *Publications of the American Sociological Society* 18 (1924).

Busaniche, Hernan, *Arquitectura de la Colonia en el Litoral.* Santa Fé: Talleres Gráficos de Castelvi Hermanos, 1941.

Butland, Gilbert J. *Latin America, a Regional Geography.* London: Longmans, Green and Co., 1961.

———. *Latin America.* New York: John Wiley & Sons, Inc., 1966.

Calderon Alvarado, Luis. *Poder Retentivo del "Area Local Urbana" en la Relaciones Sociales.* Friburgo: Oficina Internacional de Investigaciones Sociales de FERES, 1963.

Camacho, Fabio. *Aspectos de Lima.* Lima: Empresa Publicitaria Expresión, 1937.

Caplow, Theodore. "The Modern Latin American City." *Acculturation of the Americas.* Edited by Sol Tax, International Congress of Americanists, 1949. Chicago: University of Chicago Press, 1951–1952.

———. "The Social Ecology of Guatemala City." *Social Forces* 28 (1949).

———. "Urban Structure in France." *American Sociological Review* 17 (1952).

Cardenas, E., ed. *Almanaque Mundial, Diccionario Geográfico*. México: Selecciones del *Reader's Digest*, 1966.

Cardona, Ramiro. *Estudio de un Barrio de Invasion*. Universidad Nacional de Colombia, no. 2, 1969.

Carmin, Robert L. *Anapolis, Brazil*. The University of Chicago Department of Geography, Research Paper, no. 35. Chicago: University of Chicago Press, 1963.

Carroll, Douglas. "Spatial Interaction" and "The Urban-Metropolitan Regional Description." *Papers and Proceedings of the Regional Science Association* 1 (1955).

Cassinelli, Catalina. *Lima, the Historic Capital of South America*. Lima: Imprenta La Moderna, 1942.

Cavanaugh, Joseph A. *Caracteristicas Socio-Demográficas de Lima, Perú*. Lima: Servicio Cooperativo Interamericano de Salud Pública, 1955.

Centro de Investigaciones Sociales por Muestro, Ministerio de Trabajo y Comunidades, Lima. *Barriadas de Lima. Actitudes de los Habitantes Respecto a los Servicios Publicos y Privados*. Lima, 1967.

Centro de Planification y Urbanismo, Universidad de los Andes, Bogotá. *La Aguas, Plan de Ordenamiento*. Bogotá, 1967.

Centro Interamericano de Vivienda y Planeamiento, CINVA. *Suplemento Informativo*. Bogotá, September, 1965.

———. *Suplemento Informativo*. Bogotá, 1965.

Centro Latino Americano de Investigaciones en Ciencias Sociales. *Problemas de Urbanizacao na America Latina*. Rio de Janeiro, 1960.

Cespedes, Augusto. *Bolivia*. Washington, D. C.: Pan American Union, 1962.

Chapin, F. S. and Weiss, S. F. *Urban Growth Dynamics*. New York: John Wiley & Sons, Inc., 1962.

Checchi, V. *Honduras, A Problem in Economic Development*. New York: The Twentieth Century Fund, 1959.

Cieza de Leon, Pedro. *The Incas*. Norman, Okla.: University of Oklahoma Press, 1959.

Clark, C. "The Location of Industries and Population." *Ekistics* 19/110 (1965).

Cobo, Bernabe. *Historia del Nuevo Mundo*. Sociedad de Bibliófilos Andaluces. Seville: Imprenta de E. Rasco, 1893.

Cole, John P. *Geografía Urbana del Perú*. Facultad de Letras, Instituto de Etnología y Arequeología, no. 10. Lima: Universidad de San Marcos, 1955.

———. "Some Town Planning Problems of Greater Lima." *The Town Planning Review* 26 (1955–56).

Committee for Economic Development. *Economic Development of Central America*. New York, 1964.

Consejo Federal de Inversiones. *Bases Para una Política Nacional de Vivienda*. Buenos Aires, 1964.

Consejo Nacional de Desarrollo, Presidencia de la Nación. *Mapas y Estadísticas de la República Argentina*. Buenos Aires, 1962.

Consejo Nacional de Economia. *Primer Compendio Estadístico, Honduras*. Tegucigalpa, 1964.

Consejo Nacional de Politica Economica y Planeacion, Colombia. *Plan General de Desarrollo Económico y Social.* Bogotá, 1962.

Consulate General of Uruguay. *Republic of Uruguay.* London: E. Stanford, 1883.

Corporacion de Fomento de la Produccion. *Geografía Económica de Chile.* 4 vols. Santiago, 1963.

Corporacion de Fomento y Desarrollo Economico. *Estudio Preliminar de la Organización y Planes de Desarrollo de COFDET.* Tacna, Perú, 1962.

Corredor-Rodriguez, Berta. *La Familia en América Latina.* Friburgo: Oficina Internacional de Investigaciones Sociales de FERES, 1962.

Currie, Lauchlin Bernard. *Una Política Urbana para los Países en Desarrollo.* Bogotá: Ediciones Tercer Mundo, 1965.

Curtis, William Elroy. *The Capitals of Spanish America.* New York: Harper & Bros., 1888.

Damaz, Paul F. *Art in Latin American Architecture.* New York: Reinhold Publishing Corporation, 1963.

Davalos y Lisson, Pedro. *La Primera Centuria.* Lima: Librería e Imprenta Gil, 1919–26.

Davies, H., ed. *The South American Handbook.* 17th ed. London: Trade and Travel Publications, Ltd., 1940.

Davis, Kingsley. "The Origin and Growth of Urbanization in the World." *American Journal of Sociology* 60 (March, 1955).

———. "The Urbanization of the Human Population." Special Issue. *Scientific American* 213 (September, 1965).

———, and Golden, Hilda H. "Urbanization and the Development of Pre-Industrial Areas." *Economic Development and Cultural Change* 3 (October, 1954).

Dawson, G. J. *Geografía Elemental de la República del Salvador.* Paris: Hachette & Co., 1890.

Dean, William Henry, Jr. *The Theory of the Geographical Location of Economic Activities.* Ann Arbor: Edwards Brothers, 1938.

de la Rosa, Moises. *Calles de Santa Fé de Bogotá.* Ediciones del Consejo. Bogotá: Imprenta Municipal, 1938.

de las Casas, Fr. Bartolome. *Las Antiguas Gentes del Perú.* Colección de Libros y Documentos referentes a la Historia del Perú, vol. 11. 2d series. Lima: Librería e Imprenta Gil, 1939.

Demars, Vernon. "Guides to City Form." *Proceedings of the 1959 Conference, American Institute of Planners.* Seattle, Washington, 1959.

Departamento Administrativo de Planificacion Distrital, Bogotá. *Diagnosis Financiera de los Servicios Públicos Distritales.* Bogotá, 1960.

———. *La Planificación en Bogotá.* Bogotá, 1964.

———. *Bogotá, D.E. Política Urbana.* Bogotá, December, 1968.

Departamento Administrativo Nacional de Estadistica, Colombia. *Censo de Población, 9 de mayo de 1951.* Bogotá, 1954.

———. "Distrito Especial de Bogotá." *Anuario Estadístico.* Bogotá, December, 1961.

Dicke, O. A. W. "Maps in the Treatises of Roman Land Surveys." *The Geographic Journal* 126 (December, 1961).

Dickinson, Robert Eric. *City Region and Regionalism*. New York: Oxford University Press, 1947.

———. *The Growth of the Historic City*. London: Routledge & Kegan, 1951.

Diez Canseco, Ernesto. *La Red Nacional de Carreteras*. Dirección de Vias de Comunicación. Lima: Imprenta Torres Aguirre, 1929.

Dirección de Aviacion Comercial y Civil, Perú. *Boletín*. Year 1, no. 1. Lima, 1936.

Dirección de Caminos, Perú. *Informe—Carretera Marginal de la Selva*. Lima, 1964.

Dirección de Censo, Estadística, y Registro del Estado Civil, Uruguay. *Boletín Censo y Estadística*. Montevideo, July, August, 1950.

Dirección de Economia y Estadística Agropecuaria. *Immigración, Primer Semestre, 1964*. Caracas, September, 1964.

Dirección de Estadística y Censo, Panamá. "Población Urbana." *Quinto Censo de Población, 1950*, vol. 5. Panama City, 1956.

Dirección de Estadística y Censos, Republica de Chile. *XI Censo de Población 1940*. Santiago, 1941.

———. *Entidades de Población 1960*. Santiago, 1962.

Dirección de Obras Publicas y Vias de Comunicacion, Perú. *Economía y Reseña Histórica de los Ferrocarriles del Perú*. Lima: Imprenta Torres Aguirre, 1932.

Dirección General de Estadística, Chile. "Resumen de País." *XII Censo General de Población y Vivienda, 24 de Abril de 1952*, vol. 1. Santiago, 1956.

Dirección General de Estadística, Dominican Republic. *Estadística Demográfica, 1961*, vol. 19. Santo Domingo, 1964.

———. *Población de la República Dominicana Censada en 1950*. Ciudad Trujillo, 1954.

Dirección General de Estadística, El Salvador. *La República de El Salvador*. San Salvador, 1924.

Dirección General de Estadística, Guatemala. *Anuario del Comercio Exterior, 1960*. Guatemala, 1962.

———. *Censo General de la República, 1893*. Guatemala, 1894.

———. *Guía Kilométrica de la Red Vial de la Republica de Guatemala*. Guatemala, n.d.

———. *Sexto Censo de Población, 1950*. Guatemala City, 1957.

———. *Trimestre Estadístico, Enero, Febrero, Marzo*. Guatemala, 1964.

———. *Trimestre Estadístico, Abril, Mayo, Junio*. Guatemala, 1964.

———. *Trimestre Estadístico, Julio, Agosto, Septiembre*, Guatemala, 1964.

Dirección General de Estadística, Honduras. *Resumen General de Censo de Población, 18 de Junio de 1950*. Tegucigalpa, 1952.

Dirección General de Estadística, México. *VII Censo General de Población, 6 de Junio de 1950*. México, 1952.

———. *VIII Censo General de Población, 8 de Junio de 1960*. México, 1963.

Dirección General de Estadística, Perú. *Resumen del Censo General de Habitantes del Perú hecho en 1876.* Lima: Imprenta del Estado, 1878.

Dirección General de Estadísticas y Censos, Bolivia. *Proyección de la Población 1950–1962.* La Paz, 1962.

Dirección General de Estadística y Censos, Chile. *Breves Consideraciones sobre la Muestra de Población.* Santiago, 1960.

———. *Demografía Año 1961–1962.* Santiago: Servicio Nacional de Estadística, 1962.

———. *Población del País: Características Básicas de la Población (censo 1960).* Santiago, 1964.

Dirección General de Estadística y Censos, Costa Rica. *II Censo de Industrias en Costa Rica, 1958.* San José, 1962.

———. *Censo de Población de Costa Rica, 22 de Mayo de 1950.* San José, 1953.

———. *Censos de 1963, Población y Vivienda.* San José, 1965.

Dirección General de Estadística y Censos, Ecuador. *Información Censal, 1950.* Quito, 1954.

———. *Segundo Censo de Población y Primer Censo de Vivienda, 25 de Noviembre de 1962,* vol. 1. Quito, 1964.

Dirección General de Estadística y Censos, El Salvador. *Anuario Estadístico.* San Salvador, 1963.

———. *Segundo Censo de Población, 13 de Junio de 1950.* San Salvador, 1954.

———. *Tercer Censo Industrial y Comercial, 1961.* San Salvador, 1962.

———. *Tercer Censo Nacional de Población, 1961.* San Salvador, 1962.

Dirección General de Estadística y Censos, Honduras. *Anuario Estadístico, 1962.* Tegucigalpa, 1962.

———. *Cifras Definitivas de Población y Viviendas en Cabeceras Municipales y en Aldeas y Caseríos, Abril, 1961.* Tegucigalpa, 1963.

Dirección General de Estadística y Censos, Nicaragua. "Informe General y Cifras del Departamento de Managua." *Censo General de Población de la República de Nicaragua 1950,* vol. 10. Managua, 1951.

Dirección General de Estadística y Censos, Paraguay. *Anuario Estadístico, 1948–1953. Asunción,* 1957.

Dirección General de Industrias, Ecuador. *Fomento Industrial Ecuador.* Quito, 1965.

Dirección General del Censo, El Salvador. *Censo de Población del Municipio de San Salvador Levantado el 15 de Octubre de 1929.* San Salvador, 1929.

Dirección Nacional de Estadística, Perú. *Anuario Estadístico del Perú.* Lima: Dirección de Estadística del Ministerio de Fomento, 1956–1957.

Dirección Nacional de Estadística y Censos, Argentina. *Censo de Comercio 1954,* vol. 1. Buenos Aires, 1959.

———. *Censo de Población 1960, Resultados Provisionales por Departamentos y/o Partidos.* Buenos Aires, 1960–1961.

———. "Censo de Población 1947." *VI Censo General de la Nacion,* vol. 1. Buenos Aires, 1957.

————. *Censo Industrial 1960, Resultados Provisionales.* Buenos Aires, 1960.

————. *Censo Nacional 1960, Vivienda, Resultados Provisionales.* Buenos Aires, 1961.

————. *Censo Nacional Económico 1963, Resultados Provisionales.* Buenos Aires, 1964.

Dirección Nacional de Estadística y Censos, Bolivia. *Censo de Población de la República de Bolivia, 5 de Septiembre de 1950.* La Paz, 1951.

Dirección Nacional de Estadística y Censos, Perú. *Boletín de Estadística Peruana.* Year III, no. 4. Lima: Ministerio de Hacienda y Comercio, 1960.

————. *Boletín de Estadística Peruana.* Year V, no. 6. Lima: Ministerio de Hacienda y Comercio, 1962.

————. *Boletín de Estadística Peruana.* Year VI, no. 6. Lima: Ministerio de Hacienda y Comercio, 1963.

————. *Censo Nacional de Población y Occupación 1940, Vol. I, Resúmenes General.* Lima, 1944–1949.

————. *Sexto Censo Nacional de Población, 2 de Julio de 1961.* Lima, 1964.

Dirección Nacional de Estadística y Censos, Venezuela. *Noveno Censo General de Población, 1961.* Caracas, 1964.

————. "Resumen General de la República, Parte A, Población." In *Octavo Censo General de Población, 26 de Noviembre de 1950.* Caracas, 1957.

Dirección Nacional de Turismo, La Paz. *Plano Turistico de la Ciudad de La Paz.* La Paz, 1956.

Dobyns, Henry and Vazquez, Mario. *Migración e Integración en el Perú.* Monografías Andinas, no. 2. Lima: Editorial Estudios Andinos, 1963.

Dollfus, Olivier. "Lima, Quelques Aspects de la Capitale du Perou en 1958." *Les Cahiers d'Outre-Mer* 11 (1958).

Dorich, Luis. "Urbanization and Physical Planning in Peru." In *Urbanization in Latin America.* Edited by Philip Hauser. Seminar on Urbanization in Latin America, Santiago de Chile, 1959. New York: International Documents Service, 1961.

Dorselaer, Jaime and Cregory, A. *La Urbanización en la América Latina,* vol. 1. Bogotá: Central Internacional de Investigaciones Sociales, FERES, 1962.

Dotson, Floyd and Dotson, Lillian O. "Ecological Trends in the City of Guadalajara, Mexico." *Social Forces* 32 (May, 1954).

————. "La Estructura Ecologica de las Ciudades Mexicanas." *Revista Mexicana de Sociologia* 19 (January-April, 1959).

————. "Urban Centralization and Decentralization in Mexico." *Rural Sociology* 21 (March, 1956).

Duncan, Otis Dudley. *Metropolis and Region.* Baltimore: The Johns Hopkins Press, 1960.

————. "Service Industries and the Urban Hierarchy." In *Papers and Proceedings of the Regional Science Association* 5 (1959).

Dyer, Donald. "Population and Elevation in Peru." *Northwestern University Studies in Geography,* vol. 6. Evanston, Illinois: Northwestern University Press, 1962.

Eckbo, Ganet. "Form and Content in Urban Areas." *Proceedings of the 1959 Annual Conference, American Institute of Planners.* Seattle, 1959.

Elman, Service. "Indian-European Relations in Colonial Latin America." *American Anthropologists* 57/3/1 (1955).

Enock, C. Reginald. *Perú.* London: T. Fisher Unwin, 1912.

Enriquez, Eliecer. *Quito a travez de los Siglos.* Quito: Imprenta Municipal, 1938.

Ervin, Roger E. "Industry in the Concepción Area of Chile." *The American Journal of Economics and Sociology* 14/4 (April, 1955).

Espasadin, Mario Bon. *Cantegriles.* Montevideo: Ediciones Tupac Amaru, 1963.

Espinoza Gomez, Carlos. *Tres Épocas de Historia Vial Peruana.* Boletín Extraordinario. Lima: Ministerio de Fomento y O. P., Dirección de Caminos, 1964.

Fei, John C. H. and Ranis, Gustav. *Development of the Labor Surplus Economy: Theory and Policy.* New Haven: Yale University Press, 1964.

Felce, Emma. *Antiguas Ciudades de América.* Buenos Aires: Emece Editores, 1943.

Ferreira-Gubeitch, Hugo. *Geografía del Paraguay.* 5th ed. Asunción: La Colmena, 1962.

Fondo Nacional de Salud, Lima, Perú. *Barriadas de Lima Metropolitana.* Lima, 1960.

Frias V, Francisco. *Historia de Chile.* Vol. 1. Santiago Editorial Nascimiento, 1947.

Frieden, Bernard. "The Search for Housing Policy in Mexico City." *The Town Planning Review* 36 (August, 1965).

Friedmann, John. "Cities in Social Transformation." *Comparative Studies in Society and History* 1 (November, 1961).

———. "Regional Planning: A Problem in Spatial Integration." In *Papers Proceedings of the Regional Science Association* 11 (1963).

———. "Regional Planning: A Problem in Spatial Integration." In *Papers and Proceedings of the Regional Science Association* 5 (1959).

———. "Venezuela, Economic Growth and Urban Structure." *Cuadernos de la Sociedad Venezolana de Planificación.* Special Issue. (September, 1963).

Fugier, Andre. "Buenos Aires et ses problemes de croissance." *Les Cahiers d'Outre-Mer* 6 (1949).

Garcia, J. Uriel. *La Ciudad de los Incas.* Cuzco: Librería e Imprenta H. G. Rozas, 1922.

Garcia-Pelaez, F. de P. *Memorias para la Historia del Antiguo Reino de Guatemala.* Vol. 1. Guatemala: Biblioteca "Payo de Rivera," 1943.

Garcia-Ramos, Domingo. *Iniciación al Urbanismo.* México, Universidad Nacional Autónoma de México, 1961.

Garland, Alejandro. *Peru in 1906.* Lima: Imprenta "La Industria," 1907.

Gasparini, Graziano. *La Casa Colonial Venezolana.* Caracas: Ediciones Armitano, 1965.

George, Pierre. *La Ville*. Paris: Presses Universitaires de France, 1952.

Gerbi, Antonello. *Caminos del Perú*. Lima: Banco de Crédito del Perú, 1944.

Gibbs, Jack P. and Shnore, Leo, eds. "Metropolitan Growth: an International Study." *American Journal of Sociology* 66 (September, 1960).

Gibson, Charles. *The Inca Concept of Sovereignty and the Spanish Administration in Peru*. The University of Texas, Institute of Latin-American Studies, Latin American Studies, no. 4. Austin: The University of Texas Press, 1948.

Giles, Sofia. "Urbanization in Peru." Unpublished student paper, Yale University, 1965.

Gist, Noel Pitts and Fava, Sylvia Fleis. *Urban Society*. New York: Thomas Y. Crowell, 1964.

Giuria, Juan G. *Apuntes de Arquitectura Colonial Argentina*. Montevideo: Imprenta el Siglio Ilustrado, 1941.

Gobierno del Distrito Federal, Direccion de Publicaciones, Caracas. "Plan Caracas 1938–40." *Revista Municipal del Distrito Federal*. Caracas, 1945–1950.

Gomez-Quinones, J., ed. *Statistical Abstract of Latin America*. Los Angeles: Latin American Center, University of California, 1964.

Gonzalez, D. *Compendio de Geografia de Centro-America*. 2d ed. Guatemala, 1881.

González, Pedro J. "Problemes d'Habitation a Caracas." *La Vie Urbaine* (Organe de l'Institut d'Urbanisme de l'Universite de Paris) 2 (April-June, 1961).

Gonzalez-Tafur, Oswaldo. *Peru, Poblacion y Agricultura*. Lima. Imprenta Lopez, 1952.

Goode, John Paul. *World Atlas*. Edited by E. B. Espenshade. Chicago: Rand McNally, 1954.

Grinsburg, Norton. *Atlas of Economic Development*. Chicago: University of Chicago Press, 1961.

Guarda, Gabriele. *Santo Tomás de Aquino y las Fuentes del Urbanismo Indiano*. Santiago: Academia Chilena de la Historia, Facultad de Arquitectura, 1965.

Gutierrez, Ramiro Cardona. *Las Marginados Urbanos: Un Producto del Proceso de Urbanizacion*. Boletin, no. 23. Bogotá, 1968.

Guzman, Ossandon. *Guía de Santiago*. Santiago: Ediciones Zig-Zag, 1962.

Guzzardi, Walter, Jr. "The Crucial Middle Class." *Fortune* Magazine 65 (February, 1962).

Haer, Charles. "Latin America's Troubled Cities." *Foreign Affairs* 41 (April, 1963).

Hagen, Everett B. *On the Theory of Social Change*. New York: Dorsey Press, 1962.

Hanson, E. P. *The New World Guides to the Latin American Republicas*. Vol. 1. New York: Duell, Sloan & Pearce, 1943.

Harris, Walter D. and Gillies, J. *Capital Formation For Housing in Latin America*. Washington, D. C.: Pan American Union, 1963.

Harris, Walter D. and Hossé, Hans A., and Associates. *Housing in Peru.* Washington, D. C.: Pan American Union, 1963.

———. *La Vivienda en Honduras—Housing in Honduras.* Washington, D. C.: Pan American Union, 1964.

Hatt, Paul Kitchener and Reiss, Albert J., eds. *Cities and Society.* 2d ed. New York: Free Press of Glencoe, 1961.

Hauser, Philip M. *Population Perspective.* New Brunswick, N. J.: Rutgers University Press, 1960.

———. "Urbanization in Asia and the Far East." *Seminar on Urbanization in the ECAFE Region.* Calcutta: United Nations Education, Social and Cultural Organization, 1957.

———, ed. *Urbanization in Latin America.* Seminar on Urbanization in Latin America, Santiago de Chile, 1959. New York: International Documents Service, Columbia University Press, 1961.

———. and Schnore, Leo. *The Study of Urbanization.* New York: John Wiley & Sons, 1965.

Hawley, Amos. *Human Ecology.* New York: Ronald Press, 1950.

Hawthorne, Harry B. and Hawthorne, Audrey E. "The Shape of a City; Some Observations on Sucre, Bolivia." *Sociology and Social Research* 33 (November, 1948).

Hayner, Norman S. "Mexico City: Its Growth and Configuration." *American Journal of Sociology* 50 (July, 1944–May, 1945).

———. "Oaxaca: City of Old Mexico." *Sociology and Social Research,* 29 (1944).

Heabtob, Herbert. "Industrial Revolution." *Enclyclopedia of Social Sciences.* New York: Macmillan Co., 1953.

Herrick, Bruce H. *Urban Migration and Economic Development in Chile.* Cambridge, Mass.: The M.I.T. Press, 1965.

Higgins, Benjamin Howard. *Economic Development.* New York: Norton, 1959.

Hilberseimer, L. *The Nature of Cities: Origin, Growth, Decline, Pattern and Form, Planning Problems.* Chicago: Paul Theobald and Co., 1955.

Hirschman, Albert O. *Latin American Issues.* New York: The Twentieth Century Fund, 1961.

———. *The Strategy of Economic Development.* New Haven: Yale University Press, 1964.

Holmberg, Allen R. *Social Change in Latin America.* New York: Vintage Books, 1961.

Horkheimer, Hans. *Historia del Perú—Epoca Pre-Hispánica.* Trujillo: Imprenta Gamarra, 1943.

———. *El Peru Prehispánico—Intento de un Manual.* Lima: Editorial Cultura Antártica S. A., 1950.

Hoselitz, Bert F. "Cities in Advanced and Underdeveloped Countries." *Confluence* 4 (October, 1955).

———. "The City, The Factory, and Economic Growth." *American Economic Review* 45 (May, 1955).

———. *Sociological Aspects of Economic Growth.* Glencoe, Ill.: The Free Press of Glencoe, 1962.

Hoyt, Homer. "The Residential and Retail Patterns of Leading Latin American Cities." *Land Economics* 39 (November, 1963).

———. "The Structure and Growth of American Cities Contrasted With the Structure of European and Asiatic Cities." *Urban Land* 18 (September, 1959.

———. *The Structure and Growth of Residential Neighborhoods in American Cities.* Federal Housing Administration. Washington, D. C.: U.S. Government Printing Office, 1939.

———. "World Urbanization; Population in a Shrinking World." *Technical Bulletin 43.* Washington, D.C.: Urban Land Institute, April, 1962.

Hutchinson, L. *Report on Trade Conditions in Central America and On the West Coast of South America.* Document 154, House of Representatives, 59th Congress. Washington, D. C., 1906.

Imaz, Jose Luis de. *La Clase Alta De Buenos Aires.* Buenos Aires: La Imprenta de la Universidad, 1962.

Instituto Brasileiro de Geografia e Estadistica. *Censo Demografico.* Rio de Janeiro: Servico Grafico do Instituto Brasileiro de Geografia e Statistica, 1950.

———. "Ensaio para a estructura urbana do Rio de Janeiro." *Revista Brasileira de Geografia,* 22 (January-March, 1960).

———. "Estudio da populacao ativa fluminense e sua utilizacao ha delimitacao das zonas economicas do estado." *Revista Brasileira de Geografia* 21 (April-June, 1959).

———. "Expanao de espaco urbano no Dio de Janeiro." *Revista Brasileira Geografia* 22 (April-June, 1960).

———. *VI Recenseamento do Brasil: Censo Demografico, 1 de Julho de 1950.* Rio de Janeiro: Conselho Nacional de Estadistica, Servicio Nacional de Recenseamento, 1951–1955.

Instituto de Credito Territorial. *Vivienda y Desarrollo Urbano.* Cuadro no. 4. Bogotá, May 27, 1969.

———. *Informe al II Congreso Inter-Americano de Vivienda.* Bogotá, February, 1969.

Instituto de Economia, Universidad de Chile. *La Migración Interna en Chile en El Período 1940–1952.* Santiago, Chile, 1959.

Instituto de Geografia de la Universidad de Chile. *Informaciones Geografias, 1960.* Santiago, Chile: Universidad de Chile, Facultad de Filosofía y Educación, 1963.

Instituto Nacional de Planificacion, Lima, Perú. *Análisis de la Realidad Socio-Económica del Perú.* Vols. 4 & 6. Lima, 1963.

———. *Bolsa de Comercio de Lima, Memoria, 1961.* Lima, 1962.

———. *La Planificación en el Peru. Conceptos Básicos.* Vol. 1. Lima: Dirección Técnica del Instituto Nacional de Planificación, 1963.

———. *Precios e Indices para el Consumidor Medio: Lima, Callao, Arequipa.* Lima, 1963.

———. *Primer Censo Nacional Económico.* Lima, 1963.

———. *Programa de Inversiones Públicas 1964–65.* Lima, 1964–1965.

———. *Sexto Censo Nacional de Planificación, 1961.* Lima, 1964.

Inter-American Development Bank. *Social Progress Trust Fund, Fifth Annual Report, 1965.* Washington, D. C., 1951.

International Association of Universities. *International Handbook of Universities and Other Institutions of Higher Education, 1965.* Paris, 1965.

International Bank for Reconstruction and Development. *The Economic Development of Guatemala.* Washington, D. C., 1951.

International Statistical Institute. *International Statistical Yearbook of Large Towns.* Vols. 1 and 2. La Haye, 1961.

International Urban Research Institute Studies, University of California at Berkeley. *The World's Metropolitan Areas.* Berkeley: University of California Press, 1959.

Isard, Walter. *Location and Space Economy.* New York: John Wiley & Sons, 1956.

———. *Methods of Regional Analysis: An Introduction to Regional Science.* New York: John Wiley & Sons, 1960.

James, Preston E. *Latin America.* New York: The Odyssey Press, 1959.

Jefferson, Mark. "The Law of the Primate City." *The Geographical Review* 24 (April, 1939).

Jenkins, E. "Planning in Central America." *Proceedings of the 1961 Conference.* Baltimore: American Institute of Planners, 1961.

Jones, C. L. *Guatemala, Past and Present.* Minneapolis: University of Minnesota Press, 1940.

Jones, Emrys. "Aspects of Urbanization in Venezuela." *Ekistics* 18 (December, 1964).

———. *Human Geography.* New York: F. A. Praeger, 1965.

Keane, A. H. *Stanford's Compendium of Geography, Central and South America.* Vol. 2. London: E. Stanford, 1901.

Kubler, George. *The Indian Caste of Peru, 1795–1940.* Washington, D. C.: U.S. Government Printing Office, 1952.

———. "Machu Picchu." *Perspecta 6, The Yale Architectural Journal* (1960).

———. *The Quechua in the Colonial World.* Handbook of South American Indians, Bulletin 143, vol. 2. Washington, D. C.: Bureau of American Ethnology, 1946.

Lannoy, Juan Luis de. *Los Niveles de Vida en América Latina. Estudios Sociológicos,* vol. 6. Bogotá, 1963.

Larde y Larín, J. *El Salvador: Historia de sus Pueblos, Villas y Ciudades. Colección Historia,* vol. 3. San Salvador: Ministerio de Cultura, 1957.

Leite, Aureliano. *Subsidios para a historia da civilizacao Paulista.* São Paulo: Edicao Saravia, 1954.

Leonard, Olen E. "La Paz, Bolivia: Its Population and Growth." *American Sociological Review* 13 (1948).

———, and Loomis, Charles, eds. *Readings in Latin American Social Organizations and Institutions.* East Lansing, Michigan: Michigan State College Press, 1953.

Lester, Paul and Sert, Jose Luis. "La Havane." *L'Architecture D'Aujourd'hui* 88 (February, 1960).

Lewis, Oscar. *Five Families.* New York: Basic Books, 1959.

Libreria Colombiana Camacho Roldan. *Colombia en Cifras*. Bogotá: Aldita Editores, 1963.

Linder Alfredo. "Huancayo: su plan regulador." *El Arquitecto Peruano* 22 (January-February, 1958).

Linsky, A. S. "Some Generalizations Concerning Primate Cities." *Annals of the Association of American Geographers* 55 (September, 1965).

Little, Arthur D., Inc. *A Program for the Industrial and Regional Development of Peru*. A Report to the Government of Perú. Cambridge, Mass., 1960.

Lorwin, Lewis L. *National Planning in Selected Countries*. Washington, D. C.: National Resources Planning Board, August, 1941.

Luna Vegas, Emilio. *El Perú Invadido*. Lima: Ediciones Tawantinsuyo, 1962.

Lynch, Kevin. "The Form of the Cities." *Scientific American* 190 (April, 1954).

———. *The Image of the City*. Cambridge, Mass.: The M. I. T. Press, 1962.

Marbeig, P. "La Croissance de la Ville de São Paulo." *Revue de Geographie Alpine* 41 (1953).

Marchand, Bernard. "Etude Geographique de la Population du Venezuela." *Annales de Geographie* 72 (Novembre-Decembre, 1963).

Marshall, Alfred. *Principles of Economics*. 8th ed. London: Macmillan Co., 1922.

Martin, Mario E. "Urban Systems in Central America." Unpublished student paper, Yale University, 1966.

Martinez, Carlos. *Apuntes sobre el urbanismo en el Nuevo Reino de Granada*. Bogotá: Talleres Gráficos del Banco de la República, 1951.

———. *Arquitectura en Colombia*. Bogotá: Talleres Gráficos del Banco de la República, 1963.

Mason, J. Alden. *The Ancient Civilizations of Peru*. Harmondsworth, Middlesex: Penguin Books, 1957.

Matienzo, Juan. *Gobierno del Perú*. Buenos Aires: Compañía Sud-Americana de Billetes de Banco, 1910.

Mayer, Harold Melvin and Kohn, Clyde F., eds. *Readings in Urban Geography*. Chicago: University of Chicago Press, 1964.

Meade, James Edward. *A Neoclassical Theory of Economic Growth*. New York: Oxford University Press, 1961.

Means, Philip Ainsworth. *Ancient Civilizations of the Andes*. New York: C. Scribner's, 1931.

Meier, Gerald Marvin and Baldwin, Robert E. *Economic Development, Theory, History, Policy*. New York: John Wiley, 1957.

Menendez, D. Baldomero. *Manual de Geografía y Estadística del Perú*. Paris: Librería de Rosa y Bouret, 1861.

Ministerio de Fomento, Direccion General de Estadistica y Censos Nacionales, Venezuela. "Area Metropolitana de Caracas." *Noveno Censo General de Población 1961*, vol. 6. Caracas, 1964.

Ministerio de Hacienda y Comercio, Perú. *Censo Nacional de Población 1940*. Vol. 5. Lima, 1948.

Ministerio de Marina y Aviacion, Perú. *Memoria, que el Ministro de Marina Dr. Arturo Rubio presenta al Congreso Nacional de 1927*. Lima, 1927.

Ministerio de Obras Publicas, Comision Nacional de Urbanismo, Venezuela. *Plano Regulador de Caracas, Estudio Preliminar.* Caracas, 1953.

Ministry of Public Works, Colombia. *Plan for Improvements in National Transportation: Summary Report.* Bogotá, 1961.

Miro-Quesada, Aurelio. "La Ciudad en el Perú." *Mercurio Peruano* 18/181 (April, 1942).

Montecino Samperio, Jose V. *La Población del Area Metropolitana de Caracas.* Caracas: Demografía Venezuela, 1956.

Morse, Richard M. *From Community to Metropolis.* Gainesville: University of Florida Press, 1958.

———. "Latin American Cities: Aspects of Function and Structure." *Comparative Studies in Society and History* 4 (July, 1962).

———. "Some Characteristics of Latin American Urban History." *The American Historical Review* 142/2 (January, 1962).

Morua, Martin de. *Historia del Origen y Genealogía Real de los Reyes Incas del Peru, de sus hechos, costumbres, trajes y manera de Gobierno.* Colección de Libros y Documentos referentes a la historia del Perú, series 2, vol. 4. Lima, 1922–1925.

Municipalidad de La Paz, Oficina del Plan Regulador. *Reglamentos de Parcelación y Zonificacion.* La Paz, n.d.

Municipio de Barranquilla. *Código de Urbanismo, Plan Regulador, Reglamento de Zonificación—Reglamento de Parcelación.* Barranquilla, Colombia, 1958.

Musée National d'art Moderne, Paris. *Exposition Le Corbusier; oeuvres plastiques.* Paris: Editions des Musees Nationaux, 1953.

Museo de Arte, Lima. *Presencia del la Arquitectura Virreinal en Lima.* Lima: Consejo National de Conservación y Restauración de Monumentos Históricos y Artísticos, 1963.

National Geographic Society. *National Atlas of the World.* Washington, D. C., 1963.

National Resources Committee. *Our Cities in the National Economy.* Washington, D.C.: U.S. Government Printing Office, 1937.

Nicholson, Carlos. *Ensayos de geografía politica del Perú.* Arequipa: Editorial "El Orden,'" 1935.

Oficina de Estudios para la Colaboracion Economica Internacional. *America Latina: Síntesis Económica.* Vol. 1. Buenos Aires, n.d.

Oficina Nacional de Planeamiento y Urbanismo, Perú. *Guía de Ciudades del Población, Viviendas y Electoral, enero de 1953.* La Habana, 1955.

Oficina Nacional de Planeamiento y Urbanismo, Perú. *Guía de Ciudades del Perú.* Lima, 1955.

———. *Lima Metropolitana.* Lima, Diciembre, 1954.

———. *Plan de Desarrollo Metropolitano Lima-Callao, Esquema Director.* Lima, 1967.

Oficina Nacional de Urbanismo, Nicaragua. *Plànificación Urbana, Apuntes Gráficos de Proceso.* Managua: Editorial Los Angeles, 1959.

Oficina de Planificacion Distrital, Departamento de Investigaciones, Bogotá. *Planteles y Demanda Escolar en Bogotá.* Bogotá, 1958.

Ortiz de Zevallos, Luis. *Curso de Evolución Urbana.* Instituto de Urbanismo de la U. N. I. Lima: Imprenta de la Universidad de Ingeniería del Perú, 1960.

———. *Historia de las Formas Urbana y Regionales.* Lima: Instituto de Planeamiento de Lima, 1964.

Owens, Ronald Jerome. *Perú.* New York: Oxford University Press, 1963.

Palerm, A. and Wolfe, E. R. "Potencial Ecológico y Desarrollo Cultural en Mesoamerica." *Estudios Sobre Ecología Humana.* Estudios Monográficos, no. 3. Washington, D.C.: Pan American Union, 1960.

Palm, E. W. *Los Origines del Urbanismo Imperial en America.* México: Contribuciones a la Historia Municipal de América, 1951.

Pan American Union. *Bosquejo de la República Dominicana.* Washington, D. C., 1956.

———. *Informe Oficial, Misión 105 a Honduras.* Vol. 3. Washington, D. C., 1964.

———. *Selected Economic Data on the Latin American Republics.* Washington, D. C., 1948.

———. *Montevideo, the City of Roses.* American City Series, no. 20-a. Washington, D. C., 1942.

Pan American Union, Department of Social Affairs. *Economic and Social Survey of Latin America, 1961.* Vol. 2. Washington, D. C., 1964.

———. *Estudio Social de America Latina.* Washington, D. C., 1962.

———. "Tendencias de Localización y Crecimiento de la Población Urbana Latinoamericana." Unpublished mimeograph. Washington, D. C., 1964.

Pan American Union, Division of Economic Development. *Informe sobre la Integración Económica y Social del Perú Central.* Washington, D. C., 1961.

Pan American Union, Division of Economic Research. *The Peruvian Economy.* Washington, D. C., 1950.

Pani, Mario. "Conjunto Urbano Nonoalco-Tlaltelolco: Regeneración Urbanística de la Ciudad de México." *Arquitectura Mexico* 16/72 (December, 1960).

Pareja Paz Soldan. Jose. *Geografía del Peru.* Lima: Librería e Imprenta Miranda, 1943.

Parsons, Talcott. *Theories of Society; Foundations of Modern Sociological Theory.* Vol. 1. Glencoe, Ill.: The Free Press of Glencoe, 1961.

Patch, Richard W. "Life in a Callejon." *American Universities Field Staff, Reports Service.* West Coast South America Series, 8/6. Perú, June, 1961.

Peani, Gian L. "L'Architettura Moderna in Argentina." *Casabella Continuitá* 285 (Marzo, 1964).

Pepler, Elizabeth E. "Towns in Brazil." *Town and Country Planning* 29/1 (January, 1961).

Perez de Riva, Juan. *La Población de Cuba.* Habana, Cuba: Escuela de Geografía, Universidad de la Habana, 1964.

Perez Ramirez, G. "El Campesinado Colombiano." *Estudios Sociológicos Latino Americanos*, vol. 20. Friburgo: Oficina Internacional de Estudios Sociales de FERES, 1962.

Perroux, F. "Consideraciones en Torno a la Noción de 'Polo de Crecimiento.'" *Cuadernos de la Sociedad Venezolana de Planificación* 2/3 & 4 (June-July, 1963).

Picon-Salas, Mariano. *A Cultural History of Spanish America, From Conquest to Independence*. Translated by Irving A. Leonard. Berkeley: University of California Press, 1962.

Pinchas Geiger, Pedro. *Evolucao de Rede Urbana Brasileira*. Rio de Janeiro: Centro Brasilero de Pesquisas Educacionais, Instituto Nacional de Estudos Pedagogicos, Ministerio da Educacao e Cultura, 1963.

————, and, Davidovich Fany. "Aspectos do Fato Urbano do Brasil." *Revista Brasileira de Geografia* 33/2 (Abril-Junho, 1961).

Pitts, F. R., ed. *Urban Systems and Economic Development*. Eugene, Oregon: School of Business Administration, University of Oregon, June, 1962.

Plank, John Nathan. *Peru: A Study in the Problems of Nation Forming*. Unpublished Ph.D. thesis, Department of Government, Harvard University, 1958.

Polanyi, Karl. *The Great Transformation*. New York: Farrar & Rinehart, 1944.

Pons Muzzo, Gustavo. *Las Fronteras del Perú*. Lima: Talleres Gráficos Iberia, 1962.

Porras Barrenechea, Raul. "Vision Introductiva." *El Perú Virreynal*. Lima: Sociedad Académica de Estudios Americanos, 1962.

Pred, Allen. *The External Relations of Cities during "Industrial Revolution."* Department of Geography Research Paper no. 76. Chicago: University of Chicago Press, 1962.

Prendle, G. *Paraguay*. London: Oxford University Press, 1967.

Prestes, Francisco. *Plano de Avenidas para a Cidade de São Paulo. Rio de Janeiro*: Cayeiras, 1930.

Ravenstein, Ernest. "The Laws of Migration." *Journal of the Royal Statistical Society* 48/2 (June, 1885).

Regal, Alberto. "Técnica Vial del Imperio Incaico." *Ingeniería Civil* 52 (July-August, 1964).

Reissman, Leonard. *The Scope of Urban Theory*. New York: The Free Press of Glencoe, 1964.

Reuter, Edward B., ed. *Race and Culture Contacts*. New York: McGraw-Hill, 1934.

Ribero y Ustariz, Mariano E., and Tschudi, J. D. von. *Antigüedades Peruanas*. Vienna: Imprenta Imperial de la Corte y del Estado, 1851.

Roberts, Walter Adolphe. *Havana, The Portrait of the City*. New York: Coward-McCann, 1953.

Robertson, Donald. *Pre-Columbian Architecture*. New York: George Braziller, 1963.

Robinson, David A. *Peru in Four Dimensions*. Lima: Minerva, 1964.

Robson, William A. *Great Cities of the World*. New York: Macmillan, 1954.

Rodriguez-Arranz, Alfredo. "Physical Urban Form in South America." Unpublished student paper, Yale University, 1966.

Rodriguez-Camilloni, Humberto. "The Barriada Problem in Lima Today." Unpublished student paper, Yale University, 1965.

Rodwin, Lynch. "Theory of Urban Form." *American Institute of Planners Journal* 24/4 (1958).

Romero, Emilio. *Geografía Económica del Perú*. Lima: Imprenta Torres Aguirre, 1944.

Rosenstein-Rodan, Ernest. "Review of Economics and Statistics." *F.A.O. Statistical Yearbook*, vol. 43. New York: United Nations Food and Agriculture Organization, 1961.

Rostow, W. W. *The Stages of Economic Growth*. London: Cambridge University Press, 1960.

Rotary Club de Trujillo, *Monografía Geográfica e Histórica del Departamento de La Libertad*. Trujillo: Imprenta La Central, 1935.

Rother, Hans. Requierimientos de Vivienda Urbana y Politica de Realizaciones del ICT II. Seminario Nacional Sobre Urbanizacion y Marginalidad. Sogamosos, May, 1969.

Rotival, Maurice E. H. "Caracas, Reprise du Plan d'Amenagement, 1950–1965." *L'Architecture d'Aujourd'hui* 88 (February-March, 1960).

Ruiz, Fowler. *Monografía Histórico-Geográfica del Departamento de Ayacucho*. Lima: Torres Aguirre, 1924.

Rumbo, Oscar. *El Transporte Fluvial en la Argentina*. Buenos Aires: Biblioteca Cumbre, 1965.

Rycroft, Stanley W. and Clemmer, Myrtle M. *A Factual Study of Latin America*. New York: Commission on Ecumenical Mission and Relations, United Presbyterian Church of the U.S.A., 1963.

————. *A Study of Urbanization in Latin America*. New York: Commission on Ecumenical Mission and Relations, United Presbyterian Church of the U.S.A., 1962.

Saavedra. D. *Bananas, Gold and Silver*. Tegucigalpa: Talleres Tipográficos Nacionales, 1935.

Sacramento, Antenor A. *O Despertar Economico dos Sertoes Baianos*. Rio de Janeiro: Livraria Freitas Bastos, 1965.

Samuelson, Paul. *Economics*. 5th ed. New York: McGraw-Hill Book Co., 1961.

San Martin, Alberto. *Reflexiones Sobre el Planeamiento de un Sistema de Transporte Argentino*. Buenos Aires: Biblioteca Cumbre, 1965.

Santos, Milton. *A Cidade nos Paises Subdesenvolvidos*. Rio de Janeiro: Editora Civilizacao Brasileira, 1965.

————. "O Centro de Cidade do Salvador." *Estudo de Geografia Urbana*. Bahia: Instituto Brasileiro de Geografia e Estadistica, 1959.

Schneider, Ronald M. and Kingsbury, Robert C. *An Atlas of Latin American Affairs*. New York: Praeger, 1965.

Schneider, Wolf. *Babylon is Everywhere*. New York: McGraw-Hill Book Co., 1963.

Schnore, Leo. "Urban Form: The Case of the Metropolitan Community." In *Urban Life and Form.* Edited by Weiner F. Hirsch. New York: Holt, Rinehart and Winston, 1965.

Schuster, Alfred B. *The Arts of Two Worlds.* New York: Praeger, 1959.

Scobie, James R. *Argentina, A City and A Nation.* New York: Oxford University Press, 1964.

Segre, Roberto. "Introduzione Storica all'Archtettura de Buenos Aires." *Casabella Continuitá* 285 (March, 1964).

———. "Lo Sviluppo Urbanistico di Buenos Aires." *Casabella Continuitá* 285 (March, 1964).

Sellin, Thorsten, ed. "A Crowding Hemisphere: Population Change in the Americas." *Annals of the American Academy of Political and Social Science* 216 (March, 1958).

Seminario Nacional Sobre Urbanizacion y Marginalidad. *Urbanización y Marginalidad.* Asociación Colombiana de Facultades de Medicina, División de Estudios de Población. Bogotá, May 28/31, 1968.

Servicio Informativo del Banco Central de Honduras y del Banco Nacional de Fomento. *Análisis dinámico y económico-social de la población de Honduras.* Preparado par Manuel Tosio y Rubén Mondragón. Tegucigalpa: Consejo Nacional de Economía.

Servicio Nacional de Recenseamento, Brazil. *Censo Demografico 1950.* Rio de Janeiro, 1954–1958.

———. *VII Recenseamento General do Brasil 1960.* Rio de Janeiro, 1962.

The Shipping World Limited, London. *Ports of the World.* London: Benn Brothers, Ltd., 1968.

Singer, Hans Wolfgang. "Economic Progress in Underdeveloped Countries." *Social Research* 16 (March, 1949).

Sjoberg, Gideon. *The Preindustrial City.* Glencoe, Ill.: The Free Press of Glencoe, 1960.

Smith, C. T. "Aspects of Agriculture and Settlement in Peru." *Geographic Journal* 126/4 (December, 1960).

Smith, T. Lynn. "Current Social Trends and Problems in Latin America." *Latin American Monographs,* no. 1. Gainesville: School of Interamerican Studies, University of Florida, 1957.

Snyder, David. *Graphic Aids to Population and Growth Analysis.* New Haven: Yale University Press, 1964.

Sociedad Geografica de Lima. *Anuario Geográfico del Perú.* Lima: Sociedad Geográfica de Lima, 1962.

Solis, César A. *Fuentes de Migración al Puerto Industrial de Chimbote.* Lima: Oficina Nacional de Planeamiento y Urbanismo, 1960.

Solorzano, F. V. *Evolución Económica de Guatemala.* Guatemala: Ministerio de Educación Pública, 1963.

Stanislawski, Dan. "Early Spanish Town Planning in the New World." *Geographical Review* 37 (1947).

———. "The Origin and Spread of the Grid-Pattern Town." *Geographical Review* 36 (1946).

Stauber, R. L., ed. *Approaches to the Study of Urbanization.* Government Research Series, no. 27. Lawrence: University of Kansas Publications, 1964.

Steel, Robert Walter. *General Report.* International Institute of Different Civilizations, XVII meeting. Brussels, 1952.

Steward, Julian H. *The Comparative Ethnology of South American Indians.* Handbook of South American Indians, Bulletin 143, vol. 5. Washington, D. C.: Bureau of American Ethnology, 1949.

Stokes, Charles J. "The Economic Impact of the Carretera Marginal de la Selva." *Traffic Quarterly* 20/2 (April 1966).

Sudamericana Editores. *Moderna Bogotá Arquitectónica 1960.* Bogotá: Imprenta Ediciones Sudamericana, 1960.

Tamayo, Augusto. *Informe sobre las colonias de Oxapampa y Pozuzo y los rios Palcazú y Pichis.* Lima: Imprenta Liberal Unión, 1904.

Taullard, A. *Los Planos Más Antiguos de Buenos Aires, 1580–1880.* Buenos Aires: Editores Jacobo Peuser, 1940.

Taylor, Thomas Griffith. *Urban Geography.* London: Mathven, 1958.

Teichert, Pedro C. M. *Economic Policy Revolution and Industrialization in Latin America.* Oxford: University of Mississippi, Bureau of Business Research, 1959.

Terry, T. Phillip. *Terry's Guide to Mexico.* New York: Doubleday, 1934.

Terzago, Alfredo. *Geográfia de Córdoba.* Córdoba, Argentina: Assandri, 1963.

Thomsen, Charles. "Toward a New Scale." *Journal of the American Institute of Architects* 44 (August, 1965).

Toledo, R. *Geografía de Centroamerica.* Guatemala, 1874.

Tovar, Ramon A. *Venezuela, Pais Subdesarrollado.* Caracas: Universidad de Venezuela, 1963.

Tschopik, Harry. *Highland Communities of Central Peru.* Washington, D. C.: U. S. Government Printing Office, 1947.

Tschudi, J. J. *Travels in Peru during the Years 1838–1842, on the Coast, in the Sierra, across the Cordilleras and the Andes, into the Primeval Forests.* London: D. Bogue, 1847.

Tsuru, S. "The Economic Significance of Cities." In *The Historian and the City.* Edited by Handlin and Burchard. Cambridge: Harvard and MIT Presses, 1963.

Turner, John C. "Dwelling Resources in South America." *Architectural Design.* Special Number. 33 (August, 1963).

———. "Lima's Barriadas and Corralones: Suburbs versus Slums." *Ekistics* 19/112 (March, 1965).

———. "South American Housing Problems." *Architectural Design* 33 (August, 1963).

United Nations. *Demographic Yearbook, 1967.* New York, 1968.

———. *Economic Development in Selected Countries.* New York, October, 1947.

———. *Methods of Appraisal of Quality of Basic Data for Population Estimates,* Manual II. New York, 1955.

————. *Yearbook of National Account Statistics.* New York, 1963, 1964.

United Nations Bureau of Social Affairs, Secretariat. *Report on the World Social Situation.* New York, 1957.

United Nations Centro Economico para America Latina. *El Transporte en America Latina.* New York, 1965.

United Nations Department of Economic and Social Affairs. *Demographic Yearbook.* New York, 1952, 1955, 1963, 1965.

————. *The Future Growth of World Population.* New York, 1958.

————. *1963 Report on the World Social Situation.* New York, 1963.

————. *World Economic Report, 1949–1950.* New York, 1951.

————. *World Economic Survey, 1961.* New York, 1962.

————. *World Housing Conditions and Estimated Housing Requirements.* New York, December 4, 1963.

————. *World Housing Conditions and Estimated Housing Requirements.* New York, September, 1965.

————. *World Population Prospects up to the Year 2000.* New York, January 20, 1965.

————. *Yearbook of National Account Statistics, 1963.* New York, 1964.

United Nations Economic Commission for Latin America. *Análisis y Proyecciones del Desarrollo Económico: XI El Desarrollo Económico de Honduras.* México, December, 1960.

————. *Boletín Estadístico de América Latina.* Vol. 1. New York, March, 1964.

————. *The Development of Bolivia.* New York, 1958.

————. *The Development of Brazil.* New York, 1956.

————. *The Development of Colombia.* New York, 1957.

————. *Economic Bulletin of Latin America.* Vol. 6. New York, 1961.

————. *Economic Study of Latin America.* New York, 1963.

————. *Economic Survey of Latin America.* New York, 1958.

————. *General Situation and Future Outlook of the Central American Integration Programme.* New York, February 20, 1963.

————. *Geographic Distribution of the Population of Latin America and Regional Development Priorities.* New York, February 10, 1963.

————. *Human Resources of Central America, Panama and Mexico, 1950–1980, in Relation to Some Aspects of Economic Development.* New York, July 5, 1962.

————. *The Industrial Development of Argentina.* New York, 1959.

————. *The Industrial Development of Peru.* New York, 1959.

————. *The Manufacture of Industrial Machinery and Equipment in Latin America.* New York, 1963.

————. *Possibilities of Integrated Industrial Development in Central America.* New York, 1964.

————. *Preliminary Study of the Demographic Situation in Latin America.* New York, April 23, 1961.

————. *Problemas y Perspectivas del Desarrollo Industrial Latinoamericano.* Buenos Aires: Solar/Hachette, 1964.

————. *The Process of Industrialization in Latin America, Statistical Annex.* New York, January 19, 1966.

————. *The Role of Agriculture in Latin American Common Market and Free-Trade Area Arrangements.* New York, 1961.

————. *Situation of the Central American Integration Programme.* New York, 1965.

————. "Social Development of Latin America." *Ekistics* 18/109 (December, 1964).

————. *Some Aspects of Population Growth in Colombia.* New York, November 10, 1962.

————. *Statistical Bulletin for Latin America, August, 1965.* Vol. 2, no. 2. New York, 1965.

————. *Statistical Bulletin for Latin America, September, 1966.* Vol. 3, no. 2.

————. *Transportation in Central America.* New York, 1953.

————. *Urbanization in Latin America.* New York, March 13, 1963.

United Nations, Food and Agriculture Organization. *The Agricultural Development of Peru.* Washington, D. C., 1959.

United Nations Population Division. "The Past and Future Population of the World and its Continents." *World Population Conference, Rome, 1954.* Vol. 3. New York, 1955.

United States Department of Commerce. *Investment in Central America.* Washington, D. C., December, 1956.

————. *Motor Roads in Latin America.* Washington, D. C., 1925.

————. *Trade Directory of Central America and the West Indies.* Miscellaneous Series, no. 22. Washington, D. C., 1915.

United States Department of Commerce, Bureau of the Census. *Guatemala: Summary of Biostatistics.* Washington, D. C., 1944.

————. *Haiti: Summary of Biostatistics.* Washington, D. C., 1945.

————. *Honduras: Summary of Biostatistics.* Washington, D. C., 1944.

————. *El Salvador: Summary of Biostatistics.* Washington, D. C., 1944.

United States Department of Commerce, Business Information Service. *1950 Census of the Americas, Population Census—Urban Area Data.* Washington, D. C., 1954.

United States Department of State, Agency for International Development. *Housing Market Analysis in Latin America.* Washington, D. C., 1965.

Urquizo-Sossa, Carlos. *Síntesis Turística, Departamento de La Paz.* La Paz: Talleres Gráficos Bolivianos, 1963.

Valega, Jose M. *El Virreynato del Perú.* Lima: Editorial Cultura Ecléctica, 1939.

Vargas Ugarte, Ruben. *El Perú Virreynal.* Lima: Sociedad Académica de Estudios Americanos, 1962.

Vasquez, Jesus Maria. *Pucallpa: Estudio Socio-Religioso de Una Ciudad del Perú.* Madrid: Editorial O.P.E., 1961.

Villacorta, C. *Monografía del Departamento de Guatemala.* Guatemala: Tipografía Nacional, 1926.

Villanueva, Carlos R. "Caracas." *L'Architecture d'Aujourd'hui* 47 (October, 1956).

————. *La Caracas de Ayer y de Hoy.* Paris: Draeger Freres, 1950.

Villares, H. D. *Urbanismo e Problemas de São Paulo.* São Paulo: Cruzeiro do Sul, 1948.

Violich, Francis. *Cities of Latin America; Housing and Planning to the South.* New York: Reinhold Publishing Corp., 1944.

————. "Guide to Reference Collection in Latin American Urban Planning Research at the University of California." *Exchange Bibliography: Latin America* 5 (March, 1963).

Vivian, E. Charles. *Peru.* South American Handbooks. London: Sir Isaac Pitman & Sons, 1914.

Von Hagen, Victor W. *The Ancient Sun Kingdom of the Americas.* Cleveland, Ohio: The World Publishing Co., 1961.

————. *Highway of the Sun.* New York: Duell, Sloan & Pearce, 1955.

Vries, Egbert and Medina Echevarria, Jose, eds. *Social Aspects of Economic Development in Latin America.* Paris: UNESCO, 1963.

Wauchope, R. and West, R., eds. *Handbook of Middle American Indians.* Vol. 1. Austin: University of Texas Press, 1964.

Weissman, E. *The Problems of Urbanism in Developing Areas.* Conference on Urbanization. Ford Foundation, October 11, 1956.

West, R. C. "Surface Configuration and Associated Geology of Middle America." In *Handbook of Middle American Indians.* Vol. 1. Edited by R. Wauchope and R. West. Austin: University of Texas Press, 1964.

Wilgus, Alva Curtis. *An Atlas of Hispanic American History.* Washington, D. C.: George Washington Press, 1932.

————. *Maps Relating to Latin America in Books and Periodicals.* Washington, D. C.: Pan American Union, 1933.

Wilkinson, Thomas. "Urban Structure and Industrialization." *American Sociological Review* 25 (January, 1960).

Williams, Sydney H. "Urban Aesthetics." *The Town Planning Review* 25 (1954–1955).

Wissink, G. A. *American Cities in Perspective.* Assen, The Netherlands: Van Gorcum, 1962.

Wolfe, Marshall. "Some Implications of Recent Changes in Urban and Rural Settlement Patterns in Latin America." *Ekistics* 22/122 (January, 1966).

Woytinsky, W. S. and Woytinsky, E. S. *World Population and Production Trends and Outlook.* New York: Twentieth Century Fund, 1953.

Zavala, Silvio. *Programa de América en la Epoca Colonial.* México, n. d.

"Architecture Mexicain." *L'Architecture D'Aujourd'hui* 59 (April, 1955).

"Air Adventures in Peru." *National Geographic* Magazine 63 (January, 1933).

"Caracas, Cradle of the Liberator." *National Geographic* Magazine 77 (April, 1940).

"Colombia." *L'Architecture D'Aujourd'hui* 80 (October, 1958).

"Le Corbusier's 'Master Plan.'" *L'Architecture D'Aujourd'hui* 33 (December, 1950-January, 1951).

"Habitaciones Collectivos." *L'Architecture D'Aujourd'hui* 74 (October-November, 1957).

La Industria. Official organ of the Asociacion Nacional de Industriales, vol. 7, no. 147. Tegucigalpa, March 15, 1966.

"Provisions which declare the order to be kept in the Indies in new discoveries and settlements." *Laws of the Indies.* Book 4, title 7, 1573.

"Liancabur, Mountain of the Atacameños." *The Geographical Review* 45 (1955).

"The Long and Narrow Land." *Natonal Geographic Magazine* 117 (February, 1960).

"Maps of Inca Cities." *El Arquitecto Peruano* 258 (January-February, 1959).

"Mares Mexicanos." *Artes de Mexico* 119 (1965).

"Mexique." *L'Architecture D'Aujourd'hui* 109 (September, 1963).

National Atlas of the World. Washington, D. C.: National Geographic Society, 1963.

"Peru—The New Conquest." *Time* Magazine 85/11 (March 12, 1965).

"Sintesis Historica de Bolivia." *Guia de La Paz.* La Paz, 1962.

"Spectacular Rio de Janeiro." *National Geographic* Magazine 108 (March, 1955).

"Urbanisme en Amerique Latine." *L'Architecture D'Aujourd'hui* 33 (December, 1950-January, 1951).

L'Urbanisme des Capitals." *L'Architecture D'Aujourd'hui* 88 (February-March, 1960).

"Venezuela." *L'Architecture D'Aujourd'hui* 67–68 (October, 1956).

World Atlas. Chicago: Encyclopedia Britannica, 1960.

Index